ITALIAN-AMERICANS AND RELIGION:
AN ANNOTATED BIBLIOGRAPHY

ITALIAN-AMERICANS AND RELIGION:
AN ANNOTATED BIBLIOGRAPHY

SILVANO M. TOMASI
and
EDWARD C. STIBILI

With a Foreword
by
JOHN TRACY ELLIS

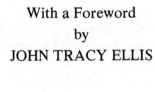
1978
CENTER FOR MIGRATION STUDIES
NEW YORK

The Center for Migration Studies is an educational, non-profit institute founded in New York in 1964 to encourage and facilitate the study of sociological, demographic, historical, legislative and pastoral aspects of human migration and ethnic group relations. The opinions expressed in this work are those of the authors.

Italian-Americans and Religion:
An Annotated Bibliography

First Edition

Center for Migration Studies
209 Flagg Place
Staten Island, New York 10304

ISBN 0-913256-25-0
Library of Congress Catalog Card Number: 76-44921
Printed in the United States of America

Foreword

Emigration from Italy belongs among the extraordinary movements of mankind. In its chief lineaments it has no like. Through the number . . . it has pursued, through its long continuance on a grand scale and its role in other lands, it stands alone.[1]

An annotated bibliography of the religious aspects of the history of those of Italian birth and descent who migrated to the United States, needs no apology. But if it did, it might well be found in the words of Robert Foerster quoted above, which were written over a half century ago. Italian emigration was, indeed, unique, and in none of the many lands where Italians sought and found a new home were they more numerous and ultimately more successful, than in the United States. Fathers Tomasi and Stibili have wisely included items from any and all religious groups with which Italians affiliated themselves on this side of the Atlantic Ocean. The principal emphasis, however, as was to be expected, centers on the great majority who remained in the traditional Catholic faith of their ancestors. And when one recalls that in the century from 1820 to 1920 — not to mention those who came later — the net Catholic immigration from Italy to this country was estimated as not far from 4,500,000, one can appreciate how pressing the so-called "Italian question" became in the life of the Catholic Church once the heavy emigration from the mother country got underway in the 1880s.

As the compilers state in their Introduction, the recent interest in ethnic history has furnished an added impetus for scholars in history, sociology, and other disciplines to seek out and to analyze critically the documentary evidence for these ethnic groups. To date hardly more than the surface has

---

[1] Robert F. Foerster. *The Italian Emigration of Our Times*. Cambridge: Harvard University Press. 1924. P. 3.

been uncovered, for an immense amount of research remains to be done before anything approaching a definitive account can be written of the role played not only by those of Italian background but too of Americans of Croatian, Ukrainian, Polish, and Hungarian origins, to mention but several of the varied ethnic strains that make up the American national pattern.

While it is true that the Italians were not as quick and insistent as, for example, the Germans and the Poles, to identify themselves with a particular church, the religious factor in time emerged as a significant part of their American experience. Thus the Italian national parish took its place in the Catholic community besides the national parishes of other ethnic groups. And with the parish came Italian social clubs, societies such as the Italian Catholic Federation, along with Italian newspapers and periodicals, all serving the immigrant communities of large urban centers with numerous Italian colonies such as New York, San Francisco, and New Orleans. Each of these enterprises accumulated files of one kind or another that today constitute the archives that describe their activities. The Tomasi-Stibili guide locates and notes the nature of these Italian parishes, societies, and newspapers.

For research workers to have at their disposal an up-to-date and annotated bibliography of 1,158 items such as is found here is an immense service to scholarship, and all whose fields of specialization touch Italian immigration to the United States will be grateful for this useful tool that will, so to speak, start them on their way with a guiding hand as they enter the vast labyrinth of scattered sources on the remarkably successful story written by those of Italian blood in the annals of American history. Finally, these same research workers will hold the Tomasi and Stibili names blessed for the eight-page Index with which they can initiate their investigations.

John Tracy Ellis
Professorial Lecturer in Church History
in
The Catholic University of America

Contents

Introduction

As in every other phase of the Republic's history, American Catholicism is still searching for the best possible expression of its national experience. It is a search that will — and should — continue as fresh approaches introduce new viewpoints and the discovery of new data colors the interpretation of events. In this way those ingredients of scholarship that are necessary to provide an enlightening historical account are gradually assembled and broadened. It is a process that operates on various levels. For example, the recent emphasis on the ethnic composition of the Catholic community of the United States is in part a response to the current interest in people's roots. But it is more, for it builds on and supplements the traditional approach employed by pioneer historians such as John Gilmary Shea, Peter Guilday, and others to whose research contemporary historians owe a basic framework for their own studies. As the frontier theory has in recent decades yielded to newer interpretations of the American past without itself losing all validity, so in American Catholic history earlier assumptions characterized by filiopietism, power centers, and the melting pot have witnessed of late a more extensive seeking out of ethnic patterns among Catholic Americans.[1] In this way the cultural contributions made by immigrant Italians, Poles, Ukrainians *et al.*, and by their descendants in this land will be neither lost nor overshadowed. The historian of late twentieth-century American Catholicism may thus be likened to the scriptural householder, "who brings out from his storeroom things both new and old."

[1] Vincent P. De Santis, "The American Historian Looks at the Catholic Immigrant," *Roman Catholicism and the American Way of Life*, edited by Thomas T. McAvoy (Notre Dame, 1960), 225-234.

The assumption of filiopietism approaches historical events in an uncritical and devotional way, with a view to their religious impact on the audience. The development of the Church, its achievements and its heroes, are the subject of historical narrative because they edify and offer the occasion of inculcating and showing reverence. In this context, popular piety expresses the relationship of the inarticulate masses to the sacred. The positive contribution of this assumption is its closeness to the religiosity of the people.

The assumption of power underlies the histories of the authority figures and controlling segments of the institutional Church. The appropriate subjects of historical writing are the bishops and the events of the hierarchical Church, i.e., councils, decision-making organisms, and the organizational strength they establish and coordinate. This assumption contributes the view of history from the top.

The melting pot is an assumption evidenced in the writings which emphasize the unique experience of American Catholicism as a Church built by various waves of immigrants successively and successfully integrated into one homogeneous community through the mediating role of Irish Catholics. The recent insistence on the persistence of ethnicity indicates that diversity is still present in the Church, that assimilation did not occur overnight, as Orestes A. Brownson demanded, that the Irish leadership was not very "catholic," and that there is a growing unity without uniformity in the American Catholic community.[2]

An adequate history of American Catholicism will have to integrate the history of elites, immigrant communities, missionary work, intellectual life, and popular religiosity. Only at that point can such crucial questions be asked as, for example, whether the popular sense of solidarity of the immigrant parish has been lost or recaptured on a higher level by the effort of Catholic schools and other church institutions to personalize the faith of the immigrants, or whether it can really be assumed that there is no incompatibility between Americanism and American attitudes on consumerism, group relations, international development and Catholicism.

The present bibliography is a part of the scaffolding needed to rewrite American Catholic history in such a way that the experience of Italian, Polish, and other East European Catholics, along with the experience of

---

[2] Daniel S. Buczek, "Polish-Americans and the Roman Catholic Church," *The Polish Review*, XXI (August, 1976), 39-61. Buczek concludes: "From the perspective of the Polish element in the Roman Catholic Church in the United States in the twentieth century, their Church's policy of Americanization and often of 'benign neglect' was particularly unfortunate" (p. 61). See also Anthony J. Kuzniewski, Jr., "Faith and Fatherland: An Intellectual History of the Polish Immigrant Community in Wisconsin, 1838-1918," (Unpublished Ph.D. dissertation, Harvard University, 1973), 470; Silvano M. Tomasi, *Piety and Power* (New York, 1975).

Catholics of all rites and origins, will be included. Indeed, the dynamic process of incorporating immigrants — and diversity — into the ecclesial community, is a continuing challenge to American Catholicism.[3]

This bibliography marks the first time an extensive survey of published and unpublished material dealing with the religious experience of Italians in the United States has been undertaken. This effort is part of the growing scholarly concern with Italian Americans and the changing approach to American Catholic history.[4]

Several limitations surfaced in the process of compiling this bibliography. For one, not all diocesan archives and repositories of religious communities could be checked and listed. Secondly, while many theses, dissertations, parish histories, books and articles have been listed, they obviously do not exhaust all the material available on this subject. Finally, annotations vary in quality, reflecting the editors' greater or lesser familiarity with the entries.[5]

[3] Elsa M. Chaney, "Colombian Migration to the United States (Part 2)," *The Dynamics of Migration: International Migration* (Washington, D.C., 1976), 117-118; Joseph P. Fitzpatrick, *Puerto Rican Americans: the Meaning of Migration to the Mainland* (Englewood Cliffs, N.J., 1971); Joseph P. Fitzpatrick, *Hispanic Americans and the Church in the Northeast* (New York, 1977; mimeo); Lydio F. Tomasi, "The Challenge of Immigration to the American Church," *Migration Today*, V (October, 1977), 9-12; Leo Grebler, Joan W. Moore, and Ralph C. Guzman, *The Mexican-American People: The Nation's Second Largest Minority* (New York, 1970), 443-485; "Somos Hispanos: Message of the U.S. Spanish-Speaking Bishops," and "Spanish-Speaking Catholics: The Difference is a Value," *Origins*, VII (September 1, 1977), 171-176.

[4] Silvano M. Tomasi, ed., *Perspectives in Italian Immigration and Ethnicity* (New York, 1976); Rudolph J. Vecoli, "European Americans: From Immigrants to Ethnics," *International Migration Review*, VI (Winter, 1972), 403-434; David J. O'Brien, "American Catholic Historiography: A Post-Conciliar Evaluation," *Church History*, XXXVII (March, 1968), 80-94; Moses Rischin, "The New American Catholic History," *Church History*, XLI (June, 1972), 225-229; Martin E. Marty, "Ethnicity: The Skeleton of Religion in America," *Church History*, XLI (March, 1972) 5-21; David O'Brien, "American Catholicism and American Religion," *Journal of the American Academy of Religion*, XL (March, 1972), 36-53; Philip Gleason, ed., *Catholicism in America* (New York, 1970), 1-9.

[5] Some parish archives may include accounts of the founding and development of the parish, e.g., "Cronaca della casa salesiana e chiesa di Maria Ausiliatrice alle 440 East 12 Street, New York City." Philip M. Hamer, ed., *A Guide to Archives and Manuscripts in the United States* (New Haven, 1961), covers more than 1300 depositories and 20,000 collections of personal papers and archival groups in the United States. Finbar Kenneally, ed., *United States Documents in the Propaganda Fide Archives, A Calendar* (Washington, D.C., 1966), is the first volume of a series published by the Academy of American Franciscan History aimed at providing a complete calendar of all American documents in the Propaganda Fide archives. Remigio U. Pane, "Doctoral Dissertations on the Italian American Experience Completed in the United States and Canadian Universities, 1908-1974," *International Migration Review*, IX (Winter, 1975), 545-556, and "Doctoral Dissertations on the Italian-American Experience, 1921-1975," *International Migration Review*, X (Fall, 1976), 395-401, lists dissertations dealing with the Italian-Americans, including several titles that deal with Italians and Religion in America. *The National Union Catalog. Pre-1956 Imprints. A Cumulative Author List Representing Library of Congress Printed Cards and Titles Reported by Other American Libraries. Compiled*

One area that is in need of much further research is the Italian American religious press, only partially referred to in this bibliography. The files of many Catholic and Protestant newspapers and periodicals have disappeared or are scattered and disorganized. Their titles can be found in a variety of books as well as the standard directories.[6] Official diocesan newspapers have not been listed here, even though they are an important source for the study of Italians in this country.[7]

All available bibliographies that contain entries on the religious experience of Italians in the United States have been listed here, even though many of the entries have been rechecked and included in this bibliography.[8]

This annotated bibliography includes material covering the three major periods of the Italian religious experience in America: the missionary period, when Italians came to work as missionaries, teachers, and explorers; the period of mass migration from 1880 to 1925, which injected a Mediterranean style into the Northern European and Irish culture of American Catholicism;

and Edited with the Cooperation of the Library of Congress and the National Union Catalog Subcommittee of the Resources Committee of the Resources and Technical Services Division, American Library Association (London, 1968), and *The National Union Catalog 1956 Through 1967. A Cumulative List Representing Library of Congress Printed Cards and Titles Reported by Other American Libraries* (Totowa, N.J., 1970-1972, and supplements), are the standard references on books.

[6] *L'Italiano in America*, published by the Italian clergy of New York City, is mentioned by Giuseppe Fumagalli, *La stampa periodica italiana all'estero* (Esposizione Internazionale di Milano, 1906). John B. Bisceglia, *Italian Evangelical Pioneers* (Kansas City, 1948), mentions several Italian Protestant publications in America on pp. 112-118. Eugene Paul Willging, *Catholic Serials of the Nineteenth Century in the United States. A Descriptive Bibliography and Union List. Second Series* (Washington, 1959), is an extremely valuable bibliographic source listing all the known Catholic periodicals, newspapers, and other serials of the nineteenth century. The first series, which covers those States with briefer histories, has been appearing at intervals in the *Records of the American Catholic Historical Society of Philadelphia* since September, 1954. Edna Brown Titus, ed., *Union List of Serials in Libraries of the United States and Canada*, 3d ed. (5 vols; New York, 1965), is the standard reference on serials and their availability in American and Canadian libraries. See also, *New Serial Titles. A Union List of Serials Commencing Publication after December 31, 1949* (4 vols.; Washington, D.C., 1973), and supplements).

[7] For example, *The New World*, Chicago archdiocesan newspaper, in a special 156-page issue on the Catholic Church in Illinois published on April 14, 1900, included some information on Italian immigrants. For a sample of the weekly coverage given by a major Catholic diocesan newspaper, see the following articles in the *Catholic News* of New York: "Great Italian Festival," July 20, 1901; "Dedication of St. Anthony's School," April 9, 1910; "No Money at the Doors of the Church," October 28, 1911; "Work Among the Italian Apostolate of New York," February 12, 1912; "Italians Honor Monsignor Ferrante," March 2, 1912; "Gala Day for Italian Children," January 17,, 1914 "Holy Week at St. Joachim's," April 14, 1914.

[8] Edward R. Vollmar, *The Catholic Church in America: An Historical Bibliography*, 2d ed. (New York, 1963), should be consulted, especially for the extensive entries from the *Lettere edificanti della Provincia Napolitana*, regarding the work of Neapolitan Jesuits in the Southwest.

the contemporary period, when Italian-Americans are reassessing their heritage and their participation in the American Catholic community.

This bibliography is divided into two major parts: primary and secondary materials. The former lists the major repositories of archival materials. The latter lists bibliographies, serials, theses and dissertations, parish histories, books and articles.

Thanks are due to the many archivists and librarians who have helped in this work, especially the directors and staffs of the Center for Migration Studies of New York and the Centro Studi Emigrazione in Rome, Professor Robert De Santis of Otero Junior College in La Junta, Colorado, Professor Joseph A. Pitti of Sacramento State University, Sr. Mary Louise Sullivan, President of Cabrini College in Radnor, Pennsylvania, and Joseph Velikonja of the University of Washington in Seattle.

Part One

Primary Materials

1

Repositories of Archival Materials

1. American Baptist Historical Society, 1108 South Goodman Street, Rochester, NY 14620.

   This archival repository contains the following materials on Italian American Baptists: ledgers and manuscripts relating to Italian Baptist churches; annual reports of the American Baptist Home Mission Society; annual reports of the Baptist Union of Philadelphia; annual reports of the Philadelphia Baptist City Mission; anniversary books of the Long Island Baptist Association and the Southern New York Baptist Association; the Papers of Edward Judson; and anniversary books on Baptist churches and missions, useful for quantitative studies.

   The repository also contains a complete file on the *New Aurora* (earlier entitled *L'Aurora*, *Il Messaggiero*, *Il Cristiano*), 1903 to the present, the monthly publication of the Italian American Baptist Association, and an incomplete file of the *Baptist Messenger*, the publication of the First Italian Baptist Church and Christian Center, Philadelphia.

   It also has the following magazines, which contain articles on Italian American Baptists: *Baptist Home Mission Monthly*, *Home and Foreign Fields*, *The Baptist*, and *Missions*.

2. Andover-Harvard Theological Library, Harvard Divinity School, 45 Francis Avenue, Cambridge, MA 02138.

   The Manuscripts Collection includes the Papers of George La Piana, a Modernist Catholic priest who taught at Harvard University from 1915 to 1947. La Piana was the John H. Morison Professor of Church History. The Papers include La Piana's memoirs, in English and Italian, manuscripts, college lecture notes, correspondence (1908-1970), subject files, biographical records, correspondence with Giuseppe Borgese (1919-1952), and Ernesto Buonaiutti (1908-1946), material on La Piana's views on Fascism, and a collection of essays on Italian immigrants in America. A register of the Papers is available.

3. The Archdiocese of St. Louis Archives, 4445 Lindell Blvd., St. Louis, MO 63108.

The Archives include the Papers of Bishop Joseph Rosati (1789-1843), the first bishop of St. Louis. They include letters, official documents, letter books, a diary, and a photocopy of the "Souvay Collection."

The Archives of St. Mary's Seminary, Perryville, MO, also contain material on Joseph Rosati.

4. Archives of the California Province of the Society of Jesus, P.O. Box 519, Los Gatos, CA 95030.

The holdings include original letters starting in 1845 and other microfilmed correspondence to 1870 of originals in the Jesuit Archives in Rome, obituaries for the California Jesuits, photographs, papers and notes of many California Jesuits. Many of these Jesuits were Italian, including most of the mission superiors and rectors of Santa Clara College (later University of Santa Clara) and St. Ignatius College (later University of San Francisco) from 1851 to 1893.

5. Archives of the Missouri Province of the Society of Jesus, 4511 West Pine Boulevard, Saint Louis, MO 63108.

The archives have the records and papers of Fr. Paul Mary Ponziglione (1817-1900), a missionary among the Osage Indians and early white settlers in southeastern Kansas. They consist of: a few letters; a Guide for missionaries; Record of Mission Stations and churches established among the Osage Indians; incomplete Osage dictionary; catechetical instructions; translation into Osage of Apostolic Letter of Pope Pius IX on the Immaculate Conception; notes on Indian customs; collection of Epistles and Gospels for Sundays in Osage; Bible History in Osage; Catechism in Osage; memoirs collected from legends, traditions and historical documents; Annals of the Mission of St. Francis Jerome.

6. Archivio di Stato, Palazzo della Sapienza, Rome.

It contains autobiographical notes of Alessandro Gavazzi, a Garibaldinian priest who stirred up much controversy in New York: 54 notebooks of 20 pages each (22x30cm) which form 1092 pages numbered — up to 1870. In 5 parts: La Famiglia, Il Chiostro, Patria, Esiglio, Ritorno.

7. The Balch Institute, 18 South Seventh Street, Philadelphia, PA 19106.

The Balch Institute focuses on American political history, North American

Immigration, Ethnic, Racial, and Minority Group History and American Folklore. Its library includes printed books, newspapers and periodicals, manuscripts, and microforms. The collection, now being processed, includes material that relates to Italian Americans and religion.

8. Cabriniana Room, Cabrini College, King of Prussia Road, Radnor, PA 19087.

The archival material housed in the Cabriniana Room at Cabrini College will be open to those who are interested in the role of St. Frances Cabrini and the Missionary Sisters of the Sacred Heart among Italian immigrants in the United States starting in 1980. The material includes letters, diaries, reports, and clippings dating from 1889. Areas covered by these materials include New York City, Newark, Philadelphia, Scranton, Chicago, New Orleans, Seattle, Denver, and Los Angeles. The documentation is mostly in Italian, though some of the material is in English.

The archives contain duplicates of the extensive correspondence of Frances Cabrini from the General Curia of the Missionary Sisters of the Sacred Heart in Rome. See *Lettere Xerografiche S. Cabrini, 1870-1917.* 13 vols. Volumes I to XI cover the period 1870 to 1907 and are numbered 1 to 4854. Volumes XII and XIII cover the years 1908 to 1917 and are numbered 4301 to 5329. Some of Cabrini's letters are included in: *Lettere di S. Francesca Saverio Cabrini.* Milano: Editrice Ancora, 1968. Pp. 628; *Letters of Saint Frances Xavier Cabrini.* Translated from the Italian by Sr. Ursula Infante, M.S.C. Privately printed, 1970. Pp. 503.

Basic documents of the Missionary Sisters of the Sacred Heart and publications and notes on the spirituality and motivations of Cabrini's life and action are also housed in these archives. See: *Regolamento per le alunne delle Missionarie del Sacro Cuore di Gesù.* Rome, 1913. Pp. 30; *Costituzioni dell'Istituto delle Missionarie del Sacro Cuore di Gesù.* Rome, 1963. Pp. 36; *Esortazioni della S. Madre Francesca Saverio Cabrini, Fondatrice delle Missionarie del S. Cuore di Gesù Raccolte dalle Sue Figlie.* Grottaferrata: Scuola Tipografica Italo-Orientale "San Nilo," 1957. Pp. 271; *La Santificazione di Madre Cabrini.* Rome: Scalice Editore, 1947. Pp. 90; *Riforme per giorni di Santo ritiro.* Rome, 1911. Pp. 244. Valuable interviews with Cabrini's contemporaries are found in the duplicates of the proceedings for Cabrini's canonization.

9. Center for Migration Studies, 209 Flagg Place, Staten Island, NY 10304.

The Center for Migration Studies of New York, Inc., has an extensive and growing collection of archival material on Italian immigration in America. See Olha della Cava, *A Guide to the Archives,* vol. I (1974) and vol. II (1977), published by the Center for Migration Studies.

The following records and papers in the collection relate to Italian-Americans and religion:

De Biasi Family Papers (1853-1973), especially Series IV: the Carlo De Biasi Papers, 32 boxes. The collection contains a complete run of the Italian language Catholic weekly *Il Crociato*, published in Brooklyn, N.Y., 1933-1973 (Carlo De Biasi, Editor); correspondence with members of the hierarchy; Carlo De Biasi's published articles; miscellaneous clippings and background information files rich in documentation pertaining to the Italian ethnic church in the United States.

Rev. Nicholas De Carlo Papers
7 boxes of newspaper clippings, photographs, personal letters, record books, sermon books and miscellaneous materials belonging to Rev. Nicholas De Carlo, pastor from 1913 to 1960 of Holy Rosary Church, the chief Italian American parish in Washington, D.C.

American Committee on Italian Migration (ACIM) Records
ACIM was organized in February, 1952, as one of the member agencies of the National Catholic Resettlement Council, part of the National Catholic Welfare Conference (NCWC). Its main objective was the liberalization of U.S. immigration policy. With passage in 1965 of the Kennedy-Johnson bill abolishing the "national origins" quota, ACIM turned to aiding immigrants reach the U.S. and adapt to their new surroundings.

General Records, 1952-1973. Entire body of files accumulated by the National Office of the American Committee on Italian Migration with the exception of bookkeeping records, subdivided into 12 series. 221 document boxes, 4 bound volumes, 7 storage boxes.

St. Raphael Society Records
The St. Raphael Society for the Protection of Italian Immigrants was established in Piacenza, Italy, by Bishop Giovanni Battista Scalabrini in 1889. It established branches in New York City (1891-1923) and Boston (1902-1907). It provided immigrants with protection and assistance.
Records, 1884-1936 with newspaper clippings through 1968. 16 document boxes, 1 storage box.

U.S. Catholic Conference Records
USCC, formerly the National Catholic Welfare Conference, is the national agency of the U.S. Catholic bishops. It carries out its activities through a variety of departments and divisions within departments. The Center for Migration Studies has accessioned from the NCWC's headquarters in Washington, D.C. the records of two of these divisions: 1. The Division of Migration and Refugee Services (formerly Immigration Bureau) of the Department of International Affairs; 2. The Division of Family Life (formerly Family Life Bureau) of the Department of Social Development.

The ca. 52.5 cu. ft. of documentation from the Division of Migration and Refugee Services spans the years 1917-1970.

Holy Ghost Parish, Providence, RI
Miscellaneous photographs, reports, diaries, clippings and souvenir journals documenting the history of this Italian-American parish.

Scalabrini Fathers in North America Records
Ca. 77.0 cu. ft. of documentation (correspondence, souvenir journals, reports, clippings, pamphlets, magazines, photographs) pertaining to the internal organization of the Scalabrinian Congregation in North America and to its pastoral and social activities among Italian Immigrants from 1887 to the present. It sheds particular light on the activities of individual Scalabrinian pastors as well as on the histories of some 60 Scalabrinian parishes, many no longer administered by the Congregation.

Italian American Churches Documentation
An artificial collection (ca. 4.0 cu. ft.) of pamphlets, photocopies of original documents, clippings, miscellaneous notes as well as some original letters dealing with Italian Catholic and Protestant churches from ca. 1880-1950.

10. Centro Studi Emigrazione Roma, Archives, via Calandrelli 11, 00153 Rome.

The most important collection in these archives are the papers and records of the "Prelate for Italian Emigration." In 1920 the Holy See reorganized the pastoral care of Italian emigrants by establishing an office dependent on the Sacred Consistorial Congregation and headed by a bishop with the task of supervising all diocesan priests engaged in the care of Italian emigrants everywhere and the Pontifical College of Migration for the preparation of these priests.

The papers include a list of 4ll Italian parishes in the United States, correspondence with several of them, occasional pamphlets and circular letters, documents on the relationship between the Church and the Italian Government on immigration matters between 1920 and 1930, and the monthly bulletin published by the office of the Prelate for Italian Emigration, *L'Informatore per l'Emigrante* (1921-1929).

11. Dominican Archives, Sinsinawa, WI 53824.

Has the papers of Fr. Samuel Mazzuchelli, O.P. (1806-1864), Italian-born pioneer missionary to the Midwest and founder of a sisters' community, the Sinsinawa Dominicans.

12. Facoltà Valdese di Teologia, Archives, via Pietro Cossa, 42, Rome.

Contains holdings relating to Alessandro Gavazzi and his activities in the United States in the form of a collection of clippings titled: Reception in New York, 1853, pp. 137; Sermons to the Italians, 1853, pp. 102; Orations in the United States, 1853, pp. 155; Orations in the United States, 1853, pp. 158; Letters consisting principally of contributions to *L'Eco d'Italia* and *The Crusader;* Brief Records of Proceedings in the United States, 1853, pp. 148; and Appendix to the American Volumes, 1853, pp. 136.

13. Immigration History Research Center, 826 Berry Street, St. Paul, MN 55114.

The Immigration History Research Center, which is part of the University of Minnesota, has a rich and growing collection of archival material on immigrant religious life in America. Material on Italians and religion includes the following collections:

St. Anthony of Padua Roman Catholic Church, Cleveland, OH
Marriage record book, August 1887-1912, 1 reel microfilm.

Pioletti, Monsignor Louis
Papers, ca. 1915-1930, 5 linear feet
Correspondence of a pastor of the Church of St. Ambrose and the Holy Redeemer Church in St. Paul, MN. Some parish records are also included. See "An Inventory of the Papers of Monsignor Louis F. Pioletti, deposited in the Immigration History Research Center of the University of Minnesota," prepared by A.C. Meloni, August 8, 1975. (Mimeographed.)

Odone, Father Nicolo Carlo, 1868-1947
Papers, ca. 1895-1947, ca. 17 linear feet
More than 90 volumes of the personal diary of an Italian-born priest who served as pastor of the Holy Redeemer parish in St. Paul, MN, from 1899 to his death in 1947. Correspondence and newspaper clippings are also included. See "An Inventory of the Papers of Nicolo Carlo Odone, deposited in the Immigrant Archives of the University of Minnesota Libraries," prepared by Nicholas Montalto, September, 1973. (Mimeographed.)

Our Lady of Mount Carmel Roman Catholic Church, Kenosha, WI, Ladies Society
Papers, ca. 1950-1975, 4 linear inches
The collection contains jubilee memorial booklets; Secretary-Treasurer's record books of the Mt. Carmel Ladies Society, and a copy of Fr. Tagliavia's (former pastor of the church) *The Italians in Milwaukee.*

Italian Evangelical Movement in Wisconsin
Papers, ca 1928-1969, ca. 1 linear inch
Essays, clippings, correspondence and programs concerning the Italian Evangelical Movement, particularly in Southeastern Wisconsin, and its leaders Rev. G. Busacca, Rev. A. Germanotta, and Rev. A. Giuliani.
First Italian Presbyterian Church, Chicago, IL
Minutes of the Session, 31 December 1891-1940, 1 reel microfilm.

14. Massachusetts Historical Society, 1154 Boylston Street, Boston, MA 02164.

This repository has a large album, containing mostly newspaper clippings and some manuscripts, relation to the work of the Rev. Gaetano Conte, an Italian Protestant minister who worked among the Italians in Boston's North End from 1893 to 1903. Conte's daughter prepared a biography of her father which remains unpublished in the Special Collections section of the New York Public Library. See Gertrude Conte. "A Modern Apostle." (A biography of the author's father, Gaetano Conte.) Pp. 232. (Typescript.)

15. Milwaukee County Historical Society, 910 N. Third St., Milwaukee, WI 53203.

Has the scrapbook of Mrs. William Hauerwas, a Protestant missionary who worked in the Italian ward. Also, various newspaper clipping files with information on Italians.

16. Missionaries of St. Charles, Scalabrinians, General Archives, via Calandrelli 11, 00153 Rome.

The papers and records of the Italian parishes staffed by the Congregation established by Bishop Scalabrini in 1887 for the care of Italian immigrants in the Americas are preserved in these archives. Reports of missionaries, requests from immigrant communities, personal memoirs, official correspondence with American bishops are a rich source of information on the religious experience of Italian Americans. Most of the documentation is in Italian. It covers the parochial and social activities of this Congregation in New York, New Haven, Boston, Providence, Buffalo, Utica, Syracuse, New Orleans, Washington, D.C., Cincinnati, Chicago, Kansas City, Milwaukee, Los Angeles and in the immigrant communities around these cities.

The archives preserve the documentation of parishes and other institutions no longer staffed by this religious Congregation, e.g., Italian parishes in West Virginia and Pittsburgh, and of individuals prominent in work with Italians in the U.S., e.g., Fr. Peter Bandini, founder of Tontitown, Arkansas, and Fr. Giacomo Gambera, reorganizer of the St. Raphael Society for the Protection of Italian Immigrants (1891-1923). The archives are indispensable for the study of the writings, life and activities of John B. Scalabrini.

17. Oregon Province Archives of the Society of Jesus, Crosby Library, Gonzaga University, Spokane, WA 99202.

The pioneer Italian Jesuits who settled the Pacific Northwest and Alaska were from the Turin Province of the Society of Jesus. They included Joseph Cataldo, John Boschi, Celestine Caldi, Joseph M. Caruana, Joseph Bandini, Philip Canistrelli, Joseph M. Chianeli, Anthony M. Chiava (who went by the English name of Keyes), Jerome D'Aste, Joseph Giorda, Anthony Morvillo, Gregory Mengarini, Edward M. Griva, Peter P. Prando, Crispinus Rossi, and Joseph M. Treca. The above archives contain original manuscripts of all of these men, and an excellent collection of dictionaries and grammars of various Indian languages and an extensive collection of books on the Church and the American Indian. E.g., the Archives hold the autobiographical notes of Fr. Cataldo, a University founder and well known missionary, dictated to Fr. O'Malley. See James O'Malley, S.J., "Northwest Blackrobe, Story of the Life and Work of Father Joseph Cataldo, S.J., 1837-1928."

The California Province of the Society of Jesus, established in 1912, was divided in 1932 into the Oregon and California Provinces. The archival materials of the southern Pacific coast are to be found at the California

Province Archives of the Society of Jesus, P.O. Box 319, Los Gatos, Ca. 95030.

18. Regis College Archives, Denver, CO 80221.

"Regis College in Denver, Colo., is the repository of the diaries and other manuscript materials of the educational and missionary activities of the Neapolitan Jesuits who in 1867 began their work throughout Colorado, New Mexico, and Western Texas. This collection is particularly valuable in view of the destruction of a large number of papers when the move was made from the old to the new cathedral in Denver, Colo." (E.R. Vollmar, "Archives, U.S. Catholic," *New Catholic Encyclopedia*, I [1967], 770-772). There are brief sketches of the following Jesuits: Dominic Pantanella, Tromby, Maffei, Montenarelli, Massa, Pandolfi; historical accounts of the activities of the Society of Jesus in New Mexico and Colorado, e.g., F.X. Tomassini, S.J., "Complete History of the Jesuit Mission of Colorado, New Mexico and West Texas administered for half a century, from the year 1967 to 1919"; Ferdinand M. Troy, S.J., "Historia Societatis Jesu in Novo Mexico et Colorado"; Vito M. Tromby, S.J., "Historia Missionis Novi Mexico et Colorati Elloria [sic] Nostrorum qui in ea Missioine defuncti sunt." The latter accurately covers the period 1867-1885. The conditions at the beginning of the mission at Conjeos and its development are reported in "Diario de la Residencia de Guadalupe (Conjeos), S.J." (9 vols. Ms. [1871-1920]). Livio Vigilante, S.J., "Diary of the Mission of New Mexico (May 27, 1867 to October 18, 1874)," gives a day-by-day account of the Neapolitan Jesuits' trip to New Mexico. The best biography of Fr. Personnè, one of the most influential missionaries, is F.X. Tomassini, "Obituary and Life of Rev. S. Personnè, S.J." (Pueblo, Colorado, 1923, unpublished Ms. in these archives). Other sketchy, but informative manuscript reports on the religious and educational activities of the Neapolitan Jesuits are: "The Jesuit College at Las Vegas, N.M. 1877 to 1886"; F.X. Tomassini, S.J., "A Brief Account of Activities, Buildings, Churches, Schools, etc., of the State of Colorado and New Mexico by the Italian Jesuit Fathers."

19. Servite Order Archives, 3041 S. Home Avenue, Berwyn, IL 60402.

The Order of Servants of Mary (Servites) is related to the history of Italian-Americans chiefly through five Italian parishes which it has staffed: Assumption, Chicago (founded in 1881; this was the first Italian parish in Chicago); Our Lady of Mt. Carmel, Denver, Colorado (founded in 1894 and entrusted to the Order in 1904); St. Philip Benizi, Chicago (founded in 1904 and suppressed in 1965); Assumption, Welby, Colorado — now in Denver (founded in 1910 and entrusted to the Order in 1912); St. Donatus, Blue Island, Illinois (founded in 1908 and entrusted to the Order in 1922). Documentation on the parishes and the priests who staffed them can be found in various repositories.

I. General Archives of the Order (viale XXX Aprile, 6 — Rome) and Provincial

Archives (Berwyn). Documents of foundation, correspondence with bishops, correspondence concerning personnel can be found in these central archives.

1874-1901. The American foundations were governed by a Vicar General. No archives of a Vicar General exist anymore. But Fr. Austin Morini, founder of the Servites in the United States, gathered together a sizeable number of letters dating from the 1870s to the 1890s. The originals are in the Servite General Archives, Rome; copies are available in the Provincial Archives of the Eastern Province, Berwyn, Illinois.

A manuscript account by Fr. Morini, "Fondazione dell'Ordine dei Servi di Maria negli Stati Uniti dell'America Settentrionale," pp. 170, is in the General Archives of the Order and reports the first years of work among the Italian immigrants in Chicago.

1901-1927. The five parishes were under the jurisdiction of the American Province.

The Provincial Registers and file folders relating to three parishes in the Chicago archdiocese are found in the Provincial Center of the Eastern Province. Folders containing correspondence, etc. with the two parishes in Denver at present are in the Provincial Center of the Western Province, in Buena Park, 5210 Somerset Street, California 90621.

In general, documentation is scanty.

1927-1948. The five parishes were under the jurisdiction of the Roman Province in whose archives some documentation may be preserved.

1948-1967. The five parishes were under the jurisdiction of the St. Joseph Province, which was composed mainly of these parishes.

The archives of St. Joseph Province are at present at the Provincial Center in Berwyn for the parishes in the Chicago area and at the Provincial Center in Buena Park, California for the two parishes in Denver.

In general the material here is also scanty.

1967-. The four parishes which still exist were divided so that the two remaining in the Chicago area became part of the Eastern Province and the two in Denver became part of the Western Province, 5210 Somerset Street, Buena Park, California 90621.

Information since 1967 should be sought from the archives of the Eastern or Western Province.

II. Local Archives.

Assumption Parish, Chicago. The local archives are still at Assumption Parish and include registers dating from the foundation of the parish and a complete set of parish bulletins starting in the early 1900s.

St. Philip Benizi, Chicago. After the suppression of the parish in 1965, its records were placed with the archives of the Eastern Province. These inlcude the following: 131 registers and ledgers dealing with financial matters, parish societies, etc. and 120 file folders.

In addition the baptismal, confirmation, and marriage registers were transferred to nearby St. Dominic's Parish.

St. Donatus, Blue Island, Illinois. Virtually nothing of importance remains in the local archives.

III. Personal Papers.

Fr. Pellegrino Giagrandi, O.S.M. (pastor of St. Philip Benizi parish, 1908-1916): 25 file folders (mostly discourses, panegyrics, and Sunday sermons from the 1890s and early 1900s).

Fr. Luigi Giambastiani, O.S.M. (pastor of St. Philip Benizi parish, 1916-1961): Fr. Luigi died in 1975, leaving correspondence, sermons, notes, etc. The material has not yet been sorted or classified.

20. **St. Bonaventure University, Friedsam Memorial Library, St. Bonaventure, NY 14478.**

This repository contains documentation pertaining to the arrival of the first Italian Franciscans in New York State in the 1850s, the founding of St. Bonaventure University, and the development of the Franciscan Custody of the Immaculate Conception. It includes records and newspaper clippings of the activities of the Franciscans among Italian immigrants and of Italian parishes in Connecticut, New York City and Boston. It also has biographical sketches of Italian Franciscans who worked in the United States.

21. **The University of Santa Clara — Archives, The University of Santa Clara, CA 95053.**

These archives contain miscellaneous materials of Italian Jesuits who served on the faculty of the college in the nineteenth century and a few letters of Fr. Michael Accolti who founded the college together with Fr. Nobili. A special collection is identified as: John Nobili, S.J., Presidential Papers, 1851-56, materials covering Nobili's presidency of the institution.

Part Two

Secondary Materials

1

Bibliographies

22. Anastos, Milton Vasil.
"Bibliography of the Works of George La Piana." *Harvard Divinity School Bulletin*, XXIII (1957-58), 103-108.

George La Piana was a Modernist Catholic priest who taught at Harvard University from 1915 to 1947.

23. Bertelli, L., G. Corcagnani and G.F. Rosoli.
Migrazioni: Catalogo della Biblioteca del Centro Studi Emigrazione — Roma. Roma: Centro Studi Emigrazione, 1972. Pp. xxxiv-806.

This is the catalogue of the library of the Center for Migration Studies in Rome (Centro Studi Emigrazione, via Calandrelli 11, 00153 Roma). It gives the table of contents for each entry. Useful for the study of Italian immigration. Contains many titles that deal with the role of the church.

24. Bettini, Leonardo.
Bibliografia dell'anarchismo. Volume I tomo 2. Periodici e numeri unici anarchici in lingua italiana pubblicati all'estero (1872-1971). Firenze: Crescita Politica Editrice, 1976. Pp. xix-351.

This bibliography lists Italian anarchist periodicals published outside of Italy during the period 1872 to 1971. Anarchist periodicals published in the United States are given in pp. 167-230. These periodicals provide a significant amount of information on anticlericalism among Italians in the United States.

25. "Bibliography." *The Assembly Herald*, XII (August, 1906), 399-400.

This is the first in a series of bibliographies on immigration which appeared in *The Assembly Herald*, the official publication of the Presbyterian Church in the United States. See "Recent Magazine Articles on Immigration." *The Assembly Herald*, XII (December, 1906), 620-621; "Immigration." *The Assembly Herald*, XIII (December, 1907), 560; "Bibliography on Immigration." *The Assembly Herald*, XIV (December, 1908), 575; "Immigration. Supplementary Bibliography." *The Assembly Herald*, XV (December, 1909), 582-585; "Immigration: Bibliography for the January Home Mission Topic." *The Assembly Herald*, XVI (December, 1910), 579-580; "Bibliography — Immigration." *The Assembly Herald*, XIX (February, 1913), 87-88. Useful for contemporary references to "new immigrants."

26. Briani, Vittorio.
Emigrazione e lavoro italiano all'estero. Elementi per un repertorio bibliografico generale a cura di Vittorio Briani. Roma: Ministero degli Affari Esteri, Direzione Generale dell'Emigrazione e degli Affari Sociali, 1967. Pp. 229.

This bibliography, while listing many official Italian documents, has limited information on the religious aspect of the emigration phenomenon.

27. Burr, Nelson R.
Religion in American Life. Vol. IV, Parts 1 and 2: *A Critical Bibliography of Religion in America.* Edited by James Ward Smith and A. Leland Jamison. Princeton, New Jersey: Princeton University Press, 1961.

Excellent bibliography on religion in America. For entries on American Catholicism, see pp. 364-366, 409-415, 443-446, and 453-486. See Nelson R. Burr. *Religion in American Life.* Vol. IV, Parts 3, 4 and 5: *A Critical Bibliography of Religion in America.* Edited by James Ward Smith and A. Leland Jamison. Princeton, New Jersey: Princeton University Press, 1961. Pp. 588-590, 720-723, 732-734, 741-743, 764-766, 805-808, 813-815, 876-879, 887-888, and 927-928.

28. Cadden, John P.
The Historiography of the American Catholic Church: 1785-1943. Washington, D.C.: The Catholic University of America Press, 1944. Pp. xi-122. Reprinted, New York: Arno Press, 1978.

Important study of American Catholic historiography. Includes: 1) Historiography of the American Catholic Church: 1785-1884; 2) John Gilmary Shea; 3) Catholic Historical Societies; 4) Historiography of the American Catholic Church: 1884-1915; and 5) Historiography of the American Catholic Church: 1915-1943.

29. Cordasco, Francesco.
The Italian-American Experience: An Annotated and Classified

Bibliographical Guide, With Selected Publications of the Casa Italiana Educational Bureau. Burt Franklin Ethnic Bibliographical Guide 1. New York: Burt Franklin & Co., 1974. Pp. xiv-179.

This guide lists 388 entires (pp. 1-96). "Religion and Missionary Work" is listed in pp. 71-77. It also contains a reprint of Columbia University Casa Italiana Educational Bureau Publications (pp. 99-169).

30. Cordasco, Francesco and Salvatore LaGumina.
Italians in the United States. A Bibliography of Reports, Texts, Critical Studies and Related Materials. New York: Oriole Editions, 1972. Pp. xvi-137.

This bibliography lists 1462 entries. "Religion and Missionary Work" is listed in pp. 91-99. Inaccuracies require that this bibliography be used with care.

31. della Cava, Olha.
"Italian American Studies: A Progress Report." *Perspectives in Italian Immigration and Ethnicity.* Edited by S.M. Tomasi. New York: Center for Migration Studies, 1977. Pp. 165-172.

This is a compilation of data on current research in Italian American studies being conducted by the members of the American Italian Historical Association. It includes course offerings in Italian-American studies, bibliographies, current research in a variety of areas, including religion, and a listing of repositories of primary documentation.

32. Dore, Grazia.
Bibliografia per la Storia dell'Emigrazione Italiana in America. Roma: Tipografia del Ministero degli Affari Esteri, 1956. Pp. 125.

This bibliography deals with Italian emigration to North and South America. An official publication of the Italian Foreign Ministry, it includes the most important works in several languages. The bibliography was reprinted in Grazia Dore, *La Democrazia Italiana e l'Emigrazione in America.* Brescia: Morcelliana, 1964, pp. 381-493.

33. Ellis, John Tracy.
A Guide to American Catholic History. Milwaukee: The Bruce Publishing Company, 1959. Pp. viii-147.

A critical annotated list of titles on American Catholic history from the earliest missions to the twentieth century. This work was a revision of John Tracy Ellis. *A Select Bibliography of the History of the Catholic Church in the United States.* New York: The Declan X. McMullen Company, 1947. Pp. 96. The *Guide* is at present being brought up to date, i.e., since 1959, by Robert Trisco.

34. English, Adrian T.
"The Historiography of American Catholic History (1785-1884)." *The Catholic Historical Review*, XI (January, 1926), 561-598.

This is one of the earliest summaries of American Catholic historiography. It lists documentary sources, printed materials, and general histories.

35. Firkins, Ina TenEyck, comp.
"Italians in the United States." *Bulletin of Bibliography and Quarterly Dramatic Index*, VIII (January, 1915), 129-132.

Old but still useful compilation of books and pamphlets, United States documents and reports, and periodical articles relating to Italians in the United States, by Firkins, reference librarian at the University of Minnesota.

36. Kenneally, Finbar, ed.
United States Documents in the Propaganda Fide Archives. A Calendar. Washington, D.C.: Academy of American Franciscan History, 1966-.

The Foreword notes: "The Academy intends to issue a complete calendar of all American documents in the Propaganda Fide archives. These will be issued in two series. The first series will end with the year 1863 approximately), and will include the various divisions, the 'Congressi,' the 'Udienza,' the 'Acta,' and so on. The present work is the first volume of the First Series. The Second Series will begin with the year 1864 (approximately), and extend to the year 1908, and will be dealt with in similar fashion." Reference to documents on Italian clerics and immigrants and the religious questions relating to them make this source a valuable research instrument.

37. McBride, Paul W.
The Italians in America. An Interdisciplinary Bibliography. Staten Island, N.Y.: American Italian Historical Association, 1976. Pp. iii-33.

This bibliography, which lists 808 titles in various disciplines, is a useful guide to Italian-American studies. It includes books, articles, theses, and dissertations.

38. Miller, Wayne Charles, ed.
A Comprehensive Bibliography for the Study of American Minorities. 2 vols. New York: New York University Press, 1976. Pp. xix-690; xix-691-1380.

This is a compilation of several bibliographies dealing with various minorities in the United States. Vol. I, 423-457, gives a bibliography on Italian-Americans, which includes entries on religion.

39. Pane, Remigio U.
"Doctoral Dissertations on the Italian American Experience Completed in the United States and Canadian Universities, 1908-1974." *International Migration Review*, IX (Winter, 1975), 545-556.

A listing of dissertations dealing with Italian-Americans. It includes several titles that deal with Italians and religion in America. See Remigio U. Pane. "Doctoral Dissertations on the Italian-American Experience, 1921-1975." *International Migration Review*, X (Fall, 1976), 395-401.

40. Reiske, Heinz.
Die USA in den Berichten italienische Reisender. Meisenheim am Glan: Verlag Anton Hain, 1971. Pp. 190.

This volume, which focuses on the reports of Italian travelers to the United States, includes an annotated bibliography on these reports. See the section "Stellung zu religiösen Fragen," pp. 102-109.

41. Rosoli, Gianfausto.
"Sources and Current Research in Italy on Italian Americans." *Perspectives in Italian Immigration and Ethnicity.* Edited by S.M. Tomasi. New York: Center for Migration Studies, 1977. Pp. 133-162.

This is a valuable guide to recent and continuing Italian scholarship on Italian immigration to the United States. It lists recent books, articles, and doctoral dissertations done in Italy on this topic. It also includes a listing of the more important libraries and archival repositories in Italy for the study of Italian immigration to the United States.

42. Smith, Fay Jackson, John L. Kessell, and Francis J. Fox.
Father Kino in Arizona. Phoenix: Arizona Historical Foundation, 1966. Pp. xvii-142.

This is a scholarly study of Fr. Eusebio Francisco Kino, Jesuit missionary and explorer in the Southwest. The first part, by Smith, is a translation of Kino's "Relaciòn Diaria." The second part, by Kessell, describes Kino's "peaceful conquest" of the Indians in southern Arizona. The third part, pp. 97-122, by Fox, gives an extensive bibliography of published books and articles dealing with Father Kino.

43. Velikonja, Joseph.
Italians in the United States (Bibliography). Department of Geography Occasional Papers 1. Carbondale, Illinois: Southern Illinois University, 1963. Pp. xi-90.

This bibliography, which lists 793 titles, attempts to list all major works that deal with the history, distribution, and adjustment of Italian immigrants in the United States. "Religion and Missionary Work" is given in pp. 20-21.

44. Vollmar, Edward R.
   The Catholic Church in America: An Historical Bibliography. 2d ed.
   New York: The Scarecrow Press, Inc., 1963. Pp. xxxix-399.

   This is the most recent and the best bibliography on American Catholic
   history. Its entries are listed alphabetically. See Edward R. Vollmar. *The
   Catholic Church in America: An Historical Bibliography.* New Brunswick,
   New Jersey: The Scarecrow Press, 1956. Lists many works that relate to
   Italians and religion in America.

2

Serials

45. *Analecta Piae Societatis Missionum* (est. Rome, Italy, January, 1910).

This publication, published by the Pallottine Fathers and written mostly in Latin, contains articles describing their work among Italians in the United States. It is available in the Pallottine archives in Rome.

46. *L'Araldo* (est. Brooklyn, New York, 1908).

This publication, published by the Presbyterian Board of Publications, lasted from 1908 to 1915. It was changed to *L'Era Nuova* in 1915 and lasted until 1927. It was then changed to *La Vita*. In 1933, it was succeeded by *Il Rinnovamento*. It is available, in incomplete files, at Columbia University, New York, Oberlin College, Oberlin, and Crozer Theological Seminary, Chester, Pennsylvania. For a history of the publicatioins, see E.R.G. Cupo, "Introduction." *Il Rinnovamento*, XX (April, 1953), 1.

47. *Bollettino della Federazione Cattolica Italiana* (est. San Francisco, California, 1924).

This monthly publication, sponsored by the Central Council of the Italian Catholic Federation, contains information on the activities of the various branches of the Federation.

48. *Il Carroccio* (est. New York, February, 1915 to April, 1935).

This publication, subtitled "Rivista Mensile di Coltura Propaganda e Difesa Italiana in America," is available at the Center for Migration Studies, New York, The New York Public Library, and several other libraries. For a history of the publication, see Agostino De Biasi. "Come Creai e Animai 'Il Carroccio.'" *Divagando*, XXXIII (April 11, 1959), 5-10.

49. *Il Crociato* (est. Brooklyn, N.Y., September 16, 1933 to January 27, 1973).

This publication, which offered detailed information on the Italian parishes of the Catholic Diocese of Brooklyn and on many other institutions and activities of the Italian Catholic community in the United States, is available in a complete file at the Center for Migration Studies, New York. For a history of the publication, see the 25th anniversary issue, October 25, 1958.

50. *L'Emigrato Italiano* (est. Piacenza, Italy, 1903).

This publication by the Scalabrinian Congregation started in 1903 with the title *Congregazione dei Missionari di San Carlo per gli Italiani emigrati nelle Americhe.* The publication was interrupted for several months after the death of Bishop Giovanni Battista Scalabrini of Piacenza in 1905, but resumed in February, 1906, with the title *L'Emigrato Italiano in America.* The publication was suspended from 1925 to 1930. From 1939 to 1953 it was published under the title *Le Missioni Scalabriniane.* It has appeared on a monthly basis since 1954 with the title *L'Emigrato Italiano.* A complete file is available at the Centro Studi Emigrazione, Rome. Incomplete files are available at the Center for Migration Studies, New York, and the Immigration History Research Center, University of Minnesota, St. Paul.

51. *Il Faro* (est. Brooklyn, N.Y., 1939).

This official monthly publication of the Christian Church of North America, founded by Vincenzo Melodia, is predominantly an Italian language publication featuring an "English Section" in the earlier issues.

The bulk of the publication is comprised of articles, poems, and exhortations regarding Christian faith and morality. There is also good coverage of the Church's missionary activities throughout the world and ample news regarding the activities of local U.S. congregations. A file from 1942 to 1968 is available at the Center for Migration Studies, New York.

52. *Fra Noi* (est. Chicago, April, 1960-).

This monthly Catholic newspaper, which reports on the activities of Villa Scalabrini and the Italian-American community in Chicago, is available at the Chicago office, the Immigration History Research Center, University of Minnesota, St. Paul, and the Center for Migration Studies, New York.

53. *L'Informatore per l'Emigrante* (est. Rome, Italy, Ufficio del Prelato per l'Emigrazione Italiana, 1921).

This publication which was published by the office of the Prelate for Emigration is available at the Centro Studi Emigrazione, Rome. Incomplete files are available at the Immigration History Research Center, University of Minnesota, St. Paul, and the Center for Migration Studies, New York.

54. *L'Italo Americano di Los Angeles* (est. Los Angeles, 1908).

This is a weekly publication written in Italian and English, which includes reports on the activities of the Italian Catholic Community in Southern California.

55. *La Lucerna* (est. New York, 1944-1954).

This publication, subtitled "Rivista Mensile Religiosa Culturale," was written chiefly in Italian, with some articles in English. Incomplete files are available at the New York Public Library, the Immigration History Research Center, University of Minnesota, St. Paul, and St. Bonaventure University, St. Bonaventure, New York.

56. *Le Mammole della Madre Cabrini* (est. Rome, Italy, 1930-1967).

This publication, subtitled "Rivista trimestrale delle Missionarie del Sacro Cuore," is available at Cabrini College, Radnor, Pennsylvania.

57. *Il Messaggero* (est. Kansas City, Missouri, January 1, 1924).

This illustrated monthly publication, first titled *Il Piccolo Messaggero*, was sponsored by Christ Presbyterian Church in Kansas City and written in Italian and English. An incomplete file is available at the Immigration History Research Center, University of Minnesota, St. Paul. For a history of the publication, see E. Barnes. "With the Messenger Through the Years." *The Messenger (Il Messaggero)*, XXXIV (October-November, 1958), 43-45.

58. *Mother Cabrini Messenger* (est. Chicago).

This bi-monthly, illustrated publication of the Mother Cabrini League, Missionary Sisters of the Sacred Heart, is available in an incomplete file at the Immigration History Research Center, University of Minnesota, St. Paul.

59. *The New Aurora* (est. Upper Darby, Pennsylvania, 1903).

This monthly publication, earlier titled *L'Aurora*, *Il Messaggiero*, and *Il Cristiano*, is sponsored by the Italian American Baptist Association. A complete file is available at the American Baptist Historical Society, Rochester, N.Y. An incomplete file is available at the Immigration History Research Center, University of Minnesota, St. Paul. For a history of the publication, see *The New Aurora*, November, 1953.

60. *Pro Emigrante* (est. Genoa, 1916).

This is an annual publication of the League Pro Emigranti, founded by the Missionaries of St. Anthony of Padua.

61. *Il Rinnovamento* (est. New York, 1933).

This illustrated bi-monthly publication, published by the Italian Evangelical

Publication Society, Inc., is available in an incomplete file at the Immigration History Research Center, University of Minnesota, St. Paul. For a history of the publication, see E.R.G. Cupo. "Introduction." *Il Rinnovamento*, XX (April, 1953), 1.

62. *Rivista Evangelica* (est. New York, 1899-1908).

This Protestant weekly publication is available in incomplete files, at the New York Public Library and Drew University, Madison, New Jersey.

63. *Veritas* (est. Cincinnati, Ohio, 1926-27).

This monthly publication of the Santa Maria Institute, Cincinnati, Ohio, changed to *The Santa Maria* in 1930. An incomplete file is available at Harvard University, Cambridge, Massachusetts.

64. *La Voce* (est. New York, 1923 to August 27, 1931).

This publication, published weekly by the Methodist Episcopal Church, Board of Home Missions and Church Extension, is available at the New York Public Library and at Drew University, Madison, New Jersey.

65. *La Voce del Popolo* (est. Dearborn, Michigan, 1910).

This is a weekly publication, sponsored by the Pious Society of St. Paul, written in English and Italian. It is available, in an incomplete file, at the New York Public Library.

66. *La Voce dell'Emigrato* (est. New York, 1924 to 1932).

This monthly publication, official organ of the Italian Auxiliary and written in English and Italian, is available in incomplete files at the New York Public Library and at Columbia University, New York.

67. *Voce Italiana* (est. Washington, D.C., June, 1961-).

This is a monthly publication, mostly in Italian, of Holy Rosary Italian parish in Washington, D.C. A complete file is available at the Center for Migration Studies, New York. An incomplete file is available at the Immigration History Research Center, University of Minnesota, St. Paul.

3

Theses and Dissertations

68. Abramson, Harold J.
"The Ethnic Factor in American Catholicism: An Analysis of Inter-Ethnic Marriage and Religious Involvement." Unpublished Ph.D. dissertation, University of Chicago, 1969.

Shows the persistence of ethnicity within Catholicism due to the length of stay of the ethnic groups in America and their historical background. See Harold J. Abramson. *Ethnic Diversity in Catholic America*. New York: John Wiley & Sons, 1973.

69. Auguardo, Maria Pia.
"Madre Cabrini, Maestra ed Educatrice." Unpublished Ph.D. dissertation, Istituto Universitario Maria SS.Assunta Parificato di Roma, 1971.

Dissertation describing Mother Frances Cabrini as a teacher.

70. Baldrigli, Leocadia.
"L'emigrazione italiana nell'U.S.A. e l'opera di S. Francesca Saveria Cabrini." Unpublished Ph.D. dissertation, Istituto Universitario Maria SS. Assunta Parificato di Magistero, Rome, 1955.

A dissertation on Cabrini's work with Italian immigrants in the United States.

71. Bick, Isabelle.
"Our Lady of Pompei: The Evolution of a Roman Catholic Nationality Parish, Bridgeport, Connecticut, 1891-1903." Unpublished M.A. thesis, Faculty of Political Science, Columbia University, 1969.

A case study of the role of an Italian national parish seen as one of the steps in the process of integration, as an acceptable social institution for further integration into American society and as a point of reference for group identity, rather than an expression of religious commitment.

72. Bohme, Frederick G.
"A History of the Italians in New Mexico." Unpublished Ph.D. dissertation, University of New Mexico, 1958. Reprinted, New York: Arno Press, 1975.

Excellent study. The author argues that "...Italian churchmen and settlers, more than any others, provided a 'bridge' between the Anglo-Saxon and Hispano cultures found here..." (p. 1). The dissertation is divided between an account of the activities of the Neapolitan Jesuits (pp. 24-100) and of the other Italian settlers (pp. 149-268). Good bibliography.

73. Brenner, M. Rebecca.
"Churchgoing Among Our Italian Immigrants." Unpublished M.A. thesis, University of Notre Dame, 1944.

The three chapters in the M.A. thesis cover the following topics: 1) survey of the historical literature dealing with the Italian problem; 2) proselytizing among our Italian immigrants; and 3) what priests and social workers think about the Italian problem.

74. Briggs, John Walker.
"Italians in Italy and America: A Study of Change Within Continuity for Immigrants to Three American Cities, 1890-1930." Unpublished Ph.D. dissertation, University of Minnesota, 1972.

A study of Italians in Rochester, New York, Utica, New York, and Kansas City, Missouri. Argues that Italians brought their traditional associations to the United States. Gives some information on the Church. See John W. Briggs. *An Italian Passage: Immigrants to Three American Cities, 1890-1930.* New Haven, Connecticut: Yale University Press, 1978.

75. Caliaro, Marco.
"La Pia Società dei Missionari di San Carlo per gli Italiani Emigrati (Scalabriniani). Studio Storico-Giuridico dalla Fondazione al Capitolo Generale dell'Anno 1951." Unpublished Ph.D. dissertation, Facultas Iuris Canonici, Pontificio Ateneo "Angelicum" (Roma), 1956.

This is a juridical study of the origin and development of the Congregation of St. Charles Borromeo. The Congregation was founded in 1887 by Bishop Giovanni Battista Scalabrini to work with Italian immigrants in the Americas.

76. Carulli, Virgil.
"Religious Life of Italians in America." Unpublished M.A. thesis,

School of Education, New York University, 1928.

This general account of Italian religious life in America is based on secondary sources.

77. Chessa, Palmerio.
"A Survey Study of the Evangelical Work Among Italians in Chicago."
Unpublished B.Div. thesis, Presbyterian Theological Seminary, Chicago, 1934.

A 51-page impressionistic review of Protestant pastoral work among Italian immigrants in Chicago.

78. Churchill, Charles W.
"The Italians of Newark: A Community Study." Unpublished Ph.D. dissertation, New York University, 1942. Reprinted, New York: Arno Press, 1975.

Chapter VIII, pp. 90-112, is titled "Religion and the Church."

79. Crispino, James.
"The Assimilation of Ethnic Groups: The Italian Case." Unpublished Ph.D. dissertation, Faculty of Political Science, Columbia University, 1977.

Chapter 11, pp. 229-246, discusses the role of religion in the process of assimilation of Italians by using the two measures of frequency of church attendance and parochial school education. The sample includes persons of various generations. Among the findings is evidence of increasing religiosity in later generation ethnics.

80. Davis, Lawrence B.
"The Baptist Response to Immigration in the United States, 1880-1925." Unpublished Ph.D. dissertation, Department of History, University of Rochester, 1968.

This dissertation includes some interesting references to Baptist work among Italian immigrants in the United States. See Lawrence B. Davis. *Immigrants, Baptists, and the Protestant Mind in America*. Urbana: University of Illinois Press, 1973.

81. De Bilio, Francis D.
"Protestant Mission Work Among Italians in Boston." Unpublished Ph.D. dissertation, Boston University, 1949.

This doctoral dissertation deals with Protestant efforts among Italian immigrants in Boston from the beginning of Italian immigration there to the 1940s. Based largely on secondary sources, the dissertation concludes that

Protestant missionary efforts among Boston's Italian immigrants were mostly a failure.

82. Easterly, Frederick J.
The Life of Rt. Rev. Joseph Rosati, First Bishop of St. Louis, 1789-1843. Ph.D. dissertation. Washington, D.C.: Catholic University of America Press, 1942. Reprinted, New York: AMS Press, 1974.

Doctoral dissertation, based on primary sources, done at the Catholic University of America on the missionary activities of Bishop Rosati.

83. Elizade, M. Caritas.
"Mother Cabrini's Educational Ideals." Unpublished M.A. thesis, University of Santo Tomas, Manila, 1949.

A cursory review of Frances Xavier Cabrini's methods and objectives in the education of Catholic girls.

84. Ferraro, Paola. "Studi sulla storia delle chiese protestanti italiane negli Stati Uniti." Unpublished Ph.D. dissertation, University of Florence, 1969.

A descriptive analysis of the activities of various Protestant denominations among Italian immigrants in the United States, with statistical data derived from their archives.

85. Fiore, Alphonse Thomas.
"History of Italian Immigration in Nebraska." Unpublished Ph.D. dissertation, History, University of Nebraska, Lincoln, Nebraska, 1938.

Chapter VI deals with religion and the Italian immigrants in Nebraska. It describes their customs and contributions.

86. Galus, Walter J.
"The History of the Catholic Italians in Saint Louis." Unpublished M.A. thesis, Saint Louis University, 1936.

The author describes religious work among Italians in St. Louis from the time of Joseph Rosati, first Bishop of St. Louis, to the period of mass migration. He gives information on the three parishes, the school and the orphanage built by Fr. Spigardi, sent to St. Louis by Bishop Scalabrini, and other Italian organizations in the city.

87. Gower, Charlotte Day.
"The Supernatural Patron in Sicilian Life." Unpublished Ph.D. dissertation, University of Chicago, 1928.

A study of the patron cult in Sicily and patrons in relationship to towns, parishes, confraternities, and individuals.

88. Hackett, Jane Katherine.
"A Survey of Presbyterian Work with Italians in the Presbytery of Chicago." Unpublished M.A. thesis, Presbyterian College of Christian Education, Chicago, 1943.

The result of a ten-month survey of Presbyterian work with Italians in the Presbytery of Chicago. Nine Presbyterian institutions serving predominantly Italian constituencies were reviewed. The author found a rapid decline in the use of the Italian language, resistance to participation in neighborhood house programs, inadequate facilities, lack of professional personnel, little insistence on formal Christian teaching, and little education of Italians toward self-support of church programs.

89. Harney, Paul.
"A History of Jesuit Education in American California." Unpublished Ph.D. dissertation, University of California, Berkeley, 1944.

Italian Jesuits were highly influential in the development of Catholic higher education in California.

90. Hinrichsen, Carl Derivaux.
"The History of the Diocese of Newark, 1873-1901." Unpublished Ph.D. dissertation, Catholic University of America, 1962.

Reference to the beginning of Italian national parishes in Newark.

91. Hoffman, George J.
"Catholic Immigrant Aid Societies in New York City from 1880 to 1920." Unpublished Ph.D. dissertation, St. John's University, Department of History, 1947.

Poorly written and inadequately researched, this dissertation contains information on the following ethnic immigrant aid societies: The Mission of Our Lady of the Rosary (Irish), The St. Raphael Society (German), The St. Raphael Society (Italian), The St. Joseph Society for Polish Immigrants, The Mission of Our Lady of Guadalupe (Spanish-speaking), French and Belgian immigrant aid societies.

92. Honig, Deborah Beatrice.
"The Church of Mary, Help of Christians, New York City: The National Parish as a solution to the 'Italian Problem'." Unpublished M.A. thesis, Faculty of Political Science, Columbia University, 1966.

This thesis reviews the "Italian Problem" and, through the history of one parish, points out how Italians had a different, less defensive, perception than the Irish of the role of Catholic schools. It also shows the role of intermediary between the immigrants and American Catholicism performed by Italian priests and the national parish. The price Honig sees as paid for the accomplishments of the national parish is the institutionalization of the division between English-speaking and non-English-speaking Catholics.

93. Juliani, Richard N.
"The Social Organization of Immigration: The Italians in Philadelphia." Unpublished Ph.D. dissertation, Sociology, University of Pennsylvania, 1971.

Reference is made to Italians and the Church. See Richard N. Juliani. "Italians and Other Americans: The Parish, The Union and the Settlement House." *Perspectives in Italian Immigration and Ethnicity.* Edited by S.M. Tomasi. New York: Center for Migration Studies, 1977. Pp. 179-186.

94. Leonetti, Donna Lockwood.
"Religion and the Life of the South Italians in Italy and America." Unpublished M.A. thesis, Anthropology, University of Washington, 1967.

This study examines the character of South Italian Catholicism, its relationship to the total social and cultural system of Southern Italians in Italy and the acculturation process of the first, second and third generation immigrants in the United States. The religious beliefs of Southern Italians in Italy and America are examined in their relationship with the people's social system. The study concludes that Southern Italians, products of a peasant society, have been acculturated into American Catholicism. The study is based on published documents and includes a bibliography.

95. Linkh, Richard Michael.
"Catholicism and the European Immigrant, 1900-1924: A Chapter in American Catholic Social Thought." Unpublished Ph.D. dissertation, Teacher's College, Columbia University, 1973.

Frequent references to the Catholic Church's view of Italian immigrants and of its work for them. See Richard M. Linkh. *American Catholicism and European Immigrants (1900-1924).* Staten Island, N.Y.: Center for Migration Studies, 1975.

96. Lo Conte, John.
"The Catholic Church and the Italian Immigrant Colony in Boston: Early Missionary Work to the Establishment of National Parishes." Unpublished M.A. thesis, Catholic University of America, 1968.

A short history of Italian Catholic immigrants in Boston with analysis of the interaction between the immigrant group and the American Catholic Church. Details are given of the San Marco Society as a Fabriceria (trustees) which was responsible for the founding of Sacred Heart in Boston as an Italian parish.

97. Lothrop, Gloria Ricci.
"Father Gregory Mengarini, An Italian Jesuit Missionary in the Transmontane West: His Life and Memoirs." Unpublished Ph.D. dissertation, History, University of Southern California, 1970.

A description of Fr. Mengarini's missionary work in the United States, mostly on the Pacific coast, and translation of his memoirs with critical comments. See Gregory Mengarini. *Recollections of the Flathead Mission: Containing Brief Observations Both Ancient and Contemporary Concerning This Particular Nation.* Translated and edited by Gloria Ricci Lothrop. Glendale, Cal.: Clark, 1977.

98. McBreen, Eileen Marie.
"The Visit of the Most Reverend Cajetan Bedini to Cincinnati in 1853." Unpublished M.A. thesis, University of Notre Dame, 1937.

Well documented work which utilizes the unpublished correspondence of Bishop John B. Purcell and Archbishop Bedini.

99. Mangano, Antonio.
"Italian Colonies of New York City." Unpublished M.A. thesis, Teacher's College, Columbia University, 1903.

Reference is made to evangelical work. See Antonio Mangano. "The Associated Life of the Italians in New York City." *Charities,* XII (May 7, 1904), 476-482. Reprinted, Cordasco, Francesco, and Bucchioni, Eugene, eds. *The Italians: Social Backgrounds of An American Group.* Clifton, New Jersey: Augustus M. Kelley, Publishers, 1974.

100. Marsh, May Case.
"The Life and Work of the Churches in an Interstitial Area." Unpublished Ph.D. dissertation, New York University, 1932.

Italians in East Harlem, New York City. Makes reference to the activities of both Catholic and Protestant churches.

101. Migliore, Salvatore.
"Half-century of Italian Immigration into Pittsburgh and Allegheny County." Unpublished M.A. thesis, University of Pittsburgh, 1928.

A chapter on the establishment of Italian parishes in Pittsburgh. Copy in Pennsylvania Room of Carnegie Library of Pittsburgh.

102. Milesi, F.
"Mons. Scalabrini e il problema dell'assistenza agli emigrati." Unpublished Ph.D. dissertation, Università Cattolica del S. Cuore, Milano, 1966.

Scalabrini's social work on behalf of Italian immigrants.

103. Moffatt, M. Eulelia Teresa.
"Charles Constatine Pise, 1801-1866. An Essay." Unpublished M.A. thesis, Catholic Univesity of America, Washington, 1930.

An essay on Father Pise, whose Italian father makes him the first American born priest of Italian background, on his literary achievements, his service as Chaplain to Congress in 1832, his poem, "American Flag" (They say I do not love thee, — Flag of my native land...), his pastoral work in Brooklyn which ended when the first immigrants from Italy began to arrive there.

104. Murphy, Mary Carmel.
"Bishop Joseph Rosati, C.M. and the Diocese of New Orleans, 1824-1830." Unpublished Ph.D. dissertation, St. Louis University, 1960.

This is a study of Bishop Joseph Rosati and his role as administrator of the Diocese of New Orleans in the second half of the 1820s. Rosati was born in Sora, Italy, in 1789, entered the Congregation of the Priests of the Mission in 1807, and came to America as a missionary in 1816.

105. North, William E.
"Catholic Education in Southern California." Unpublished Ph.D. dissertation, Catholic University of America, Washington, D.C., 1936.

Indicates the role of Italian religious communities in education.

106. O'Brien, Thaddeus John.
"Attitudes of Suburban Italian-Americans Towards the Roman Catholic Church Formal Education and the Parochial School." Unpublished Ph.D. dissertation, Sociology, University of Chicago, 1972.

After a presentation of theories of cultural change, the author analyzes life in Southern Italy and among Italians in America, concentrating on their community and family in Melrose Park, Illinois. By studying the cultural heritage of this ethnic group, he attempts an interpretation of their present attitudes and behavior toward sex and religion.

107. Palisi, Bartolomeo J.
"The Changing Attitudes and Values of Sicilian Americans Toward Religion and Superstition." Unpublished M.A. thesis, Brooklyn College, 1960.

A report on the changes in attitudes and values toward religion and superstition across three generations of Sicilian-Americans. The report summarizes cultural institutions in Sicily and relates the changes in attitudes and values among Sicilian-Americans in reference to their exposure to, and experience with equivalent institutions in American society. The findings are related to theories of immigrant adjustment by which newcomers either modify their attitudes and values as an accommodation to their new surroundings, or attempt to set up exclusive ethnic enclaves.

108. Perrotta, Christopher.
"Cahtolic Care of the Italian Immigrant in the United States." Unpublished M.A. thesis, School of Philosophy, Catholic University of America, 1925.

This unpublished master's thesis, based on secondary sources, gives a general view of Italian immigration and the efforts made to care for the religious needs of the immigrants. The author's presuppositions as well as his conclusions are unsupported, thus limiting the value of this work.

109. Piccinni, Gaetano M.
"Blessed Frances Xavier Cabrini in America." Unpublished M.A. thesis, Columbia University, 1942.

A study of the social and religious conditions of Italian immigrants at the turn of the century and the motives that prompted Cabrini and Scalabrini to become interested in them. See Gaetano Michael Piccinni. *Blessed Frances Xavier Cabrini in America*. New York: The Missionary Sisters of the Sacred Heart, 1942.

110. Pockstaller, Theodore.
"Juan Maria Salvatierra and the Establishment of the First Permanent Settlements in California." Unpublished Ph.D. dissertation, University of California, 1919.

A study of Salvatierra (Giammaria Salvaterra), an Italian Jesuit missionary in California and other parts of the West, in the late 1600s.

111. Pozzetta, George E.
"The Italians of New York City, 1890-1914." Unpublished Ph.D. dissertation, University of North Carolina at Chapel Hill, 1971.

This unpublished dissertation focuses on the Italian settlements in New York City. Chapter VIII, "The Religious Accommodation," gives a good summary of the role of the Church in the Italian community of the city. The author concludes that by 1914 the New York Church had accommodated to the Italian immigrants and that the extensive and expensive Protestant efforts to convert the immigrants had largely failed.

112. Roniger, M. Stella Maris.
"Contributions of the Missionary Sisters of the Sacred Heart to Education in Italy and the United States." Unpublished M.A. thesis, Education, Fordham University, 1938.

This thesis presents an historical development of the origin, growth, and educational activities of the Missionary Sisters of the Sacred Heart, in an evaluation of the contributions of their community to the field of Christian education in Italy and the United States. Much of this thesis is centered on the biography of the foundress of the Order, St. Frances Xavier Cabrini.

113. Rosoli, Gianfausto.
"L'emigrazione italiana in America dal 1861 al 1915 e l'organizzazione assistenziale e religiosa di Scalabrini." Unpublished Ph.D. dissertation, Università Cattolica del S. Cuore, Milano, 1970.

A critical study of Bishop Scalabrini's religious and social understanding and strategies of intervention regarding Italian mass migration.

114. Russo, Nicholas J.
"The Religious Acculturation of The Italians in New York City." Unpublished Ph.D. dissertation, St. John's University, Department of Sociology, 1968.

The author concludes: "In sum, the findings of this study have indicated that three generations of American-Italians have gone through the process of absorbing the cultural patterns of American society, while retaining some of their own 'social identity' " (p. 298). See Nicholas J. Russo. "Three Generations of Italians in New York City: Their Religious Acculturation." *The Italian Experience in the United States.* Edited by S.M. Tomasi and M.H. Engel. New York: The Center for Migration Studies of New York, Inc., 1970.

115. Shanabruch, Charles H.
"The Catholic Church's Role in the Americanization of Chicago's Immigrants: 1833-1928." Unpublished Ph.D. dissertation, University of Chicago, 1975.

This study, based on archival material and newspaper accounts, examines the work of the Catholic Church among immigrants in Chicago, including the Italians. It shows how the Church joined together more than twenty-five nationalities and fostered a new identity that was more American than foreign.

116. Shumway, Felice.
"The Social Contribution of Mother Cabrini in the United States with Emphasis on the Immigrant." Unpublished M.A. thesis, Catholic University of America, 1950.

Short narration of Mother Cabrini's pastoral and social activities throughout the United States in favor of Italian immigrants and their children.

117. Sterbick, Mary Elizabeth.
"The Social Thought of St. Frances Xavier Cabrini as Exemplified in the Sacred Heart Orphanage at Seattle." Unpublished M.A. thesis, School of Social Science, Seattle University, 1948.

Historical development of Sacred Heart Orphanage in Seattle.

118. Stibili, Edward C.
"The St. Raphael Society for the Protection of Italian Immigrants, 1887-1923." Unpublished Ph.D. dissertation, Department of History, University of Notre Dame, 1977.

Detailed study, based largely on archival sources, of an emigrant aid society established in Italy by Bishop Giovanni Battista Scalabrini. The society, which gave newly arrived immigrants protection and assistance, developed branches in New York City and in Boston. See Edward C. Stibili. "The Interest of Bishop Giovanni Battista Scalabrini of Piacenza in the 'Italian Problem.' " *The Religious Experience of Italian Americans.* Edited by Silvano M. Tomasi, Staten Island, New York: The American Italian Historical Association, 1975. Pp. 11-30.

119. Sullivan, Edwin Vose.
"An Annotated Copy of the Diary of Bishop James Roosevelt Bayley, First Bishop of Newark, New Jersey, 1853-1872." Unpublished Ph.D. dissertation, Department of History, University of Ottawa, 1956.

A two-volume dissertation which gives valuable information on the activities of Italian-American priests in the diocese of Newark, New Jersey. Volume I, 219 pages, contains the text of the Diary. Volume II, 365 pages, contains critical annotations.

120. Tangarone, Adam Abel.
"An Intensive Study of the Torrington Italian Mission Connected with the Center Congregational Church, Torrington, Connecticut." Unpublished M.R.E. thesis, Hartford School of Religious Education, 1935.

A general work of Protestant apologetics.

121. Tomasi, Silvano M.
"Assimilation and Religion: The Role of the Italian Ethnic Church in the New York Metropolitan Area, 1880-1930." Unpublished Ph.D. dissertation, Department of Sociology, Fordham University, 1972.

Description of growth and development of Italian parishes in the New York City metropolitan area. Silvano Tomasi. *Piety and Power: The Role of the Italian Parishes in the New York Metropolitan Area.* Staten Island, N.Y.: Center for Migration Studies, 1975.

122. Valletta, Clement Lawrence.
"A Study of Americanization in Carneta. Italian-American Identity through Three Generations." Unpublished Ph.D. dissertation, University of Pennsylvania, 1968. Reprinted, New York: Arno Press, 1975.

A detailed study of the changing identities of three generations of Italian-Americans living in the small town they founded in eastern Pennsylvania. Chapter 10, pp. 281-315, is titled: "Religion in Carneta: Mary, The Great Mother, and the Word."

123. Vollmar, Edward R.
"History of the Jesuit Colleges of New Mexico and Colorado, 1867-1919." Unpublished M.A. thesis, St. Louis University Graduate School, 1939.

A fairly complete study, based mainly on Regis College archival material. See Edward R. Vollmar. "Donato Gasparri, new Mexico — Colorado Mission Founder." *Mid-America*, N.S., IX (April, 1938), 96-102.

124. Walsh, John P.
"The Catholic Church in Chicago and Problems of an Urban Society, 1893-1915." Unpublished Ph.D. dissertation, University of Chicago, 1948.

This study of the Catholic Church in Chicago from 1893 to 1915 contains some information on the work of the Church among immigrant groups, including the Italians.

125. Wehmhoff, Mary Walter.
"Educational Activities of the Santa Maria Institute." Unpublished M.A. thesis, University of Dayton, 1944.

This is an account of the foundation and work of "The Santa Maria Educational and Industrial Home," later known as "The Santa Maria Institute," founded in 1897 in Cincinnati, Ohio, by two Sisters of Charity of Mount St. Joseph, Sisters Blandina Segale and Justina Segale. The Institute, a Catholic social settlement for Italians, was established to provide a variety of social services and to counter the influence of Protestant social work among the Italians of Cincinnati.

126. Weisz, Howard Ralph.
"Irish-American and Italian-American Educational Views and Activ-

ities, 1870-1900: A Comparison." Unpublished Ph.D. dissertation, Columbia University, 1968.

An excellent chapter (pp. 376-419) on Italian schools in the United States and their history. Public and parochial schools and the attitudes of Italian-Americans toward them in comparison to the attitudes of Irish-Americans are carefully analyzed.

127. White, M. Afra.
"Catholic Indian Missionary Influence in the Development of Catholic Education in Montana, 1849-1903." Unpublished Ph.D. dissertation, St. Louis University, 1940.

Reference is made to the contribution of Italian Jesuits.

128. Williams, Phyllis H.
"The Religious Mores of the South-Italians in New Haven." Unpublished M.A. thesis, Yale University, 1933.

Attempts to level out differences by education between Italian immigrants in New Haven and their American-born children have been in a large measure unsuccessful because of the lack of knowledge of their particular religious mores. The author, therefore, presents her findings on the background of the immigrants and their beliefs on: Souls and Ghosts; Spirits and Gods; the Evil Eye; Right and Wrong; Magic and his Workers; Religion and Change. See Phyllis H. Williams. *South Italian Folkways in Europe and America, a Handbook for Social Workers, Visiting Nurses, School Teachers, and Physicians.* New Haven: Published for the Institute of Human Relations by Yale University Press, 1938. Reprinted, New York: Russell & Russell, 1969.

129. Yans-McLaughlin, Virginia.
"Like the Fingers of the Hand: The Family and Community Life of First-Generation Italian-Americans in Buffalo, New York, 1880-1930." Unpublished Ph.D. dissertation, State University of New York at Buffalo, 1970.

Italian parishes and Italian parish schools as centers for Italian social and religious life in Buffalo are mentioned. The public school system was often biased towards Italian culture, so that Italians sent their children to Catholic schools of the Italian parishes. St. Anthony's parochial school performed a dual function by informing the second generation Italians of their heritage and by keeping the young within the protective control of the Italian community. See Virginia Yans-McLaughlin. *Family and Community. Italian Immigrants in Buffalo, 1880-1930.* Ithaca, N.Y.: Cornell University Press, 1977.

130. Zaloha, Anna.
     "A Study of the Persistence of Italian Customs Among 143 Families
     of Italian Descent. Members of Social Club at Chicago Commons."
     Unpublished M.A. thesis, Northwestern University, 1937.

     Study of the persistence of social, cultural, and religious customs among
     Italian families in Chicago.

4

Parish Histories

131. Blessed Virgin of Pompei Church, Milwaukee, Wis. *Golden Jubilee, 1904-1954*. Milwaukee: 1954.

132. Bolzan, Louis.
Memories of an Italian Parish. A History of the Sacred Heart Italian Church of Cincinnati, Ohio. Cincinnati, 1974. (From its foundation in 1890 to 1974.)

133. Briggs, E.B.
Anniversary Year, 1907-1957, of the Catholic Church of Monongah, West Virginia: St. Stanislaus Church, Our Lady of Pompei Church and Monongah Disaster. Monongah, W.Va.: 1957.

134. *Centennial Booklet. Our Lady of Sorrows Parish, 1874-1974*. (Basilica of Our Lady of Sorrows, 3121 Jackson Boulevard, Chicago, Illinois 60612).

135. *Chiesa di S. Antonio da Padova, Buffalo, New York. Brevi note storiche in commemorazione del 30.mo anniversario della sua fondazione, 1891-1921*.

136. Ciaburri, Alfred.
The Story of a Parish. Our Lady of Assumption R.C. Church. Bayonne, New Jersey, 1953.

137. Ciufoletti, Manlio.
Storia della Parrocchia Italiana di S. Gioachino in New York pubblicata in occasione del suo giubileo d'oro. 1938.

138, Committee for the 50th Anniversary of St. Bartholomew's Parish. *Golden Jubilee — 50th Anniversary, 1907-1957.* Providence, R.I.: St. Bartholomew's Parish, 1957.

139. Committee of the Golden Jubilee. *Santa Maria Addolorata Parish: 50th Anniversary, 1903-1953.* Chicago: 1953.

140. *Diamond Jubilee of the Assumption Parish, 1881-1956.* Chicago: 1956.

141. *Eco delle feste giubilari pel XXV° Anniversario della Missione Italiana del S. Cuore in Boston, Mass., 25-26-27 Gennaio, 1914.* Firenze: Tipografia Barbera, Alfani & Venturi Proprietari.

142. *Fifty Years of Grace — 1952 — A Historical Sketch and Souvenir Commemoration of the Golden Jubilee of the Blessing of the Church of the Immaculate Conception.* Iron Mountain, Michigan: 1952.

143. The First Italian Baptist Church, Brooklyn, New York. *Its Heritage of Thirty-five Years of Service and Its Future.* New York: 1939.

144. Flynn, Paul V.
History of St. John's Church. Newark: Press of the New Jersey Trade Review, 1908.

145. Fusco, Nicola.
Mount St. Peter. Story of Saint Peter's Church in New Kensington, Pennsylvania. Pittsburgh, Pa.: St. Joseph's Protectory, 1944.

146. *Golden Anniversary, 1908-1958. Most Holy Rosary Parish, Perth Amboy, N.J.*

147. *Golden Jubilee Year, 1893-1943. Sacred Heart Italian Church, 527 Broadway, Cincinnati, Ohio.*

148. *Historical Review: St. Ambrose Church, Fortieth Anniversary, 1903-1943.* St. Louis, Mo.: 1943.

149. *History of Transfiguration Parish, Mott Street, New York, 1827-1897.* New York: 1897.

150. Holy Rosary Church, Bridgeport, Conn. *Golden Jubilee, 1903-1953.* Bridgeport, Conn.: 1953.

151. Holy Rosary Church, Cleveland, Ohio. *1909-1959: Holy Rosary Church Golden Jubilee.* Cleveland, Ohio: 1959.

152. Holy Rosary Church, Kansas City, Mo. *Historical Holy Rosary Parish, Kansas City, Missouri. Holy Rosary Parish Golden Jubilee, 1942.* Kansas City: 1942.

153. Holy Rosary Church, Washington, D.C. *45th Anniversary Celebration, April 19, 1959.* Washington, D.C.: 1959.

154. Holy Rosary Church, Washington, D.C. *The Parish of the Holy Rosary in Washington, D.C., Twenty-Five Years of Mission Work, 1913-1938. Some Records of the Parish of the Queen of the Most Holy Rosary.* Washington, D.C.: 1938.

155. Holy Rosary Parish. *Golden Jubilee 1942.* Kansas City, Missouri: Oct. 25, 1942.

156. Holy Rosary Parish. *Golden Jubilee 1913-1963.* Washington, D.C.: Holy Rosary Church, 1963.

157. *Nel Cinquantesimo Anniversario della Fondazione della Chiesa di S. Antonio di Padova, Prima Parrocchia Italiana negli State Uniti, e della venuta dei Francescani italiani in New York.* New York: Emporium Press, 1916.

158. *The New San Antonio Italian Church, Queen City Avenue and White Street, Cincinnati, Ohio.* 1940.

159. "Our Lady Help of Christians Church" (New York). *The Vigo Review,* II (February, 1938), 12-13.

160. "Our Lady Help of Christians Church, Pittsburgh, Pa." *The Vigo Review,* II (February, 1939), 12-13, 16.

161. Our Lady Help of Christians' Church, St. Louis, Mo. *Twenty-fifth Anniversary (Silver Jubilee) of the Società di mutuo soccorso Maria SS. della Misericordia (Misericordia Society): Brief Local History, 1920-1945.* St. Louis, Mo.: 1945.

162. Our Lady of Mount Carmel Church, Bristol, R.I. *Silver Jubilee Celebration, 1916-1941.* Bristol, R.I.: 1941.

163. "Our Lady of Mt. Carmel Church in Jersey City." *The Vigo Review*, I (May, 1938), 12-13.

164. Our Lady of Mt. Carmel Church, Meriden, Conn. *Church Re-Dedication, (1936-1961), November 5, 1961.* Meriden, Conn.: 1961.

165. "Our Lady of Mount Carmel Church of Newark, N.J." *The Vigo Review*, I (July, 1938), 12-13.

166. *Our Lady of Mount Carmel, Denver, Colorado.* Hackensack, N.J.: Custombook, Inc., 1975.

167. *Our Lady of Mount Carmel Golden Jubilee, 1917-1967* (141 State Street, Bristol, Rhode Island).

168. Our Lady of Mt. Carmel Parish, Melrose Park, Ill. *Golden Jubilee and 50th Anniversary, 1903-1953.* Melrose Park, Ill.: 1953.

169. Our Lady of Pompeii Church. *Golden Jubilee 1911-1961.* Chicago: 1961.

170. Our Lady of the Most Holy Rosary Church, Jersey City, N.J. *Our Lady of the Most Holy Rosary Church Commemorates the Seventy-Fifth Anniversary of Its Foundation, 1885-1960.* Jersey City, N.J.: 1960.

171. Parolin, Pio.
     Ricordo del venticinquesimo anno della fondazione della Chiesa di S. Pietro in Syracuse, N.Y. 6 Ottobre, 1895-1920. Syracuse: Fulco Publishing Co., 1920.

172. *"Pati non Mori": il 14 ottobre 1883 ed il 28 Giugno, 1891.* Philadelphia, Pa.: Printing House, 1891. (St. Mary Magdalen de Pazzi, Philadelphia, Pa.).

173. Pisani, Lawrence F.
"Oldest Italian Church in Connecticut, St. Michael's Marks 75th Anniversary." *New Haven Register Features*, May 16, 1965, 5.

174. Pizzoglio, William.
Fortieth Anniversary, 1927-1967, St. Anthony's Church of Everett. Its History and Progress from the Beginning to the Present. Everett, Mass.: 1967.

175. Pizzoglio, William.
St. Mary of Mt. Carmel Church, Utica, N.Y.: Its History and Progress from the Beginning to the Present (1896-1936). Utica, N.Y.: 1936.

176. Reeves, W.H.
Our Lady Help of the Christians' Parish. History of the Parish. St. Louis Register, 1946.

177. *Ricordo degli italiani di Iron Mountain, Mich.* Calumet, Mich.: Tipografia del "Minatore italiano," 1903.

178. *Ricordo Giubilare ed Inaugurale della chiesa dei Sacri Cuori in Brooklyn, N.Y., 1882-1907.*

179. Sacred Heart Church, Cincinnati, Ohio. *History of Sacred Heart Italian Church, Cincinnati, Ohio. Golden Jubilee Year (1893-1943).* Cincinnati: 1943.

180. Sacred Heart Italian Church, Cincinnati, Ohio. *Diamond Jubilee, 1893-1968.* Cincinnati, Ohio: 1968.

181. *Saint Rocco's Church, 1952.* Cleveland: Star Calendar and Printing Co., 1952.

182. "Saint Roch's Church, Bronx, New York." *The Vigo Review*, I (June, 1938), 12-13, 19.

183. Sassi, Costantino.
Parrocchia della Madonna di Pompei in New York. Notizie storiche dei primi cinquant'anni dalla sua fondazione: 1892-1942. Marino: Santa Lucia, 1946.

184. *75th Anniversary, Our Lady of Pompei in Greenwich Village, May 7th, 1967.* New York: The Tenny Press, 1967.

185. *Solenne Dedicazione della Nuova Chiesa di Maria SS. Ausiliatrice. New York City, 10 Febbraio 1918.* New York: Nardone Press, 1918.

186. *Solenne Dedicazione della Nuova Chiesa di Nostra Signora del Carmelo. Bronx, New York, 14 Ottobre, 1917.* Bronx, New York: Mt. Carmel Press, 1917.

187. Souvenir. *History of Transfiguration Parish — Mott Street, New York, 1827-1897.* New York: 1897.

188. St. Ambrose Church, St. Louis, Mo. *Fortieth Anniversary: Historical Review, Brief Historical Sketches and Data of Saint Ambrose Park, 1903-1943.* St. Louis, Mo.: 1943.

189. St. Anthony Church, Everett, Mass. *Silver Jubilee Celebration, 1928-1953.* Everett, Mass.: 1953.

190. St. Anthony Church, Fredonia, N.Y. *History of St. Anthony Church, Fredonia, New York. Golden Jubilee (1906-1956).* Fredonia, N.Y.: 1956.

191. *St. Anthony of Padua Church, New York City.* South Hackensack, N.J.: Custombook, Inc., 1967.

192. St. Anthony's Church, Buffalo. *Golden Jubilee, 1891-1941.* Buffalo, N.Y.: 1941.

193. "St. Anthony's Church, East Newark N.J." *The Vigo Review*, I (November, 1938), 12-13.

194. St. Anthony's Church, New Haven, Conn. *50th Anniversary 1904-1954.* New Haven, Conn.: 1954.

195. St. Anthony's Church, Somerville, Mass. *Grand Reunion Commemorating the Thirtieth Anniversary of the Founding of St. Anthony's Church, Somerville, Mass.* Somerville, Mass.: 1946.

196. St. Bartholomew's Parish, Providence, R.I. *50th Anniversary.* Providence: 1957.

197. St. Callistus Church, Chicago, Ill. *Silver Jubilee (1919-1944).* Chicago: 1944.

198. St. Francis of Assisi Church, Hoboken, New Jersey. *Seventy-Fifth Anniversary Celebration.* Hoboken, N.J.: 1963.

199. St. Joachim's Church. *May God Bless Your Jubilee: 1905-1930.* New York: St. Joachim's Church, 26 Roosevelt St., 1930.

200. St. Joachim's Church, New York, N.Y. *Il venticinquesimo della prima chiesa italiana sorta per Mons. Scalabrini su terra de l'Unione.* New York: 1913.

201. St. John's Baptist Church and Christian Center. *Directory, 1964-1965.* Philadelphia: 1965.

202. St. Joseph's Parish, Fairmont, W.Va. *Golden Anniversary, 1909-1959.* Fairmont, W.Va.: 1959.

203. St. Lazarus Church, East Boston, Mass. *Brief History of St. Lazarus Parish during Its Fifty Years from 1892-1942, Golden Jubilee,* East Boston: 1942.

204. St. Maria Addolorata Church, Chicago, Ill. *50th Anniversary, 1903-1953, Souvenir Book.* Chicago: 1953.

205. St. Maria Incoronata Church, Chicago, Ill. *Golden Anniversary, 1904-1944.* Chicago: 1944.

206. *St. Mary of Mount Carmel Church, Diamond Jubilee* (648 Jay Street, Utica, New York).

207. St. Mary of Mount Carmel, Utica, N.Y. *50th Anniversary, 1896-1946.* Utica: 1946.

208. St. Michael Church, Chicago, Ill. *Golden Anniversary, 1903-1953.* Chicago: 1953.

209. St. Michael's Church, New Haven, Conn. *75th Anniversary.* New Haven: 1965.

210. St. Peter's Italian Church, Duluth, Minn. *Dedication.* Duluth, Minn.: December 18, 1927.

211. St. Rocco's Church, Thornton, R.I. *50th Anniversary, 1903-1953.* Thornton, R.I.: 1953.

212. St. Tarcisius Church. *50th Anniversary, 1907-1957.* St. Tarcisius Church, Framingham, Mass.: 1957.

213. *Tu es Petrus.* Dedication of Saint Peter's Church, September 18, 1955. Syracuse: 1955.

5

Books and Articles

214. Abel, Theodore.
Protestant Home Missions to Catholic Immigrants. New York: Institute of Social and Religious Research, 1933. Pp. xi-143.

This book is divided into two parts. Part one deals with various aspects of Protestant missionary work among Catholic immigrants in the United States. Part two gives an excerpt from an autobiography written by an Italian Protestant minister describing his missionary work in a large Italian urban settlement.

215. Abeloe, William N.
To the Top of the Mountain. Hicksville, New York: Exposition Press, 1976. Pp. xiii-160.

This biography, subtitled "The Life of Father Umberto Olivieri, 'Padre of the Otomis,' " recounts the life of Umberto Olivieri, born in Rome in 1884 and educated in law at the University of Rome. Olivieri pursued several careers in Italy and the United States, married an American, and at the age of 74 was granted permission to become a priest.

216. Abramson, Harold J.
"Ethnic Diversity Within Catholicism: A Comparative Analysis of Contemporary and Historical Religion." *Journal of Social History*, 4 (Summer, 1971), 359-388.

Italian-American Catholics are included in this analysis.

217. Abramson, Harold J.
Ethnic Diversity in Catholic America. New York: John Wiley & Sons, 1973. Pp. xvi-207.

"Most of the data in this book is secondary analysis, derived from a survey research conducted by the National Opinion Research Center at the University of Chicago in the winter of 1963-1964..." (p. vii). The study, based on the author's Ph.D. dissertation, University of Chicago, 1969, aims to show the persistence of ethnicity within Catholicism due to the length of stay and the historical background of the ethnic groups in America.

218. Abramson, Harold J.
      "The Social Varieties of Catholic Behavior: The Italian Experience Viewed Comparatively." *The Religious Experience of Italian Americans.* Edited by Silvano M. Tomasi. Staten Island, New York: The American Italian Historical Association, 1975. Pp. 53-70.

      Sociological study assessing the diversity of Catholicity on a few measures of religious involvement and association, comparing Italian Catholic levels with those of the Irish, Polish, German, and other Catholic backgrounds in the United States.

219. Accolti, Biagio.
      Padre Michele Accolti. Bari: ed. Accolti-Gil, 1915. Pp. 148.

      Biography of a leading Italian Jesuit in San Francisco and a co-founder of the University of San Francisco. Includes two letters by Fr. Accolti and Fr. DeSmet.

220. *Acta et Decreta Concilii Plenarii Baltimorensis Tertii, A.D. MDCCCLXXXIV.* Baltimore: Typis Joannis Murphy et Sociorum, 1886. Pp. 321.

      These proceedings and decrees of the Third Plenary Council of Baltimore are useful to document the first official discussions in the Church about immigrants and their religious needs (pp. 131-133). The debate was provoked by the massive arrival of Italians.

221. Adams, Joseph H.
      "The Italian Quarters of New York City." *The Baptist Home Mission Monthly,* XXXI (September, 1909), 379-384.

      Description of Italian section in New York City.

222. Agnew, W.H.
      "Pastoral Care of Italian Children in America." *The Ecclesiastical Review,* XLVIII (March, 1913), 257-267.

      The author, a Jesuit with personal experience in the West Side Italian district in Chicago and the Italian settlements in St. Louis, argues that many children of Italian immigrants will be lost to the Church if something is not done to educate them in the basics of the Catholic faith. He praises the work of a lay Sunday School Association, founded in Chicago at the turn of the century by Fr. Edmund M. Dunne, first pastor of Guardian Angel Italian Church.

223. "Alaska, An Account of the Mission Brought Down to June, 1889." *Woodstock Letters*, XIX (1890), 55-63.

Account of Jesuit missions in Upper Alaska. Includes information on the various Christian sects, the spread of prejudice toward Alaskans among Catholics, the progress of the Jesuit missions and the work of the Italian Jesuit missionaries Tosi, Treca, Negro and Giordano.

224. Alba, Richard D.
"Social Assimilation Among American Catholic National-Origin Groups." *American Sociological Review*, 41 (December, 1976), 1030-1046.

This paper, using data about Catholic national-origin groups in the early 1960s, finds little support for recent assertions of ethnic vitality. Includes data on Italian-Americans.

225. Alderson, Jo Bartels and J. Michael Alderson.
The Man Mazzuchelli. Madison, Wisconsin: Wisconsin House, Ltd., 1974. Unpaged.

This is the first complete biography in English of Fr. Samuel Mazzuchelli, O.P., a pioneer Catholic priest in the Midwest. It is based in large part on archival materials.

226. Algardi, Filippo.
"Il centenario di un pioniere: P. Pasquale Tosi, esploratore e missionario nell'Alasca." *Vie d'Italia e del mondo*, 3 (1935), 745-769.

Brief article on Fr. Pasquale Tosi, missionary and explorer in Alaska.

227. Allen, Adrian.
"Man Against the Wilderness." *Sign*, XXXII (October, 1952), 36-38.

This article deals with the Jesuit missionary Anthony Ravalli and his work at the Indian mission of St. Mary's, Montana, during the middle 1880s.

228. Allen, Harold.
Father Ravalli's Missions. Chicago: The Good Lion, 1972. Pp. 31 of text and additional pages with photographs.

Father Anthony Ravalli came from Italy to the Catholic missions of the early Northwest in 1844 and for 40 years worked among the Flathead and Coeur d'Alene Indians. His two outstanding missions were the "Old Mission" at

Cataldo, Idaho, and Old St. Mary's in Stevensville, Montana, including many of their furnishings. Harold Allen has photographed these churches and written the story of their creation. He includes an account of the decade-long effort by the Flathead Indians to get the "Black Robes" (Jesuits), their remarkable conversion, and a bibliography.

229. Amberg, Mary Agnes.
Madonna Center. Chicago: Loyola University Press, 1976. Pp. 220.

This chronicle of Madonna Center, subtitled "pioneer Catholic social settlement," was written between 1940-42, though published in 1976. Based largely on personal recollections and newspaper clippings, it describes the center's development and its work among the Italian in Chicago.

230. Amfitheatrof, Erik.
The Children of Columbus. An Informal History of Italians in the New World. Boston: Little, Brown and Company, 1973. Pp. 371.

This popularly written informal history of the Italians in America includes some references to Italian religiosity.

231. Anderson, Floyd.
"The Pope's U.S. Representatives." *Ave Maria,* LXXXI (May 21, 1955), 15-17.

This is a brief biographical sketch of Archbishop Amleto Giovanni Cicognani, Apostolic Delegate to the United States from 1933 to 1958.

232. Arrighi, Antonio.
"Christian Work Among the Italians of New York City. Fourth Annual Report." The New York City Missions and Tract Society, *59th Annual Report.* New York: 50 Bible House, 1886. Pp. 57-60.

This is the annual report for 1885. Though titled "Fourth Annual Report," this is the first report to be signed "Antonio Arrighi, Pastor." The Italian Congregation worshipped in the Chapel of the Five Points House of Industry, 155 Worth Street, New York.

233. Arrighi, Antonio.
"The Calvary Italian Evangelical Church, 151 Worth Street, New York." The New York City Mission and Tract Society, *60th Annual Report.* New York: 50 Bible House, 1887. Pp. 61-64.

This is the annual report for 1886 of the Calvary Italian Evangelical Church, 151 Worth Street, New York. Arrighi was the pastor.

234. Arrighi, Antonio. "The Calvary Italian Evangelical Church, 155 Worth Street, New York." New York City Mission and Tract Society, *61st Annual Report*. New York: 50 Bible House, 1888. Pp. 71-74.

This is the annual report for 1887 of the Calvary Italian Evangelical Church, 155 Worth Street, New York City. Antonio Arrighi was the pastor.

235. Arrighi, Antonio. "Italian Evangelical Church of the City Mission, 155 Worth Street, New York." New York City Mission and Tract Society, *62nd Annual Report*. New York: 50 Bible House, 1889. Pp. 68-71.

This is the annual report for 1888 of the Italian Evangelical Church of the City Mission, 155 Worth Street. Antonio Arrighi was pastor.

236. Arrighi, Antonio. "Italian Evangelical Church." New York City Mission and Tract Society, *63d Annual Report*. New York: 106 Bible House, 1890. Pp. 74-78.

This is the annual report for 1889 of the Italian Evangelical Church, 155 Worth Street, New York City. Antonio Arrighi was the pastor.

237. Arrighi, Antonio. "Italian Evangelical Church." New York City Mission and Tract Society, *64th Annual Report*. New York: 106 Bible House, 1891. Pp. 97-102.

This is the annual report for 1890 of the Italian Evangelical Church at 155 Worth Street, New York City. Antonio Arrighi was the pastor.

238. Arrighi, Antonio. "Italian Evangelical Church. 155 Worth Street." New York City Mission and Tract Society, *65th Annual Report*. New York: 106 Bible House, 1892. Pp. 131-135.

This is the annual report for 1891 of the Italian Evangelical Church at 155 Worth Street, New York City. Antonio Arrighi was the pastor. This report marks the Church's tenth anniversary. The mission was first started on June 19, 1881, in the chapel of the Five Points House of Industry.

239. Arrighi, Antonio. "Italian Evangelical Church. 395 Broome Street." New York City Mission and Tract Society, *69th Annual Report*. New York: Press of Albert A. Ochs, 1896. Pp. 45-51.

This is the annual report for 1895 of the Italian Evangelical Church at 395 Broome Street, New York City. Antonio Arrighi was the pastor.

240. Arrighi, A.
"Italian Evangelical Church. 395 Broome Street." New York City Mission and Tract Society, *70th Annual Report*. New York: Press of Albert A. Ochs, 1897. Pp. 45-49.

This is the annual report for 1896 of the Italian Evangelical Church at 395 Broome Street, New York City. The Rev. A. Arrighi was pastor.

241. Arrighi, Antonio.
"Italian Evangelical Church. 395 Broome Street." New York City Mission and Tract Society, *72nd Annual Report*. New York: Press of Albert A. Ochs, 1899. Pp. 49-51.

This is the annual report for 1898 of the Italian Evangelical Church at 395 Broome Street, New York City. Antonio Arrighi was the pastor.

242. Arrighi, Antonio.
"Italian Evangelical Church. 395 Broome St." New York City Mission and Tract Society, *Annual Report*, January, 1902. Pp. 22-27.

This is the annual report for 1901 of the Italian Evangelical Church at 395 Broome Street, New York City. Antonio Arrighi was the pastor.

243. Arrighi, A.
"Italian Evangelical Church. Broome Street Tabernacle." The New York City Mission and Tract Society, *Annual Report*, January, 1909. Pp. 7-11.

Account of Arrighi's work in establishing Evangelical Churches in various parts of the United States.

244. A. S. R.
"Italian Mission Work, Buffalo, N.Y., Conducted by Mrs. May." *The Baptist Home Mission Monthly*, XXII (May, 1900), 145-146.

Describes work among Italians carried on at Cedar Street Baptist Church and in downtown Buffalo. The work, which was prospering, was supported by the Home Mission Society.

245. Astori, Guido.
"Scalabrini e Bonomelli fraternalmente uniti nell'assistenza agli emigrati italiani." *Studi Emigrazione*, V (Ottobre, 1968), 579-586.

Brief article, based on correspondence between Bishop Geremia Bonomelli of Cremona and Bishop Giovanni Battista Scalabrini of Piacenza, describing early attempts at collaboration between them on assistance to Italian immigrants.

246. *Atti del primo congresso cattolico italiano dell'America del Nord tenuto nella città di New York il 5 dicembre 1917.* New York: Polyglot Publishing House, 1918. Pp. 84.

Text of the talks and resolutions of the first Italian Catholic Congress held in the United States. The Congress, attended by 338 Italian priests from the ecclesiastical provinces of Baltimore, Philadelphia, New York and Boston, stressed the need for social action among Italian immigrants, for an Italian Catholic newspaper, and for a union of Italian Catholic clergy and laity in North America.

247. Bacigalupo, L.F.
"Italians in the U.S." *New Catholic Encyclopedia*, VII (1967), 746-747.

Brief account of Italian immigration to the United States, with a summary of the Italian contribution to American Catholic life.

248. Bacigalupo, Leonard.
"The Franciscans and Italian Immigration in America." *The Religious Experience of Italian Americans.* Edited by Silvano M. Tomasi. Staten Island, New York: The American Italian Historical Association, 1975. Pp. 105-119.

Brief and sketchy survey of the work of the Franciscan Order among Italian immigrants in the United States and in Canada.

249. Bacigalupo, Leonard F.
The Franciscans and Italian Immigration in America. Hicksville, N.Y.: Exposition Press, 1977. Pp. 80.

The author describes the urban mission of the Franciscan Friars and their relation to the Italian immigrant community. He also describes the activities of the Franciscan Province of the Immaculate Conception from its foundation in 1855 to 1977. The bibliographical essay lists the Franciscan archival material used.

250. Bandini, Albert R.
"Concerning the Italian Problem." *The Ecclesiastical Review*, LXII (March, 1920), 278-285.

The author analyzes the Italian immigrants as a "problem" in the American Catholic Church. He concedes that the Italian immigrants were deficient in religious instruction and often failed to support the Church. Yet, he argues that there was "a sound basis of Catholicity in their souls."

251. Bandini, A.R.
"The Italian Catholic Federation of California." *Atlantica* (October,

1931), 116-118.

Brief sketch of the "Italian Catholic Federation" of California, founded in 1924 in San Francisco "to gather in a strong organization having a central directive body and subsidiary branches, the Catholic Italians of California (and eventually of other States) in order to encourage them in the practice of religion by a cultural, religious and social propaganda."

252. Bandini, J.
"Montana. St. Ignatius' Mission. Letter of Father J. Bandini to Father Cataldo." *Woodstock Letters*, XI (1882), 275-279.

Work among the Nez-Percé Indians and conversion of their chief.

253. Bandini, P.
First Annual Report of St. Raphael's Italian Benevolent Society. (July 1st, 1891 to June 30th, 1892). New York: 1892. Pp. 27.

This first annual report presents the purpose of the Society, established by the Missionaries of St. Charles (Scalabrinians), and the statistics of the work it carried out, especially for Italian immigrant women and children. The last annual report was published in 1922 for the Society's activities of that year.

254. Bandini, Pietro.
"Origine della Colonia Italiana di Tontitown nell'Arkansas." *Bollettino dell'Emigrazione*, 1 (1903), 61-62.

A brief description of the Italian colony of Tontitown, Arkansas, by its first pastor and mayor.

255. Bandini, Pietro.
"Il Ritorno ai Campi. Per La Salvezza dei Nostri Emigranti." *Italica Gens*, II (Giugno-Luglio, 1911), 258-279.

Fr. Pietro Bandini, pastor of the Italian Colony of Tontitown, Arkansas,· argues that the immigrants should be encouraged to settle in agricultural areas of the United States.

256. Banfield, Edward C.
The Moral Basis of a Backward Society. New York: The Free Press, 1958. Pp. 188.

Important sociological study of a single village in southern Italy done in 1954-55. The author concludes that the villagers, for a variety of reasons, are incapable of acting together for the common good. This inability he terms "amoral familism," since the primary loyalty of the peasants is to the family and not to the community. There are several references to the peasants and religion.

257. Bannon, John F.
"Kino: Agent for Both Majesties." *The Historical Bulletin*, XXV (March, 1947), 55-56, 62-63.

This is a brief article on the work of Fr. Eusebio Kino among the Pima, the Pàpago, the Yuma and other Indian tribes in the American Southwest in the latter part of the seventeenth century.

258. Barberio, G. Chiodi.
Il Progresso degl' Italiani nel Connecticut. New Haven, Conn.: Maturo's Printing and Publishing Co., 1933. Pp. 802.

History of Italians in Connecticut. Includes biographies of priests and churches.

259. Barcelo, G.
"Letter of Fr. Barcelo to Fr. Cataldo—Helena, October 7, 1880." *Woodstock Letters*, X (1881), 138-139.

Work among the Crow Indians between Fort Custer and Terry's Landing. Refers to interference by the Government.

260. Bardaglio, P.W.
"Italian Immigrants and the Catholic Church in Providence, 1890-1930." *Rhode Island History*, XXXIV (May, 1975), 47-57.

The author argues that Providence's two major Italian parishes, Holy Ghost and St. Ann's, tended to aggravate differences between the Italians themselves, rather than with the Irish Catholics. He notes that the eruption of "regional differences among Italians created a difficult and sensitive situation in the diocese from early years through the 1920s, severely hampering the ability of these parishes to retain Italian loyalties and thereby facilitate the assimilation process."

261. Barr, Alfred H.
"Work Among South Italians and Sicilians in Detroit." *The Assembly Herald*, XV (January, 1909), 29-30.

Brief report on Protestant work among Italians in Detroit. The sixty to seventy man congregation is viewed very positively.

262. Barry, Colman J.
The Catholic Church and German Americans. Milwaukee: The Bruce Publishing Company, 1953. Pp. xii-348.

This is the standard study of German Americans and the Catholic Church in the United States. It includes a few references to Italian immigrants and the Catholic Church.

263. Basile Green, Rose.
The Cabrinian Philosophy of Education. Radnor, Pa.: Cabrini College, Inc., 1967. Pp. 29.

St. Frances Cabrini is portrayed as an example of Catholic principles and methods in education.

264. Basso, Ralph.
History of Roseto, Pa., 1882-1952. Easton, Pa.: Tanzella Printing, n.d. Pp. 67.

A short history of Roseto with accurate description of the important role of the Church in this small town settled by southern Italian immigrants.

265. Baudier, Roger.
The Catholic Church in Louisiana. New Orleans: A.W. Hyatt Stationery Mfg. Co., Ltd., 1939. Pp. 605.

This is a general history of the Catholic Church in Louisiana, based largely on archival sources. It includes material relevant to Italian immigrants and the Church.

266. Bayard, Ralph.
Lone-Star Vangard. The Catholic Re-Occupation of Texas (1838-1848). St. Louis: The Vincentian Press, 1945. Pp. xiii-453.

The author notes in his Preface that in "this book, one of several studies designed to tell the story of the Congregation of the Mission in the United States, a broadly biographical pattern of portrayal has been adopted." Several Italian Vincentians are included in this study, including Bishop Joseph Rosati.

267. Beccherini, Francesco.
Il fenomeno dell'emigrazione negli Stati Uniti d'America. 1906. Pp. 35.

Text of a conference given in Italy by Fr. Beccherini, pastor of the Italian Church of St. Francis in Detroit, Michigan. Beccherini describes the miserable conditions of the immigrants, the proselytizing of Protestant sects and the necessary unity between faith and ethnicity. He describes his successful experience, foresees great success for the children of the immigrants, and advocates a new concern for emigration on the part of the clergy and the government in Italy.

268. Belcredi, G.G.
"Gli italiani nel Nord America (un colloquio con Monsignor Scalabrini)." *L'Italia coloniale*, 1 (January, 1902), 33-38.

An interview with Scalabrini on Italians in North America.

269. Bellò, Carlo.
"La pastorale dell'emigrazione nelle opere di Mons. Scalabrini e di Mons. Bonomelli." *Studi Emigrazione*, IV (Giugno, 1967), 286-292.

The author compares the efforts of Bishop Giovanni Battista Scalabrini of Piacenza and Bishop Geremia Bonomelli of Cremona on behalf of Italian immigrants. Scalabrini was concerned with overseas emigration while Bonomelli was concerned with emigration to Europe.

270. Bellondi, Ariel B.
"Another Italian Mission." *The Baptist Home Mission Monthly*, XX (December, 1898), 423-424.

Describes the founding of a new Baptist mission among the Italians of Barre, Vt.

271. Bellondi, Ariel.
"Italian Immigration and Missions." *The Baptist Home Mission Monthly*, XXIII (February, 1901), 40-41.

Brief article which cites the number of Italian immigrants in 1900, notes that Italians "are generally Republicans," and mentions work of several Baptist Italian missions.

272. Bellondi, Ariel.
"The Brothers of Columbus and Garibaldi." *The Watchman*, XCV (May 22, 1913), 16-19.

Description of Baptist work among the Italian in the northeastern states.

273. Benedictus PP. XV.
"Ad R.P.D. Thomam Josephum, Episcopum Trentonensem, Cuius Paternas Curas Erga Italos Commigrantes Dilaudat." *Acta Apostolicae Sedis*, XIII (February 10, 1921), 89-90.

Letter written by Pope Benedict XV to Bishop Thomas J. Walsh of Trenton, New Jersey, on December 10, 1920, praising him for his pastoral care on behalf of Italian immigrants.

274. Berger, Mary.
"Catholic Settlement Workers." *Extension*, IV (June, 1909), 7-8, 27.

This is an account, with photographs, of Guardian Angels' Mission in Chicago's "Little Italy."

275. Bertoglio, Tommaso.
Missioni salesiane d'America. Fossano: Tip. Rossetti, 1901. Unpaged.

Small pamphlet describing the Salesians' work in America, including care of Italian immigrants.

276. Biagi, Ernest L.
The Italians of Philadelphia. New York: Carlton Press, Inc., 1967. Pp. 289.

Chapter 4, pp. 89-106, is titled "The Italians and the Church." Chapter 5, pp. 107-113, is titled "Italian Protestants in Philadelphia."

277. Bianchi, Enrico.
Guida per gli Stati Uniti. Norme e Consigli. Genova: Tipografia C. Mascarello, 1926. Pp. 255.

Information and counseling for Italian emigrants. A list of Italian churches in the United States is also included.

278. Bianco, Carla.
The Two Rosetos. Bloomington: Indiana University Press, 1974. Pp. 234.

A study of the folkways of Roseto, Pennsylvania, founded in 1882 by immigrants from the Southern Italian village of Roseto Valfortore. Folk beliefs and fantasies are described in the section "Magic and Religion: The Evil Eye and a New Madonna," pp. 84-106.

279. Biasotti, Roberto.
Rapporto della Scuola Italiana S. Carlo Borromeo in Boston, Mass. S.U.A., 1903-1904. Roxbury: Angel Guardian Press, 1904. Pp. 32.

A description of the activities and finances of the parish school attached to Sacred Heart Italian parish in Boston.

280. Biasotti, Roberto.
La Società San Raffaele per la protezione degli immigranti italiani in Boston. New York: Tipografia V. Ciocia, 1906. Pp. 96.

History of the founding and work of the Boston St. Raphael Society for the Protection of Italian Immigrants prepared for the Exposition in Milan.

281. Bisceglia, John B.
Italian Evangelical Pioneers. Kansas City, Missouri: Brown-White-

Lowell Press, Inc., 1948. Pp. 143. Reprinted, *Protestant Evangelism Among Italians in America*. New York: Arno Press, 1975.

Brief biographies of the following Italian-American Evangelical missionaries: Rev. Antonio Andrea Arrighi, Rev. Michele Nardo, Rev. Francesco Pesaturo, Rev. Thomas Fragale, Rev. Agide Pirazzini, Rev. Filippo Ghigo, Rev. Pasquale R. DeCarlo, Cerchiara-Fresina, Dr. Antonio Mangano, Rev. Joseph Brunn, Rev. Joseph Vilelli, M.D. Isabella Fragale Bisceglia, Lydia Tealdo, Rev. Francis J. Panetta, Rev. Gennaro Gustavo D'Anchise, Charles Fania, M.D., and Rev. Andrew S. Solla.

282. Bischoff, William N.
The Jesuits in Old Oregon. Caldwell, Idaho: The Caxton Printers, Ltd., 1945. Pp. xvii-258.

This book deals with the work of the Turin province Jesuit missionaries in the Rocky Mountains region.

283. Bohme, Frederick G.
"The Italian in New Mexico." *New Mexico Historical Review*, XXXIV (April, 1959), 98-116.

Reference is made to Italian Jesuits.

284. Bolognani, Bonifacio.
Dalle Dolomiti all'Arizona. Biografia di P. Eusebio Francesco Chini Gesuita Trentino Pioniere Scopritore Missionario in Arizona. Sherbrooke, Canada: Edizioni Paoline, 1960. Pp. 255.

Popularly written biography of Father Kino, based on his writings and standard secondary sources.

285. Bolognani, Bonifacio.
Un Grande Pioniere Trentino. P. Eusebio F. Chini S.J. Nei Suoi Scritti. Trento: Arti Grafiche Saturnia, 1964. Pp. 139.

Brief biography of Father Chini and the text of his various writings.

286. Bolton, Herbert E.
"Kino, Eusebio Francisco." *Dictionary of American Biography*, X (1933), 419-420.

Brief biography of Kino, born at Segno, Italy, c. 1645. He became a Jesuit in 1665. He arrived in Mexico in 1681 and from 1687 to his death in 1711 he worked among the Pimas in Pimería Alta, a district now embraced in northern Sonora and southern Arizona. He established many towns and missions.

287. Bolton, Herbert E.
Rim of Christendom. A Biography of Eusebio Francisco Kino, Pacific Coast Pioneer. New York: Macmillan Company, 1936. Pp. xvi-644.

Vast biography of the Italian Jesuit missionary and explorer in the southwestern part of the United States. It includes a short essay on the work of the Jesuits in New Spain.

288. Bonomelli, Geremia.
Questioni Religiose, Morali e Sociali del Giorno. 2 vols. Roma: Desclèe, Lefebvre e C. Editori Pontifici, 1903.

In vol. II, pp. 422-466, Bonomelli, Bishop of Cremona, reprints his pastoral letter on the problems of Italian emigration and the social and religious consequences of emigration.

289. Borden, Lucille Papin.
Francesca Cabrini. Without Staff or Scrip. New York: The Macmillan Co., 1945. Pp. x-402.

This is a popular biography of Frances Xavier Cabrini, who worked among the Italian immigrants at the turn of the century.

290. Bortolucci, G.
Una Rassegna dell'opuscolo di S.E. Mons. G.B. Scalabrini Vescovo di Piacenza sopra l'Emigrazione Italiana in America. Modena: Tip. Rossi, 1887. Unpaged.

A pamphlet reviewing Scalabrini's booklet entitled *L'emigrazione italiana in America.*

291. Bosi, Alfredo.
Cinquant' Anni di Vita Italiana in America. New York: Bagnasco Press, 1921. Pp. xix-530.

This study of Italian life in the United States during the half century prior to 1920 includes a chapter on the Italian immigrants and the Catholic Church titled "Il Cattolicismo e gli Italiani in America" (pp. 370-379). The chapter includes a survey of the development of the Catholic Church in the United States as well as brief sketches of outstanding Italian Catholic priests in the American Church.

292. Bove, Antonio.
Controversia circa il Proselitismo fra i cattolici Italiani di Providence, R.I., Praticato dei Protestanti Battisti. Roma: Tip. del "Roma e Provincia," 1911. Pp. 33.

A pamphlet by Fr. Bove, pastor of a large Italian national parish in Providence, Rhode Island (St. Anne's), against Baptist proselytizing among Italian immigrants in that city.

293. Bove, Antonio.
L'Ordine Figli d'Italia di Fronte alla Coscienza Cattolica. Lettera Aperta alle Associazioni Italiane negli Stati Uniti. Providence, R.I.: Joseph M. Tally, 1918. Pp. 18.

An open letter to Italian-American societies on the relationship between Catholicism and the Order Sons of Italy.

294. Boville, Robert G.
"Italian Evangelization." *The Baptist Home Mission Monthly*, XXIX (April, 1907), 134-135.

Points to opportunities for evangelization among Italians and argues for better efforts by the Baptists.

295. "Br. Ralph Vezza." *Woodstock Letters*, XVIII (1889), 248-250.

Vezza (1826-1889), a Neapolitan Jesuit, accompanied Frs. Gasparri and Bianchi in the founding of the new mission in New Mexico in 1867. Worked at Woodstock College from its beginning.

296. Branchi, E.
Il primato degli italiani nella storia e nella civiltà americane. Breviario degli italiani in America. Bologna: Cappelli, 1925. Unpaged.

This volume includes several sketches of Italian missionaries in the United States.

297. Brann, Henry A.
"Rev. Charles Constantine Pise, the Only Catholic Chaplain of the Congress of the United States." United States Catholic Historical Society, *Historical Records and Studies*, Vol. II, Part I. New York: The United States Catholic Historical Society, 1900. Pp. 354-357.

Copies of original documents relating to the Rev. Charles C. Pise.

298. Bressani, Francesco Giuseppe.
Breve Relatione d'alcune Missioni De' PP. della Compagnia di Gesù nella Nuoua Francia. Macerata: Heredi D'Agostino Grisei, 1653.

Born at Rome in 1612, Bressani joined the Society of Jesus in 1626. In 1642 he arrived in Canada to work among the Indians. Poor health forced him back to Europe in 1650. After his return to Italy, he published this account of his experiences in New France. The account, whose English title is *A Brief Account of Certain Missions of the Fathers of the Society of Jesus in New France*, was also published in *The Jesuit Relations*, vol. XXXVIII, 203-287, vol. XXXIX, 11-263, vol. XL, 13-65. The Index (vols. LXXII-LXXIII) of *The Jesuit Relations* includes many references to Bressani and his activities in New France. See "Bressani," vol. LXXII, 109-110.

299. "Brief Addressed to Fathers Mazzella and DeAugustinis." *Woodstock Letters*, VIII (1879), 44-45.

Leo XIII addressed a brief to these two Italian Jesuits teaching at Woodstock College, Maryland, for their support of Thomism. Mazzella became a Cardinal.

300. Briggs, John W.
An Italian Passage: Immigrants to Three American Cities, 1890-1930. New Haven, Conn.: Yale University Press, 1978. Pp. xxii-348.

This study, based on archival material and dealing with Italians in Rochester, Utica, and Kansas City, portrays the typical immigrant as an active agent, capable of both initiative and accommodation, and the possessor of a viable culture that gave a sense of continuty between his old and new lives.

301. "Brother Bartholomew Tortore." *Woodstock Letters*, XXXV (1906), 288-289.

Tortore (1832-1906), born in Piedmont, was an architect and painter and taught fine arts in California and Washington.

302. "Brother Joseph Pirisi." *Woodstock Letters*, XXXVI (1907), 350-351.

Pirisi, a Jesuit missionary, worked as a tailor and as a catechist for over 50 years in several institutions and missions on the West Coast.

303. Browne, Henry J.
"The 'Italian Problem' in the Catholic Church of the United States, 1880-1900." United States Catholic Historical Society, *Historical Records and Studies*, Vol. XXXV. New York: The United States Catholic Historical Society, 1946. Pp. 46-72.

This is a good summary of the "Italian Problem," based mostly on secondary sources. The author concludes that "racial antipathies, political-religious conceptions brought from Italy, inadequate churches, Protestant proselytizing, immigrant priests of poor quality, and over and above all this a woefully uninstructed people — these elements went to make up the 'Italian problem' for the Church in the United States."

304. Bruce, James M.
"The Italian Advance in New Haven." *The Baptist Home Mission Monthly*, XXVIII (February, 1906), 68-69.

Bruce, Superintendent of work among Foreign Populations, describes the new chapel for Italian Baptists in New Haven.

305. Bruce, James M.
"Italian Baptist Convention." *The Baptist Home Mission Monthly*, XXVIII (June, 1906), 253.

Account of the Eighth Annual Convention of the Italian Churches and pastors, held at the Bethel Church, Boston, on May 8, 9 and 10, 1906.

306. Bruce, J.M.
"A New Italian Mission." *The Baptist Home Mission Monthly*, XXX (January, 1908), 24-25.

Describes the new Italian Baptist Mission at Uniontown, Pennsylvania, where Mr. Hector Schisa has taken charge of the work. Page 24 has a photograph of Schisa with the first three converts baptized.

307. Bruce, J.M.
"Ordination of Italian Missionary." *The Baptist Home Mission Monthly*, XXX (September, 1908), 354.

Account of ordination to the ministry of Mr. Giuseppe Petrelli on June 18, 1908, at the Mariners' Temple in New York.

308. Bruce, James M.
"The Hartford Italian Mission." *The Baptist Home Mission Monthly*, XXX (December, 1908), 474-477.

Describes dedication of a hall in the basement of the First Baptist Church in Hartford to be used for Italians. The Rev. Antonio Roca is the pastor of the Italian mission.

309. Bruce, J.M.
"Italian Chapel at Barre." *The Baptist Home Mission Monthly*, XXXI (November, 1909), 467-468.

Description of the formal opening and dedication of the Italian Baptist chapel at Barre, Vermont, on September 17, 1909. The Rev. A.B. Castellini is the pastor.

310. Budenz, Louis.
"A Survey of Conditions in 'Dago Hill,' St. Louis." *Central Blatt and*

Social Justice, 8 (1915), 126-128.

Survey of social and religious needs of Italian immigrants.

311. Buonocore, O.
L'Emigrazione. Napoli: Tipografia Protosalvo, 1923. Pp. 40.

A pamphlet written by a Catholic, advocating lay participation in the care of Italian migrants, but also lamenting Protestant proselytizing, scarcity of clergy among immigrants and praising the work of Bishops Scalabrini and Bonomelli.

312. Burlingame, Merrill G.
The Montana Frontier. Helena, Montana: State Publishing Company, 1942. Pp. xiii-418.

In the Foreword, the author notes: "This story of 'The Montana Frontier' picks out certain movements which fit most closely into the early period: the Indian, the fur trade, the mining camps, the empire of the cattlemen, the frontier army, the frontier church, and the pioneer settlement." Chapter XIII, pp. 290-309, deals with "Religion on the Montana Frontier," and refers to the work of Italian missionaries in Montana.

313. Burns, James A.
The Growth and Development of the Catholic School System in the United States. New York: Benziger Bros., 1912. Pp. 421. Maps. Tables.

This general study of Catholic schools in the United States has information on Italian national parishes, the number of Italian Catholic schools and pupils (48 schools and 13,838 pupils in 1912), and notes the little concern Italians have for the retention of their language. Reprinted, New York: Arno Press, 1970.

314. Burns, Robert I.
"The Jesuits, the Northern Indians, and the Nez Perce War of 1877." *Pacific Northwest Quarterly*, 42 (January, 1951), 40-76.

It includes the activity of Italian Jesuits.

315. Burns, Robert I.
The Jesuits and the Indian Wars of the Northwest. New Haven: Yale University Press, 1966. Pp. xvi-512. Illustrations.

Detailed, well-documented description of Jesuit involvement in Indian-White troubles in the Northwest from 1840 to 1880. Includes much information that relates to the role of Italian Jesuits.

316. Burrus, E.J.
"Francesco Maria Piccolo (1654-1729), Pioneer of Lower California,

in the Light of Roman Archives." *The Hispanic American Historical Review*, XXXV (February, 1955), 61-76.

Account of Piccolo's "contribution to the advance of civilization along the northwestern rim of New Spain, as reflected in the letters and reports that reached headquarters in Rome." Burrus notes that the "principal significance of this Jesuit missionary in the history of the West Coast is that his arrival in Lower California late in 1697 consolidated the beachhead established by Juan Maria Salvatierra earlier in the same year."

317. C.
"Mission for the Italians in New York." *Woodstock Letters*, XVII (1888), 234-235.

Describes work among the Italians at Transfiguration parish. The Archbishop is confident in the promise of "the Bishop of Piacenza" (Scalabrini) that he will send his missionaries soon.

318. Cabrini, Frances Xavier.
Parole sparse della Beata Cabrini. Roma: Istituto Grafico Tiberino Editore, 1938. Pp. 269.

Personal retreat notes of Cabrini along with comments on spiritual topics. It includes a 76-page commentary on the notes by Giuseppe DeLuca.

319. Cabrini, Francesca Saverio.
Terzo Viaggio delle Suore Salesiane Missionarie del S. Cuore di Gesù in America. Relazione del Medesimo fatta dalla Superiora Generale dell'Istituto M. Francesca Saverio Cabrini in due lettere alle sue Figlie. Genova: Tipografia arcivescovile, 1894. Pp. 47.

Narrative of the trip to New York from LeHavre, September 5-13, 1891, and from there to Central America.

320. Cabrini, Francesca Saverio.
Viaggio delle Suore Missionarie del Sacro Cuore nel Pacifico attraverso la Cordigliera e nell'Atlantico. La Superiora Generale Francesca Saverio Cabrini al Noviziato di Cologna ed alla Casa Madre in Roma, via Montebello. Roma: Scuola Tipografica Salesiana, 1898. Pp. 79.

Cabrini's 1896 trip in the Pacific through parts of Latin America, across the Andes and to the Atlantic.

321. Cabrini, Francesca Saverio.
Fondazione di una casa delle Missionarie del S. Cuore di Gesù in Denver, Colorado. La Superiora Generale Francesca Saverio Cabrini

*al Noviziato di Codogno ed alla Casa Madre in Roma, via Montebello,
1*. Roma: Tipografia Cooperativa Sociale, 1903. Pp. 15.

Opening of the Cabrini Sisters' school in Denver and description of the
Italians in that city.

322. Cabrini, Francesca Saverio.
     *Lettera della Superiora Generale M. Francesca Saverio Cabrini alle
     Alunne del Magistero Superiore Convittrici delle Missionarie del Sacro
     Cuore de Gesù*. Roma: Tipografia A. Beffani, 1906. Pp. 32.

     A letter from Chicago with references to Italian immigrant workers in the
     United States and the activities of the Sisters of the Sacred Heart among
     them.

323. Cabrini, Francesca Saverio.
     *Viaggi della Madre Francesca Saverio Cabrini Fondatrice delle
     Missionarie del Sacro Cuore de Gesù narrati in varie sue lettere*.
     Milano: Stab. Pont. Arti Grafiche Sacre Bertarelli, S.A., 1935. Pp.
     410.

     Most of these narratives are translated in *Travels of Mother Frances Xavier
     Cabrini Foundress of the Missionary Sisters of the Sacred Heart of Jesus*.
     Chicago: The Missionary Sisters of the Sacred Heart of Jesus, 1944. Pp. 277.
     An earlier Italian edition was published in Turin in 1922 by Società Editrice
     Internazionale. Frances Cabrini's accounts of her ocean crossings, her efforts
     to interest the Italian government in the welfare of its emigrants, the obstacles
     she met in dealing with factions in Italo-American communities, and the
     difficulties she encountered with a not always sympathetic Roman Catholic
     hierarchy will provide immigration historians with new insights. The English
     language edition contains a biographical sketch of Cabrini by Amleto
     Giovanni Cicognani, Apostolic Delegate to the United States. For a more
     recent publication on this topic, see *Tra un'onda e l'altra: Viaggi di S.
     Francesca Saverio Cabrini*. Milano: Editrice Ancora, 1967.

324. Caliaro, Marco and Mario Francesconi.
     John Baptist Scalabrini, Apostle to Emigrants. Translated by Alba I.
     Zizzamia. New York: Center for Migration Studies, 1977. Pp. 555.

     This well researched study is the best biography of Bishop Scalabrini, founder
     of the Missionaries of St. Charles Borromeo. Scalabrini's role as a leader in
     the Italian church at the turn of the century and as an organizer for social and
     religious assistance to Italian emigrants is well documented. This volume is a
     translation of the Italian version by Caliaro and Francesconi: *L'Apostolo
     degli Emigranti, Giovanni Battista Scalabrini, Vescovo di Piacenza. La Sua
     Opera e la Sua Spiritualità*. Milano: Editrice Ancora, 1968. A detailed
     bibliography on archival and published sources on Scalabrini as well as a
     listing of his published and unpublished writings are included in this biography.

325. Callahan, Adalbert.
Medieval Francis in Modern America. The Story of Eighty Years, 1855-1935. New York: The Macmillan Co., 1936. Pp. 494.

Account of the coming and work of Italian Franciscans in New York State and elsewhere. Recounts activities of Fr. Pamfilo da Magliano and other Italian Franciscans.

326. "The Camaldolese come to America." *Jubilee*, VI (December, 1958), 36-43.

Photographic essay on the first Camaldolese foundation in the United States established by Italian religious in 1958 at Big Sur, California. The Camaldolese originated in Camaldoli, Italy.

327. Caminada, Constantino.
Un'italiana per le vie del mondo. 2ª edizione riveduta e aumentata. Torino: L.I.C.E., R. Berruti & Co., 1946. Pp. 206.

A popularly written biography of St. Frances Cabrini.

328. Campbell, Thomas J.
"The Maryland-New York Province." *The Catholic Church in the United States of America.* 3 vols. New York: The Catholic Editing Company, 1912-1914. I, 253-265.

Brief account of the founding and development of the Maryland-New York Province of the Society of Jesus. The account refers to several Italian Jesuits who played an important part in the history of the province.

329. Campbell, Thomas J.
"Eusebio Kino, 1644-1711." *The Catholic Historical Review*, V (January, 1920), 353-376.

Brief sketch of the life of Fr. Kino, a Jesuit missionary in the Southwest.

330. Cannelli, Antonio, ed.
La Colonia Italiana di New Haven, Connecticut. New Haven, Conn.: Stabilimento Tipografico A. Cannelli Co., 1921. Pp. 312.

History of Italians in New Haven, Connecticut. Pp. 101-116 include sketches of religious institutions in New Haven.

331. Cantelmo, Ercole.
"Usi, Costumi e Feste degli Italiani negli Stati Uniti." *Gli Italiani negli Stati Uniti D'America.* New York: Italian American Directory Co., 1906. Pp. 156-163.

Customs observed during the rites of passage and special patronal feasts.

332. *Capita praecipua quae emi. Cardinales S.C. de Propaganda Fide censuerunt a rmis. archiepiscopis et episcopis Foederatorum Statuum A.S. Romae congregatis praeparanda esse pro futuro Concilio.* Roma: 1883. Unpaged.

Agenda of the meeting of the American Archbishops in Rome who had convened there in preparation of the Third Plenary Council of Baltimore (1884). It mentions the pastoral needs of Italian immigrants.

333. Capitani, Pacifico.
La Questione Italiana negli Stati Uniti d'America. Cleveland: M.E. M'Cabe, Printer, 1891. Pp. 44.

This pamphlet deals with the religious problems of Italians in the United States in the early stages of mass migration. Much of the pamphlet, which is written in Italian, originally appeared in a series of six English-language articles written by Capitani and published in the *New York Freeman's Journal and Catholic Register*, April 27 to June 1, 1889. See also the editorial, "Our Iatlian [sic] American Co-Religionists," June 1, 1889, p. 4 of that newspaper.

334. Capra, Giuseppe.
"*L'Italica Gens* negli Stati Uniti." *Italica Gens*, VI (Ottobre-Dicembre, 1915), 255-261.

This article gives a good overview of the role and objectives of the *Italica Gens*. Capra visited for 3 months the more than 100 offices and secretariats of the *Italica Gens* in the United States. He found these offices normally directed by Italian priests and "that abroad religion and fatherland are more than ever tightly united." He favors rural settlements for Italian emigrants.

335. Capra, Giuseppe.
"L'Opera dei Padri Francescani negli Stati Uniti d'America." *Italica Gens*, VII (Gennaio-Giugno, 1916), 39-56.

A cursory description of the work, churches, schools and spirit of *Italianità* of the Franciscan Fathers among the Italian immigrants in the United States.

336. Capra, Giuseppe.
"I Padri Scalabriniani nell'America del Nord." *Italica Gens*, VII (Gennaio-Giugno, 1916), 57-68.

A brief and superficial account of the work of the Congregation of St. Charles Borromeo in various parishes throughout the United States.

337. Capra, G.
"Le scuole in America." *Italica Gens*, VII (Luglio-Dicembre, 1916), 117-133.

Capra discusses Italian schools in America and points out the little support received from the Italians. Lack of Italian schools means lack of *Italianità*. More Italian parochial schools are advocated.

338. Caruana, J.M.
"Indian Missions. The Rocky Mountains. Attanam, Washington Territory. Letter of Father J.M. Caruana to Father Cataldo, Superior General of the Mission." *Woodstock Letters*, XI (1882), 269-275.

Spreading of Christianity in the Kichital Valley.

339. Caruana, J.M.
"Extract from a Letter of Father J. Caruana to Father J. Cataldo. Colville, W.T., January 21, 1882." *Woodstock Letters*, XII (1883), 43-49.

Describes hostilities between Whites and Indians and the public execution of a young white man.

340. Caruana, J.M.
"Letter of Fr. Caruana to Father Cataldo, Colville, W.T., April 17, 1882." *Woodstock Letters*, XII (1883), 49-51.

Holy Week celebration among the Indians.

341. "Una Casa a New York per i Marinai italiani." *Italiani nel Mondo*, XXVI (January 10, 1970), 20-22.

Description of a club for Italian seamen in New York run by the Missionaries of St. Charles (Scalabrinians).

342. Casagrandi, Salvatore.
De Claris Sodalibus Provinciae Taurinensis Societatis Jesu Commentarii Conscripti et Exornati. Augustae Taurinorum: Iacobus Arneodus Eques, 1906. Pp. xii-333.

A series of biographical sketches, written in Latin, of prominent members of the Turin Province of the Society of Jesus with bibliographical references. Includes Fr. Giuseppe Giorda, who worked in the Northwest, and Fr. Pasquale Tosi, who worked in Alaska.

343. Cassigoli, B.R. and H. Chiariglione, eds.
Libro d'Oro degli Italiani in America. Pueblo, Colorado: By the

Editors, 1904. Pp. 606.

Biographical sketches of Italians, with photographs, listed state by state. It includes biographies of Italian priests in various states. This is volume one of a projected series.

344. Castañeda, Carlos E.
Our Catholic Heritage in Texas, 1519-1936. 7 Vols. Austin: Von Boeckmann-Jones Co., 1936-58. Reprinted, New York: Arno Press, 1977.

Standard history of the Catholic Church in Texas, prepared under the auspices of the Knights of Columbus of Texas. It includes some information on Italian priests in Texas. Excellent bibliographies at the end of each volume.

345. Castellani, Giuseppe.
"Una vittima ignorata degli irochesi, F.G. Bressani, S.J." *Civiltà Cattolica*, 4 (1934), 473-484.

On the Italian Jesuit missionary Bressani among the Iroquois Indians.

346. Cataldo, J.M.
"Coeur d'Alêne Mission, Idaho Territory, April 2, 1872." *Woodstock Letters*, II (1873), 57-58.

A letter to Fr. DeSmet, S.J., expressing the gratitude of these Indians for his kindness.

347. Cataldo, J.
"Our Missions in Alaska As it is Today. A Letter from Father Cataldo. Spokane, Washington, Nov. 17, 1903." *Woodstock Letters*, XXXIII (1904), 28-35.

Description of places, methods, missions and progress of the Jesuits' missions since their inception. Missions in Upper Alaska: Eagle, Nulato, Koserefky, Kuskakwin, Akulurak, St. Michael, Nome, Council. The Missions of Eagle, Nome and Council were for white settlers; St. Michael, both for whites and Eskimos; and all others for the Eskimos.

348. "Catholic Italian Losses." *The Literary Digest*, XLVII (October 11, 1913), 636.

This article is based on an editorial that appeared in *The Catholic Citizen*, Milwaukee diocesan newspaper, on September 27, 1913, p. 4. The editorial, titled "Our Biggest Catholic Question," was one in a series of five editorials published by that newspaper from September 6 to October 4, 1913, dealing with the question of massive leakage by Italian immigrants from the Catholic

Church. All five editorials were reprinted in one article in the November 8, 1913 issue of the newspaper. D. Lynch, "The Religious Conditions of Italians in New York," *America*, X (March 21, 1914), 558-559, takes issue with the editorials, claiming that their figures are exaggerated. The editorial, "As to Our Italian Catholics," *The Catholic News*, November 22, 1913, New York diocesan newspaper, also takes issue with the editorials and points out the inaccuracies in their statements on Italian Catholic losses.

349. Cerrati, Michael.
"Pastoral Care of Italian Immigrants." *American Ecclesiastical Review*, LXIV (March, 1921), 279-284.

A statement of concern for Italian immigrants by Bishop Cerrati, the Prelate for Italian Emigration in the 1920s.

350. Cerruti, G.B.
"Sulla Colonia Italiana in California." *Bollettino Consolare*, VII (1872), 46-56.

Refers to the assistance to Italians in California by Italian priests and to the educational activity of Italian Jesuits.

351. Charlston Street Memorial Church. *Thirtieth Anniversary of the Religious and Social Work Among the Italians of this Community and the Fifteenth Anniversary of the Charlston Street Memorial Church*. New York: Società Tipografica Italiana, 1927. Pp. 15.

A brief historical outline of New York's Charlston Street Memorial Church and its beginnings. English and Italian.

352. Chivers, E.E.
"Our Baptist Mission Work." *The Baptist Home Mission Monthly*, XXVII (May, 1905), 187-200.

Chivers has written an introduction describing Baptist Italian Mission work to a series of reports from every Italian mission of the American Baptist Home Mission Society. The reports include the following places: First Italian Mission, Brooklyn, New York; Mt. Vernon, New York; Providence, Rhode Island; Boston; Haverhill, Massachusetts; Monson, Massachusetts; New Haven; Hartford, Connecticut; Stamford, Connecticut; Barre, Vermont; Springfield, Massachusetts; Troy, New York; Albany, New York; Buffalo; Passaic, New Jersey; and Camden, New Jersey. This is part of a section titled "The Italians in America."

353. Cianci, Salvatore.
Il lavoro sociale in mezzo agli Italiani. Conferenza data in Milwaukee,

Wis., l'11 Agosto 1913, in occasione del XII Congresso della Federazione Americana delle Società Cattoliche. Pp. 22.

Cianci, Italian pastor in Grand Rapids, Michigan, notes in this pamphlet that the Italian immigrants are generally good and hard-working and, although uneducated, men of faith. He brands the series of abuses and prejudices Italians are exposed to and advocates that all children be sent to Catholic schools, that workers be fully defended in their rights, and that more Italian priests be sent to America. He sees the Italian priests as the best vehicles of *Italianità*.

354. Cinel, Dino.
"La voce degli esuli." *L'Emigrato Italiano*, LXVI (November, 1970), 17-27.

The history of the origin and development of Holy Rosary Church, the Italian national parish of Washington, D.C. Contains information on the Italian community of Washington, D.C.

355. Cirigliano, D.
"Protestant Activities in Our Parish." *Woodstock Letters*, XLVIII (1919), 222-231, 340-349; XLVIX (1920), 216-222, 335-340.

Protestant proselytism among the Italian immigrants in Loreto Nativity Parish, New York, at the turn of the century. Issues and response. The Catholic Church and the immigrants in "Little Italy." An interesting detailed description of this typical phenomenon in the period of Italian mass immigration.

356. Ciufoletti, Manlio.
"Le scuole parrocchiali negli Stati Uniti ed in particolare le italiane." *L'Emigrato Italiano*, IX (October-December, 1917), 9-30. Reprinted, Roma: Tipografia Pontificia dell'Istituto Pio IX, 1918. Pp. 28.

An important article describing the American parochial schools to an Italian audience. Reports official statistics on Italian-American schools, pupils and teachers. Surveys the causes of their limited numbers and advocates the maintenance of an Italian ethnic identity through the teaching of the Italian language and culture. It concludes with a brief historical reference to Italian priests who pioneered in promoting Catholic schools in the United States.

357. Ciufoletti, Manlio.
"Il XX Settembre...passato, presente, futuro." *L'Emigrato Italiano*, XIII (January-March, 1919), 17-29.

A description of how the Italian-American press reported the celebration of the 20th of September, the day Rome was annexed to Italy. Includes a plea for reconciliation between patriotism and religion among Italian-Americans.

358. Ciufoletti, Manlio.
"Importanza sociale delle parrocchie italiane in America." *L'Emigrato Italiano*, XVIII (October-December, 1924), 1-6.

Describes three historical stages in the development of the Italian-American parish: 1) before formal organization; 2) the actual organization; and 3) the development. Then, the "social importance of the Italian parishes in America" is deduced from their charitable, educational and assistential activities.

359. Ciufoletti, Manlio.
John Baptist Scalabrini, Bishop of Piacenza, Apostle of the Italian Immigrants. New York: Congregation of St. Charles Borromeo, 1937. Pp. 72.

A brief biography of Scalabrini and his initiatives on behalf of Italian migrants.

360. Claghorn, Kate Holladay.
"Our Italian Immigrants." *The Baptist Home Mission Monthly*, XXVII (May, 1905), 177-182.

Claghorn, the Assistant Registrar, New York Tenement House Department, gives a general description of Italian immigration to the United States. This is part of a section titled "The Italians in America."

361. Clark, Elmer T.
The Latin Immigrant in the South. Nashville: The Cokesbury Press, 1924. Pp. 57.

Published under the auspices of the Home department of the Board of missions, Methodist Episcopal Church, South. Chapter III, pp. 23-27, deals with "Methodism and the Italians."

362. Clark, Francis E.
Our Italian Fellow Citizens in Their Old Homes and Their New. Boston: Small, Maynard & Company Publishers, 1919. Pp. ix-217. Reprinted, New York: Arno Press, 1975.

In the introduction, the author says that his "purpose in this volume is chiefly to make my raders sympathetically acquainted, so far as I am able, with the Italian of to-day in his old home and his new." Chapter XVI, pp. 160-167, is titled "Education and Religion."

363. Clot, Alberto.
Guida e consigli per gli emigranti negli Stati Uniti e nel Canada. New York: Amer. Waldensian Aid Society, 1913. Pp. 64.

Guide written for those emigrating to the United States. Mentions the Waldensian missions in the United States.

364. Coats, A.S.
"First Italian Baptist Church, Buffalo, N.Y." *The Baptist Home Mission Monthly*, XXII (March, 1900), 94-95.

Gives history and work of the First Italian Baptist Church in Buffalo, New York, which claimed "to be the First Italian Baptist Church organized in the United States."

365. Codella, Pasquale.
Patriottismo, morale e religione. Patriotism, moral and religion. Waterbury, Conn.: P. Codella, 1937. Pp. 384.

A poorly organized, repetitious, anecdotal account on Italian-Americans. The selections, part Italian and part English, include songs with music.

366. "Il Columbus Hospital delle Missionarie del Sacro Cuore; come l'anticlericalismo resta 'merce d'esportazione' solo per gli Italiani." *La Civiltà Cattolica*, XLII (26 Gennaio, 1921), 281-282.

Response to anticlerical attacks against New York's Columbus Hospital, operated by the Cabrini Sisters.

367. Comitato del Clero Italiano di New York Pro Famiglie dei Soldati Italiani. *Serata pro Patria Concerto e Conferenza.* New York: 1916. Pp. 24.

Italian priests in New York respond to the needs of the families of soldiers in the Italian Army during World War I.

368. Comitato Romano.
Venticinquesimo Anniversario dei Missionari di Mons. Scalabrini per gli Emigrati Italiani. Roma: Tipografia Poliglotta Vaticana, 1912. Pp. 44.

Description of activities for Italian immigrants in various parts of the world, including the United States, by the Scalabrini Missionaries.

369. *Commemorating the Twenty-fifth Anniversary of Rev. Father Nicola Fusco as Pastor of Mt. St. Peter's Congregation, New Kensington, Pa. 1923-September 6, 1948.* Pittsburgh: St. Joseph's Protectory, 1948. Pp. 93.

A booklet on the career of Fr. Fusco, active among Italians in the United States.

370. Condon, Peter.
"Rev. Anthony Couvin, Founder of the Church of 'Our Lady of Grace' of Hoboken, New Jersey." *United States Catholic Historical Records and Studies*, III (January, 1903), 155-167.

Fr. Couvin, an Italian priest from Piedmont, was active among Italians in the New York area in the 1850s and 1860s.

371. Condon, Peter.
"Monsignor Bedini's Visit to the United States. The Official Correspondence." United States Catholic Historical Society, *Historical Records and Studies*, Vol. III, Part I (1903), 149-154.

This is a copy of the correspondence between the Papal Government and the government of the United States on the occasion of Archbishop Bedini's visit, taken from the files of the Department of State in Washington, D.C.

372. Connelly, James F.
The Visit of Archbishop Gaetano Bedini to the United States of America (June, 1853-February, 1854). Rome: Libreria Editrice dell'Università Gregoriana, 1960. Pp. xiii-307.

Published doctoral dissertation. Includes the text of Bedini's reports on his visit presented to the Holy See in July 1854. Describes, inadequately, Bedini's conflict with Gavazzi.

373. Conte, Gaetano.
Dieci Anni in America: Impressioni e Ricordi. Conferenze riguardanti l'emigrazione italiana nell'America del Nord. Palermo: G. Spinnato, 1903. Pp. 223.

Gaetano Conte was an Italian Protestant minister who left Italy in 1893 to work among the Italians of Boston. This book, written in 1903, is a reflection of his ten years of work in the United States.

374. Conte, Gaetano.
Le Missioni Protestanti ed i nostri emigrati. Venezia: Tipografia dell'Istituto Industriale, 1906. Pp. 31.

Important pamphlet on Protestant religious and social work among Italian immigrants in the United States. Conte lists 144 places where Protestant work is carried out among the Italians.

375. Coppo, Ernest.
"Salesians of Don Bosco." *The Catholic Church in the United States of America*. 3 vols. New York: The Catholic Editing Company, 1912-1914. I, 388-390.

Brief account of founding and development of the Salesians of Don Giovanni Bosco in the United States, starting in New York City in 1898.

376. Corley, Patricia.
     The Story of St. Mary's Mission. Oakland, Calif.: Tribune Press, c. 1941. Pp. 29.

     Regarding St. Mary's Mission, Stevensville, Montana, founded by Italian Jesuits.

377. Cornaggia Medici, Luigi.
     Le caratteristiche di Mons. Giovanni Battista Scalabrini, Vescovo di Piacenza. Nel 30° anniversario della sua morte. Reggio Emilia: Frate Francesco, 1935. Pp. 23.

     Analysis of Scalabrini's character published on the occasion of the 30th anniversary of his death.

378. Cornaggia Medici, Luigi.
     "Un Profilo di Mons, Scalabrini Vescovo di Piacenza." *Rassegna Romana,* 6 (Luglio-Agosto, 1930), 1-17.

     A profile of Scalabrini from one who knew him personally.

379. Cornelio, A.M.
     "L'emigrazione italiana e l'abate Villeneuve." *La Rassegna Nazionale,* 67 (September 16, 1892), 241-258.

     Gives a summary of the Abbè Alphonse Villeneuve's conference in Rome on the Italians in the United States. Villeneuve was a friend of Bishop Giovanni Battista Scalabrini of Piacenza and supported his work on behalf of Italian immigrants.

380. Costa, Joseph.
     "Institute of Charity." *The Catholic Church in the United States of America.* 3 vols. New York: The Catholic Editing Company, 1912-1914. I, 252-253.

     Brief account of founding and work of the Institute of Charity, founded by Antonio Rosmini in 1828. Italian-born Father Joseph Costa established the Institute's first permanent American settlement at Galesburg, Illinois, in 1877.

381. Covello, Leonard.
     "Cultural Assimilation and the Church." *Religious Education,* 39 (July-August, 1944), 229-235.

An important statement of the social role of the church for first generation immigrants and their children.

382. Covello, Leonard.
The Social Background of the Italo-American School Child. A Study of the Southern Italian Family Mores and Their Effect on the School Situation in Italy and America. Leiden: E.J. Brill, 1967. Pp. xxx-490. Reprinted, Totowa, New Jersey: Rowman and Littlefield, 1972.

This is a comprehensive study of Southern Italian life at the time of mass migration to the Americas. Pp. 103-145 give an excellent portrayal of Southern Italian religious thought and practice. Pp. 399-400 give the author's conclusions on the Italian immigrants and religion.

383. C.R.
"La Missione Italiana del S. Cuore in Boston." *Italica Gens*, V (Settembre-Dicembre, 1914), 221-224.

Historical note on the Church of the Sacred Heart in the North End of Boston on the occasion of its 25th anniversary. Mentions the social services carried out by the church.

384. Cushing, Richard J.
"Italian Immigrants." *The Catholic Mind*, LII (October, 1954), 604-609.

Text of an address to the American Committee on Italian Migration, New York City, given on December 3, 1953 by Archbishop Cushing of Boston.

385. "The Cyreneans, A New Association for Immigrant Welfare Work." *The Catholic Charities Review*, VI (October, 1922), 277-280.

This article describes the founding and organization of The Cyreneans, a society whose aim is to coordinate the societies that provide moral and religious support to Italian immigrants and their children in the United States and Canada.

386. Damiani, P.
"Indian Missions. Mission of the Rocky Mountains. Letter of Father P. Damiani to Father J.M. Cataldo, Superior General of the Mission." *Woodstock Letters*, XI (1882), 179-183.

A journey to the Milk River area to visit the "Half-Breeds" and the Assinniboine Indians.

387. D'Amico, Silvio.
Scoperta dell'America Cattolica. Seconda edizione. Firenze: R. Bemporad & Figlio, 1928. Pp. 177.

These are the author's notes and impressions during a visit to the United States from May to July, 1926 on the occasion of the Eucharistic Congress in Chicago.

388. D'Aponte, John.
"Letter of Fr. D'Aponte to Very Rev. Fr. D. Palomba, Provincial of the Neapolitan Province. Las Vegas, April, 1874." *Woodstock Letters,* IV (1875), 75-78.

Describes missions given by himself, Fr. Gasparri and Fr. Carrozzini in New Mexico and Colorado.

389. D'Aponte, J.
"St. Mary's, Montana Ty. Letter of E. D'Aponte, May 6th, 1878." *Woodstock Letters,* VII (1878), 179-184.

Missions among the Flathead Indians of St. Mary's Valley in Montana. Conflicts between Indians, settlers and soldiers.

390. Davis, Lawrence B.
Immigrants, Baptists, and the Protestant Mind in America. Urbana: University of Illinois Press, 1973. Pp. 230.

Includes useful information on the work of the Baptists among Italian immigrants in the United States.

391. Davis, Ruth Edward.
"Pietro in Search of the Sun." *The Vigo Review,* I (April, May, June, 1938), 15-16, 20, 10-11, 22, 14-16.

Account of the Italian agricultural colony at Tontitown, Arkansas.

392. "Dean Street Mission in Providence R.I." *The Baptist Home Mission Monthly,* XXVIII (March, 1906), 110-111.

Photograph of the Italian Mission in Providence, under the pastoral charge of Mimi C. Marseglia, and information from the last quarterly report put out by the Mission.

393. DeBiasi, Agostino.
"La Morte di Padre Bandini." *Il Carroccio*, V (Febbraio, 1917), 103-104.

This is a brief tribute to Fr. Pietro Bandini (born 1852) at the time of his death. Bandini was an Italian missionary in the Rocky Mountains, New York City, and Tontitown, Arkansas.

394. DeBiasi, Agostino.
"La Nightingale Italiana: Suor Francesca Saverio Cabrini." *Il Carroccio*, VII (Gennaio, 1918), 41-47.

Description of Mother Cabrini's work among the sick, followed by a sonnett in honor of Cabrini by Nicola Fusco.

395. DeBiasi, Agostino.
"Il Sacerdote dell'Italianità, Roberto Biasotti." *Il Carroccio*, XXIV (Luglio, 1926), 66-67.

This is a tribute to Fr. Roberto Biasotti (born 1863) at the time of his death. Biasotti worked in Boston and New York City, where he directed the "Apostolato Italiano." He established the St. Raphale's Society in Boston and founded parishes and other institutions for Italian immigrants.

396. DeConcilio, Gennaro.
Su Lo Stato Religioso degl'Italiani negli Stati Uniti d'America. New York: Tipografia J.H. Carbone, 1888. Pp. 32.

This important pamphlet on the religious conditions of Italian immigrants in the latter part of the nineteenth century is divided into three main parts: 1) a statistical study of Italian immigrants and Italian priests in the United States; 2) an outline of the reasons why the religious condition of Italian immigrants in the United States is deplorable; and 3) a statement of what can be done to improve the situation. See "Delle condizioni religiose degli emigrati italiani negli Stati Uniti d'America." *La Civiltà Cattolica*, Serie XIII, Vol. XI (3 Settembre, 1888), 641-653, a description of the condition of Italian immigrants in the United States based on DeConcilio's pamphlet.

397. DeConde, Alexander.
Half Bitter, Half Sweet. An Excursion into Italian-American History. New York: Charles Scribner's Sons, 1971. Pp. vii-466.

This is a comprehensive study of relations between Italy and the United States from the beginning to recent times. The role of the Church in the Italian-American community is briefly discussed in pp. 92-94.

398. DeCourcy, Henry.
The Catholic Church in the United States: Pages of Its History.
Translated and Enlarged by John Gilmary Shea. Second edition,
revised. New York: Edward Dunigan and Brother, 1857. Pp. 591.

Early history of the Catholic Church in the United States. Chapter XXVII, pp.
499-520 deals with the mission of Archbishop Cajetan Bedini. The Appendix,
pp. 560-591, includes documents relating to Bedini.

399. Delaney, Mary C.
"Albany Concludes Citizenship Course. Efforts of Catholic Women's
Service League Successful." *National Catholic Welfare Council
Bulletin*, III (June, 1921), 6.

Describes Americanization work among Italians in Albany.

400. "Della Emigrazione Europea in America." *La Civiltà Cattolica*, Serie
XV, VI (1893), 641-652.

This article gives a general overview of emigration from Europe to the
Americas. It contains some comments on immigration to the United States
and the leakage of immigrants from the Church.

401. "Della Emigrazione Italiana." *La Civiltà Cattolica*, Serie XIII, XI (1888),
385-403.

This is a general account of the increase in Italian emigration during the
period 1876-1886. The article makes reference to the Crispi emigration bill of
1887-1888.

402. DeLuca, Giuseppe.
Francesca Saverio Cabrini: la Madre degli Emigrati. Roma: Società-
Anonima "La Nuova Antologia," 1937. Pp. 8.

This short essay by a famous author is a reprint (*Nuova Antologia*, 16
December, 1937) and also a sample of the many pamphlets which have
appeared over the years on St. Frances Xavier Cabrini. See Augusto Grossi
Gondi. *Una grande italiana in America: M. Francesca Saverio Cabrini.* Roma:
Scuola Tipografica Salesiana, 1919. Pp. 32; Maria Luisa Perduca. *Santa
Francesca Cabrini protettrice degli Emigrati italiani.* Pavia: Tipografia Fusi,
1950. Pp. 21; *La Beata Francesca Saverio Cabrini.* New York: The Missionary
Sisters of the Sacred Heart, 1938. Pp. 29; Sister Joan Mary. *Mother Cabrini.*
Staten Island, N.Y.: Apostolate of the Press, 1952. Pp. 223; Nello Vian.
Madre Cabrini. Brescia: Morcelliana, 1938. Pp. 284; A Benedictine of
Stanbrook Abbey. *Frances Xavier Cabrini.* London: Burns, Oates, &
Washbourne Ltd., 1944.

403. Desmond, Humphrey J.
The Neglected Italians, A Memorial to the Italian Hierachy [*sic*].
Milwaukee: The Author, 1899. Pp. 11.

Humphrey J. Desmond, editor of *The Milwaukee Citizen*, first published this memorial in both Italian and English in the September 30, 1899, issue of that newspaper. The memorial is very critical of the lack of priests among the Italians of the United States. It calls for "the organization of a band of Italian priests consecrated to the work of following their emigrating countrymen." See the editorial, "Let Italy Awaken!" which appeared on p. 4 of the September 30, 1899, issue of the *Citizen*

404. DeVille, John.
"Italians in the United States." *The Catholic Encyclopedia*, VIII (1910), 202-206.

A summary article on Italian immigration and its distribution in the United States with special emphasis on religious organization and a diocese-by-diocese report on the number of Italian churches, priests, and schools.

405. DeVille, John.
"The Italian Problem." *The Extension Magazine*, XII (September, 1917), 3-4.

A concise statement on the Church and Italian immigrants.

406. DiBrazzà Savorgnan, Detalmo.
"Ricordi personali su Padre Angelo Secchi." *Il Carroccio*, IX (February, 1919), 150-153.

Personal recollections on the well-known Jesuit astronomer A. Secchi, who taught at Georgetown University.

407. DiDomenica, A.
"Work Among Italians." *The Baptist Home Mission Monthly*, XXIII (May, 1901), 143-144.

Brief article describing the work of the Italian Baptist Mission of Newark, New Jersey.

408. DiDomenica, Angelo.
"How I was Converted." *The Baptist Home Mission Monthly*, XXVI (March, 1904), 84-85.

Story of his conversion from Catholicism to the Baptist faith by DiDomenica, a Baptist minister among the Italians in Newark, New Jersey, and New Haven, Connecticut.

409. DiDomenica, Angelo.
"The Sons of Italy in America." *The Missionary Review of the World*, XLI (March, 1918), 189-195.

A leading Italian immigrant convert and Protestant minister defends Italian immigrants.

410. DiDomenica, A.
"Conditions Among Italians in America." *The Missionary Review of the World*, LVIII (February, 1935), 71-73.

Brief description of condition of Italian immigrants by a Protestant minister.

411. DiDomenica, Angelo.
Protestant Witness of a New American. Mission of a Lifetime. Chicago: The Judson Press, 1956. Pp. 172.

Autobiography with an underlying apologetic, polemic flavor. Makes interesting observations on Italian-American Baptists, their view of Americanization, his experience as a convert and Protestant minister within the American Baptist Church and the Italian immigrant communities.

412. DiDomenica, Vincenzo.
"Italian Work in Rhode Island." *The Baptist Home Mission Monthly*, XX (October, 1898), 359-360.

DiDomenica, a Baptist missionary, describes his work among Italians in Rhode Island.

413. DiDonato, Pietro.
Immigrant Saint, The Life of Mother Cabrini. New York: McGraw Hill, 1960. Pp. 246.

A biography of St. Frances Xavier Cabrini by novelist DiDonato.

414. DiGiura, G. Favoino.
"La difesa della nostra nazionalità. Il Vescovo Walsh e le scuole di Trenton." *Il Carroccio*, XVIII (October, 1923), 394-397.

Defense of Italian contribution to the Church in New Jersey.

415. Dilhet, Jean.
Beginnings of the Catholic Church in the United States Being État De L'Église Catholique ou Diocèse des États-Unis de L'Amérique Septentrionale. Translated and Annotated by Patrick W. Browne. Washington, D.C.: The Salve Regina Press, 1922. Pp. xxii-261.

First historical account of the Catholic Church in America. French and English on opposite pages. Refers to a "Mr. Zocchi, an Italian priest, a Roman, of the new Italian Company of the Jesuits, [who] resides here [Frederick County, Maryland] and his flock is rapidly increasing owing to the conversion of several Protestants" (p. 48). Zocchi is again listed in the "List of Catholic Priests in the United States" (p. 52).

416. "Diocesan Bureaux for the Care of Italian, Slav, Ruthenian, and Asiatic Catholics in America." *The Ecclesiastical Review*, XLVIII (February, 1913), 221-222.

This brief article notes the establishment in the Archdiocese of New York of special governing bureaux for Italians, Slavs, Ruthenians and Asiatics. These bureaux were established to help meet the special needs of these four immigrant groups.

417. Diomedi, A.
"Indian Missions. Fort Colville, Washington Ty., July 20th, 1878." *Woodstock Letters*, VIII (1879), 32-41.

Work in the Columbia and Colville valleys. Indian customs described.

418. Diomedi, A.
"Sketches of Modern Indian Life." *Woodstock Letters*, XXII (1893), 231-256, 353-378; XXIII (1894), 23-49.

Paganism, vices, government, language, Indian rights, conversion and civilization, work of the missionary, response to the faith. Written in 1879.

419. Diorio, F.P. and J. DeCarlo.
La Storia delle Assemblee Italiane in America. Brooklyn, N.Y.: The Elite Press, 1945. Pp. 20.

Gives history of Italian Assemblies in the United States and Canada. Lists Assemblies in Connecticut, Massachusetts, Michigan, New York, Oregon, Pennsylvania, and Canada, and notes the publication of a Christian monthly magazine, *La Voce Nel Deserto*, in Brooklyn, New York.

420. DiPalma, Castiglione, G.E.
"La protezione degli emigranti in New York." *Rivista Popolare*, X (May 30, 1904), 150-155.

Description of the social work of the three private associations to which the Commissariat of Emigration has given responsibility for Italian immigrants in New York City: the Society for the Protection of Italian Immigrants, The Italian Benevolent Society, and La Società di S. Raffaele. The author argues that the Italian government should finance only the first association since the

Società di S. Raffaele is entrusted to a religious congregation (the Missionaries of St. Charles) and has as its main scope the moral and religious assistance of immigrants.

421. Dixon, John.
"Our Church and the Foreigners." *The Assembly Herald*, XIV (January, 1908), 30.

Refers to money spent by the Presbyterian Church in proselytizing among new immigrants like the Italians.

422. "Don Bosco's Teaching in the U.S." *The Vigo Review*, I (April, 1938), 12-13.

Account of Don Bosco's educational methods, known as "the Preventive system, for they aim to transform the students of each Salesian school into one big family, the boys treating familiarly with their superiors as with elder brothers, and with the Rector as the common and beloved father of the entire community."

423. "Il Dovere dei Cattolici degli Stati Uniti Verso i Loro Correligionarii Italiani." *La Civiltà Cattolica*, Serie XVIII, IX (1903), 467-472.

This article summarizes the article by Thomas F. Meehan, "Evangelizing the Italians," *The Messenger*, XXXIX (January, 1903), 16-32.

424. Dragoni, Ladislao.
"I Francescani Italiani negli Stati Uniti dal 1855 al 1925." *Visioni Serafiche*. Edited by Ladislao Dragoni. New York: Catholic Polyglot Publishing House, 1926. Pp. 178.

A review of Franciscan work among Italian immigrants.

425. Dragoni, Ladislao.
"L'attività dei Francescani Italiani negli Stati Uniti." *Il Carroccio*, XXIV (October, 1926), 389-397.

Good account of the work of Italian Franciscans in the United States, 1855 to 1920s.

426. Dragoni, L.
"Arte Italiana in California. Il pittore P. Luigi Sciocchetti." *Il Carroccio*, XXXII (Settembre, 1930), 138-141.

Brief account of the paintings of Fr. Sciocchetti in some California churches.

427. Drayer, Allen.
"Italy in the Ozarks." *American Fruit Grower*, XLIII (September, 1923), 6, 14.

On Tontitown and Fr. Bandini.

428. Drury, Clifford M.
"Church-Sponsored Schools In Early California." *The Pacific Historian*, 20 (Summer, 1976), 158-166.

Lists 64 church-sponsored schools founded in California, including schools founded by Italian missionaries.

429. Dunn, R.
"Salesian Sisters." *New Catholic Encyclopedia*, XII (1967), 982.

The Daughters of Mary Help of Christians, or Salesian Sisters, were founded in Italy by John Bosco in 1872, mainly for the Christian education of youth. They arrived in the United States in 1908, establishing their first center in Paterson, New Jersey.

430. Dunne; E.M.
"Memoirs of 'Zi Pre.' " *The Ecclesiastical Review*, XLIX (August, 1913), 192-203.

This article includes some interesting recollections by Father Edmund M. Dunne on his work and life with the Italians of Guardian Angel parish in Chicago. The South Italian parishioners referred to Dunne as "Zi Prè" or Uncle Priest. Dunne was second Bishop of Peoria.

431. Dunne, Edmund M.
"The Church and the Immigrant." *Catholic Builders of the Nation*. 5 Vols. Edited by C.E. McGuire. Boston: Continental Press, Inc., 1923, II, 1-15.

This is an important statement of the relationship of the American Catholic Church to the immigrants. Dunne argues that the American Church has been guided by three key principles in its work with the immigrants: 1) the immigrant must be kept faithful to his religion; 2) through his own language as long as necessary; and 3) he must at the same time be made a good American citizen. The author concludes by stating that the Church is the best agency for americanizing the various immigrant groups.

432. Dunne, John J.
"Work of NCWC Community House at Utica." *NCWC Bulletin*, V (May, 1924), 5.

Americanization work at the Italian Church of Our Lady of Mt. Carmel in Utica, New York.

433. Dunne, Peter M.
"Salvatierra's Legacy to Lower California." *The Americas*, VII (July, 1950), 31-50.

Account of the work of the Jesuit missionary Juan Maria Salvatierra in Lower California from 1697 to 1717.

434. Earle, E. Lyell.
"Character Studies in New York's Foreign Quarters." *The Catholic World*, LXVIII (March, 1899), 782-793.

This is a sketch of various immigrant sections of New York City in the 1890s. It includes comments on "Little Italy" and Italian religious life.

435. "Eastern Catholics in America. IV. The Italo-Greeks." *The Lamp*, XLVII (July, 1949), 198-200.

This brief article deals with Our Lady of Grace chapel in the lower East Side of New York City and the work of Father Ciro Pinnola among the Italo-Greek Catholics of New York about 1900 to 1940.

436. Eckert, Robert P., Jr.
"A Missionary in the Wilderness." *Catholic World*, CXLIV (1937), 590-595.

Biography of Mazzuchelli based on his *Memoirs*.

437. Editorial.
"The Italian Problem." *Extension Magazine*, XII (September, 1917), 3-4.

This editorial focuses on the "Italian problem," i.e., the failure of the first generation of Italian immigrants to support their own churches. It calls for donations to the Church Extension Society to be used on behalf of the Italian immigrants.

438. Editorial.
"Our Duty to Our Fellow Catholic Italians." *The Messenger*, XXXIX (January, 1903), 89-92.

This editorial points out that Protestants in large cities like New York are very active in missionary work among the large masses of incoming Italian immigrants. It urges American Catholics to help preserve the immigrants' Catholic faith. The editorial makes reference to Thomas F. Meehan, "Evangelizing the Italians," *The Messenger*, XXXIX (January, 1903), 16-32.

439. E.E.C.
"Dedication of an Italian Church." *The Baptist Home Mission Monthly*, XXVII (February, 1905), 80.

Account of dedication of a new Italian Baptist Church in Camden, New Jersey, on December 18, 1904. Vincenzo Lomonte was the pastor.

440. Einaudi, Luigi.
"Un missionario apostolo degli emigranti." *Studi Emigrazione*, III (Ottobre, 1966), 66-69.

These are Einaudi's impressions of Fr. Pietro Maldotti, sent in August, 1894 by Bishop Scalabrini of Piacenza to investigate the conditions of the immigrants at the port of Genoa. This article originally appeared in Turin's *La Stampa*, September 9, 1898.

441. Einaudi, Luigi.
"Il problema dell'emigrazione in Italia." *Studi Emigrazione*, III (Ottobre, 1966), 70-73.

In this report on the Turin exposition of September, 1898, the author focuses on the section of the exposition that dealt with immigration and a meeting in which Bishops Bonomelli and Scalabrini gave lectures on emigration. It originally appeared in Turin's *La Stampa*, March 16, 1899.

442. Eliot, Ada.
"Two Italian Festivals." *Charities*, VII (1901), 321-322.

Description of two festivals showing how Italians mingle joy and gaiety with their worship. Author says that if the immigrants can impart this lesson to the Americans, "they will have amply justified themselves in this country."

443. Ellis, John Tracy.
The Life of James Cardinal Gibbons, Archbishop of Baltimore, 1834-1921. 2 vols. Milwaukee: The Bruce Publishing Company, 1952. Pp. xix-707, vii-735.

This is the standard biography of Cardinal Gibbons, the leading Catholic prelate during the period 1880-1921. It includes some information on the relationship between immigrants and the American Catholic Church.

444. Ellis, John Tracy.
American Catholicism. Second Edition, Revised. Chicago: The University of Chicago Press, 1969. Pp. xviii-322.

Brief history of the Catholic Church in the United States. See John Tracy Ellis. *American Catholicism*. Chicago: The University of Chicago Press, 1956. Pp. xiii-207.

445. Ellis, John Tracy, ed.
Documents of American Catholic History. Revised Logos ed. 2 vols.
Chicago: Henry Regnery Company, 1967. Pp. xxii-385, xxii-387-702.

Contains selections which trace the development of the American Catholic
Church from the days of Columbus to the twentieth century. Includes some
references to Italians in the United States. See John Tracy Ellis, ed. *Documents
of American Catholic History.* Milwaukee: The Bruce Publishing Company,
1956. Pp. xxiv-677.

446. "Gli Emigranti Italiani a Nuova York." *La Civiltà Cattolica,* 55, II
(1904), 172-179.

This article discusses some of the efforts made by Archbishop John M. Farley
of New York and other priests in the city to protect the Italians, especially the
children, from Protestant missionary efforts.

447. "Emigrazione dei Cattolici negli Stati Uniti d'America." *La Civiltà
Cattolica,* LV (9 July, 1904), 252-253.

Rome's concern for Catholic immigrants, especially Italian, in the United
States of America.

448. Espinosa, Jose Manuel.
"Documents: Account of the First Jesuit Missionary Journey Across
the Plains to Santa Fè." *Mid-America,* N.S., IX (January, 1938), 51-62.

Account of the journey of Father Donato M. Gasparri, S.J., to found the New
Mexico mission in 1867. Gasparri's account appeared in Italian in the *Lettere
Edificanti* of the Neapolitan Province in 1886.

449. Espinosa, Jose Manuel.
"The Neapolitan Jesuits in the Colorado Frontier." *Colorado Magazine,*
XV (January, 1938), 64-73.

A literal translation of parts of Jesuit Father Troy's unpublished history
(written in Latin) concerning the Neapolitan Jesuits in the Southwest.

450. Espinosa, Jose Manuel.
"The Opening of the First Jesuit Mission in Colorado: Conejos Parish."
Mid-America, XVIII (October, 1936), 272-275.

Excerpt from "Diario" of the mission, translated and edited by Espinosa.

451. *Estratto di alcune lettere del P. Giuseppe Giorda Superiore delle
Missioni della Compagnia di Gesù nelle Montagne Rocciose al R.P.
Provinciale della Provincia Torinese, scritte dal 1863 al 1865.* Roma:

coi tipi della "Civiltà Cattolica," 1866. Pp. 24.

Reprint of letters sent by Fr. Giuseppe Giorda, superior of the Jesuit Rocky Mountain mission, to the provincial of the Turin Province, from 1863 to 1865.

452. Evans, Mary Ellen.
The Seed and the Glory. The Career of Samuel Charles Mazzuchelli, O.P., on the Mid-American Frontier. New York: McMullen Books, Inc., 1950. Pp. 250.

Popularly written biography of Charles Mazzuchelli, a Dominican missionary in the Midwest.

453. Faccenna, D. Filippo.
Al Di Là Dell'Oceano. Tivoli: Tipografia Tivoli, 1913. Pp. 203.

A guide for potential migrants written by a priest. Gives detailed information on customs, norms, demographic data. Numerous are the references to Church activities, and the addresses of religious institutions working in North and South America among migrants. The Scalabrini Fathers are often mentioned.

454. Farnham, Edwin P.
"Rev. Antonio Mangano." *The Baptist Home Mission Monthly*, XXIX (September, 1907), 315-318.

Sketch of the Rev. Antonio Mangano, pastor and missionary among the Italians in Brooklyn. Page 314 has a photograph of Mangano, and pp. 316-317 contain a photograph of the "Young People's Society — First Italian Baptist Church of Brooklyn."

455. "Father Aloysius M. Folchi." *Woodstock Letters*, XXXIX (1910), 238-239.

Fr. Folchi, a Jesuit born in Rome (1834-1909), spent his life working in Washington, Montana, and Idaho among Indians, railroad men, miners and lumbermen.

456. "Father Aloysius Romano." *Woodstock Letters*, XLIV (1915), 220-227.

Obituary of Fr. Romano, born in 1842 in Positano (Amalfi). He arrived in the United States in 1873, was involved in teaching and worked among the Italian immigrants at Loreto parish in New York City.

457. "Father A.M. Marigliano." *Woodstock Letters*, IX (1880), 59-62.

Obituary of Antonio Marigliano (1842-1879), a Neapolitan Jesuit who came to America in 1872, gave several missions in Washington, D.C., Philadelphia and Wilmington, and left a "memoir" of his work.

458. "Father Angelo Coltelli." *Woodstock Letters*, XXXVII (1908), 108-111.

Fr. Coltelli (1850-1907), from Tuscany, worked as a Jesuit missionary for 34 years in California seminaries and missions.

459. "Father Angelo M. Paresce." *Woodstock Letters*, VIII (1879), 186-187.

Obituary of Fr. Paresce (1817-1879), a Neapolitan Jesuit who came to America in 1845, where he worked as Novice Master and Provincial of the Maryland Province. Undertook the building of Woodstock College and became its first Rector.

460. "Father Anthony Ciampi." *Woodstock Letters*, XXIII (1894), 154-155.

Obituary of Fr. Ciampi, a Jesuit born in Rome in 1816. He was Rector of Holy Cross College and worked as a missionary in the eastern United States.

461. "Father Anthony M. Mandalari." *Woodstock Letters*, XXXIV (1905), 413-415.

Mandalari (1842-1902), a Jesuit from Calabria, was a professor at Woodstock.

462. "Father Bartholomew Calzia." *Woodstock Letters*, XXXV (1906), 279-281.

A Jesuit born in Genoa (1844-1906), came to California in 1865 and spent his life in teaching and pastoral work.

463. "Father Benedict Piccardo." *Woodstock Letters*, XXVI (1897), 485.

Piccardo (1819-1897), a Jesuit missionary from Liguria, worked among the Spanish-speaking in the Santa Clara Valley, California.

464. "Father Caesar A. Barchi." *Woodstock Letters*, XXXV (1906), 137.

Barchi (1828-1906), a Jesuit missionary from Genoa, came to the United States in 1860. Worked at St. Ignatius College and ministered in San Francisco and San Jose, California.

465. "Father Carmelus Polino." *Woodstock Letters*, XVII (1888), 385-386.

Obituary of a Jesuit missionary, Polino, who came to the United States in

1876, worked in Denver, Pueblo and Las Vegas and was editor of *Revista Catolica.*

466. "Father Charles Piccirillo. A Sketch." *Woodstock Letters,* XVII (1888), 339-350.

Piccirillo was a contributor to the *Civiltà Cattolica* from its inception. Born in Naples in 1821, he came to the United States in 1875 as a teacher at Woodstock College and as Dean of Studies. Participated in the third council of Baltimore as a Theologian.

467. "Father Domenic Pantanella." *Woodstock Letters,* LI (1922), 406-410.

Fr. Pantanella (1831-1922) was born near Naples. He taught at Woodstock College, worked in New Mexico and, for 33 years, in Denver, Colorado.

468. "Father Francis B. Andreis. Father Charles Mary Pollano. Father Celestine Galliano." *Woodstock Letters,* XXVIII (1899), 315-320.

Obituaries of three Jesuit missionaries from Piedmont who labored in the missions of the West Coast in the second half of the nineteenth century.

469. "Father Francis I. Prelato." *Woodstock Letters,* XXXVII, 255-259.

The Jesuit Fr. Prelato (1829-1907), born in Liguria, spent 49 years in California as professor and missionary. He was called the Apostle of San Francisco.

470. "Father John Pinasco." *Woodstock Letters,* XXVI (1897), 487-490.

Obituary of Fr. Pinasco (1837-1897) professor, rector and parish priest in California. A native of Chiavari, near Genoa.

471. "Father Joseph Caruana." *Woodstock Letters,* XLIII (1914), 109-111.

Fr. Caruana (1836-1913) was born in Malta and educated in Rome. In 1862 he arrived in California where he became one of the pioneer Italian missionaries in the Rocky Mountains among the Spokane and Flathead Indians.

472. "Father Joseph Giorda." *Woodstock Letters,* XI (1882), 322-323.

Fr. Giorda (1823-1882), a native of Piedmont, came to America in 1858. During his term as superior in Montana, many churches and missions were established among both whites and Indians.

473. "Father Joseph M. Marra." *Woodstock Letters,* XLIV (1915), 389-392.

Marra (1844-1914), from Catanzaro, came to the United States in 1870. He was a professor in California, editor of *Revista Catolica*, and fought for the teaching of Spanish in the public schools of New Mexico.

474. "Father Joseph N. Neri." *Woodstock Letters*, XLIX (1920), 242-246.

An ingenious and talented man, Neri wrote treatises on chemistry and electricity, developed the spectroscope, invented the track electric power system for trains, and laid plans for the new lighting system of the city of San Francisco. In California from 1858 as Jesuit missionary and teacher. He died in 1919.

475. "Father Mengarini." *Woodstock Letters*, XVI (1887), 93-97.

Obituary of one of the three founders of the Rocky Mountains missions. Mengarini was born in Rome in 1811. He composed the first grammar of the Flathead Indians' language.

476. "Father Nicholas Russo — Father Henry Imoda." *Woodstock Letters*, XXXI (1902), 281-287.

Obituaries of two Italian Jesuit missionaries. Fr. Russo active for many years among the Italian immigrants of New York and, Fr. Imoda, active among the Indians of the Northwest.

477. "Father Peter Paul Prando." *Woodstock Letters*, XXXVI (1907), 349-351.

Fr. Prando (1845-1906) worked in the Indian Mission of the Rocky Mountains for over 30 years. Baptized more than 3,000 Indians.

478. "Father Philip Rappagliosi." *Woodstock Letters*, VIII (1879), 97-109.

Obituary of Fr. Rappagliosi (1841-1878), an Italian Jesuit missionary among the Flathead and Black-feet Indians in the Rocky Mountains starting in 1873. Noted for a holy and dedicated life.

479. "Father Pius Massi." *Woodstock Letters*, XL (1911), 93-99.

Obituary of a Roman Jesuit missionary, a very knowledgeable and ingenious man, chaplain to workers in the Panama Canal, Cuba, Jamaica and most of all in the eastern United States. Died in 1910 after years of teaching and work at Georgetown and in New York City.

480. "Father Salvatore Personè." *Woodstock Letters*, LIII, 124, 387-390.

Obituary of Fr. Personè, a pioneer of the New Mexico-Colorado Mission. Born in Lecce in 1833, he died in 1923 in Trinidad, Colorado. In the 1860s he arrived as a missionary in the United States. He was the first rector of Las Vegas College, now Regis College, and a very able organizer of the Jesuit missions in the Southwest.

481. "Father Sanctus Traverso." *Woodstock Letters*, XXXVI (1907), 363-367.

A native of Genoa, Traverso came as a Jesuit missionary to California in 1856. He was a professor of modern languages and was active in the apostolate at San Jose.

482. "Father Theodore Sebastiani — Father Aloysius Varsi." *Woodstock Letters*, XXX (1901), 127-128, 131-132.

Obituaries of Italian Jesuit missionaries in the United States.

483. Felici, Icilio.
Father to the Immigrants: The Life of John Baptist Scalabrini. Translated by Carol della Chiesa. New York: P.J. Kenedy & Sons, 1955. Pp. viii-248.

Popular biography of Bishop J.B. Scalabrini of Piacenza and his activities on behalf of Italian immigrants.

484. Femminella, Francis X.
"The Impact of Italian Migration and American Catholicism." *The American Catholic Sociological Review*, XXII (Fall, 1961), 233-241.

The author sums up his article in these words: "I have attempted in this paper to describe analytically the coming together — the impact — of Italian immigrants and American Catholicism. I adumbrated a social-psychological interpretation of the three major adjustive responses of Italians, and I described the significant negativism of one aspect of this impact. Finally, I have hypothesized that out of this negation comes a real positive Italian influence on American Catholicism" (p. 241). For a brief critique of this paper, see Andrew Greeley, Letter to the Editor of *The American Catholic Sociological Review*, XXII (Winter, 1961), 333.

485. Ferrante, Gherardo.
"Chiese e Scuole Parrocchiali Italiane." *Gli Italiani Negli Stati Uniti D'America.* New York: Italian American Directory, Co., 1906. Pp. 89-95.

Describes the difficulties and successes of Italian parishes in the New York metropolitan area. Points out the need for parochial schools and notes that with the coming of the Scalabrinian Missionaries to New York, exclusively Italian parishes are established.

486. Ficarra, Bernard J.
Zappatori. Boston: The Christopher Publishing House, 1953. Pp. 112.

Popularly written account of Italian life in America. Chapter VII, pp. 82-90, is titled "Our Religion." "Zappatori" is the Italian word for "The Ditch Diggers."

487. Fidelis.
"Nationalism and Catholicity of the Clergy in the United States." *The Ecclesiastical Review,* LXX (March, 1924), 295-298.

In this article the author makes a strong case for the need to americanize Catholic immigrants in the United States. He argues that the foreign clergy has been a chief obstacle to the process of americanization.

488. *Fiftieth Anniversary Annual of the Italian Baptist Association of America, 1898-1948.* Mount Vernon, New York: 1948. Pp. 64.

It contains a history of the Italian Baptist Association of America (pp. 9-52) and its various churches written by Angelo DiDomenica.

489. Fiorentino, Joseph.
In the Power of His Spirit. A CCNA publication. n.p., n.d. Pp. 17.

This pamphlet is subtitled "a summary of the Italian Pentecostal movement in the U.S.A. and abroad." The introduction states that this "account of the Italian Pentecostal Movement is concerned mainly with that body of people which, at present, is called the Christian Church of North America [CCNA] and with those churches which comprise the Assemblies of God in Italy. However, mention will be made incidentally of the Italian Assemblies of God in the U.S.A., the Italian Pentecostal Church of Canada, and the Christian Congregations in Brazil." The CCNA published two periodicals: *The Lighthouse* for the English-speaking constituency and *Il Faro* for the Italian-speaking members.

490. "The First Church Built in California: Sketch of the Life and Labor of Father Giovanni Maria Salvatierra, the Apostle of California." *Woodstock Letters,* X (1881), 28-42.

Fr. Salvatierra, born in Milan in 1644, became a Jesuit and was sent to Mexico in 1675. In 1697 he founded Our Lady of Loreto mission in San Dionigio Bay, worked for 20 years in California and New Mexico, and died in California in 1717. A reprint from the San Francisco *Monitor.*

491. "The First Italian Priest in New York." *Atlantica* (November, 1931), 176-177.

Account of the coming of a group of Franciscan missionaries in 1855 —

Fathers Panfilo da Magliano, Sisto da Graffagliano, Samuele da Prezza, and Salvatore — to found an Italian Franciscan Mission in the Diocese of Buffalo, New York. Taken from an article in *Il Legionario* of Rome.

492. Flamma, Ario, comp.
Italiani di America. Enciclopedia Biografica Compilata da Ario Flamma. 3 Vols. New York: Cocce Brothers, 1936-1949. Pp. 367, 331, 370.

Brief biographical sketches of Italians in the United States, listed alphabetically in each volume. Includes biographies of Catholic priests and Protestant ministers.

493. Flynn, Joseph M.
The Catholic Church in New Jersey. Morristown, N.J.: By the Author, 1904.

Occasional reference to Italian priests and immigrant communities in New Jersey.

494. Folchi, Luigi.
"The Indian School of St. Ignatius' Mission. Extract of a Letter from Fr. Luigi M. Folchi to Father Piccirillo. St. Ignatius' Mission, Missoula Co., Montana. December 26, 1880." *Woodstock Letters*, X (1881), 140.

Refers to government harassment of the school and the Indians.

495. "Fr. Aloysius Masnata." *Woodstock Letters*, XIX (1890), 100-101.

Obituary of Fr. Masnata (1823-1889), a Jesuit missionary from Genoa who had come to the United States in 1850. He spent many years in the California missions with Frs. Canio and Bixio.

496. "Fr. Aloysius Valente." *Woodstock Letters*, XVIII (1889), 245-246.

Valente (1835-1888) was one of the first professors at Woodstock. A Neapolitan Jesuit who came to the United States in 1869.

497. "Fr. Anthony Maraschi." *Woodstock Letters*, XXVI (1897), 490-492.

Fr. Maraschi (1820-1897) was a missionary who came to California from Italy in 1849.

498. "Fr. Basil Pacciarini." *Woodstock Letters*, XIII (1884), 409-412.

Pacciarini (1816-1884), born in Umbria, came to America in 1846, ministered in Maryland, preached missions to the Italians on the West Shore Rail Road where he had some difficulties with the "Garibaldini," to whom he brought the sacraments.

499. "Fr. Benedict Sestini." *Woodstock Letters*, XIX (1890), 259-263.

Obituary of Fr. Sestini, born in Florence in 1816. He came to the United States as a Jesuit missionary in 1849 together with the astronomer Fr. Secchi, with whom he taught mathematics and natural sciences at Georgetown College. Published scientific books, started the *Messenger of the Sacred Heart* in 1866, and remained very active until his death in 1890.

500. "Fr. Camillus Imoda." *Woodstock Letters*, XV, 322-323.

Obituary of Fr. Imoda (1829-1886) missionary in Montana among the Black-Feet Indians. Born in Turin, came to the United States in 1858.

501. "Fr. Camillus Vicinanza." *Woodstock Letters*, XIII (1879), 114-116.

Obituary of Fr. Vicinanza (1814-1878), a Neapolitan Jesuit who came to America in 1845, and was professor and missionary at St. Charles Co. and St. Mary's Co., Maryland.

502. "Fr. Joseph Bixio." *Woodstock Letters*, XVIII (1889), 246-247.

Fr. J. Bixio (1819-1889), brother of the Italian General Nino Bixio who captured Rome in 1870, was a self-appointed chaplain of both the Union and Confederate soldiers during the Civil War. He worked at San Jose, California.

503. "Fr. Joseph Tadini." *Woodstock Letters*, XVIII (1889), 109-110.

Tadini (1816-1888) worked in California, where he arrived in 1857, and also in the Rocky Mountains with Fathers Mengarini and DeSmet.

504. "Fr. Nicholas Cangiato." *Woodstock Letters*, XXVI (1897), 492-495.

Obituary of Fr. Cangiato (1816-1897), superior of the missions in California and instrumental in the opening of several parishes. Born in Sardinia, came to the United States in 1849.

505. "Fr. Urban Grassi." *Woodstock Letters*, XIX (1890), 266-270.

Obituary of Fr. Grassi, a Jesuit from Piedmont, who labored for many years in the Rocky Mountains missions. He was born in 1830.

506. Francescon, Luigi.
Autobiography of Luigi Francescon. Oak Park, Illinois: The Author, 1952. Pp. 16.

A biographical sketch of Francescon, an Italian Pentecostal, and his activities in the United States and Brazil.

507. Francesconi, Mario.
Inizi della Congregazione Scalabriniana (1886-1888). Roma: Centro Studi Emigrazione, 1969. Pp. 179.

This is the first in a series of volumes on the history of the Society of St. Charles Borromeo written by Francesconi. This volume limits itself to the study of the beginnings of the Society, 1886-1888. It is based on archival material at the Archivio Generalizio Scalabriniano in Rome.

508. Francesconi, Mario.
Storia della Congregazione Scalabriniana. Vol. II: *Organizzazione Interna-Prime Missioni negli Stati Uniti (1888-1895)*. Roma: Centro Studi Emigrazione, 1973. Pp. 310.

This is the second volume in Francesconi's multi-volume study of the Society of St. Charles Borremeo. It deals with the internal development of the Society after its founding in 1887 and with the development of Scalabrinian missions in the United States. Volume III deals exclusively with the Society of St. Charles Borromeo in Brazil.

509. Francesconi, Mario.
Storia della Congregazione Scalabriniana. Vol. IV: *Le Missioni nel Brasile e negli Stati Uniti (1905-1919)*. Roma: Centro Studi Emigrazione, 1973. Pp. 390.

This volume continues Francesconi's multi-volume history of the Society of St. Charles Borromeo, an Italian community established in 1887 to work among Italian immigrants in the New World. This volume covers the missions in Brazil and the United States during the period 1905-1919.

510. Francesconi, Mario.
Storia della Congregazione Scalabriniana. Vol. V: *Il Primo Dopoguerra (1919-1940)*. Roma: Centro Studi Emigrazione, 1975. Pp. 468.

Continuation of the history of the Scalabrinian Congregation. A special section of this volume reports on the growth and activities of Italian parishes run by the Scalabrinians in the United States between the two World Wars. The characteristic of Francesconi's history is the abundant use of original archival sources previously unutilized, although he often limits his writing to descriptive and chronological historical reporting.

511. Frangini, A.
Italiani in Cincinnati, O. Strenna Nazionale. Cincinnati, Ohio:

Tipografia del "Corriere dell'Ohio," n.d. Pp. 68.

Biographies of prominent Italians and a brief sketch of the "Santa Maria Institute, 534 West Seventh Street."

512. Frangini, A.
Italiani in Detroit, Mich. Strenna Nazionale. Cincinnati, Ohio: Tipografia del "Corriere dell'Ohio," n.d. Pp. 69.

Biographies of prominent Italians, including work of the Presbyterian Church in Detroit.

513. Frangini, A.
Italiani in St. Louis, Missouri. Strenna Nazionale. New York: Tipografia Paolo Vitagliano, n.d. Pp. 69.

Biographies of prominent Italians and brief sketches of various churches.

514. Frangini, A.
Italiani in Boston, Mass. Strenna Nazionale. Cenni Biografici. Boston: Stamperia Commerciale, 1907. Pp. 99.

Brief biographical sketches of prominent Italians in Boston. Includes sketches on the churches of St. Leonard and Sacred Heart in Boston's North End.

515. Frangini, A.
Italiani nel Connecticut. Strenna Nazionale. Cenni Biografici. New Haven, Conn.: Tipografia Sociale, 1908. Pp. 103.

Biographies of prominent Italians in New Haven and histories of several churches.

516. Frangini, A.
Italiani nel New Jersey. Strenna Nazionale. Cenni Biografici. Rutherford, New Jersey: Stamperia Italiana, 1908. Pp. 106.

Biographies of prominent Italians and histories of churches.

517. Frangini, A.
Italiani in Cleveland e Dintorni. Strenna Nazionale. New York: Tipografica Commerciale, 1910. Pp. 60.

Biographies of prominent Italians and brief histories of churches.

518. Frangini, A.
Italiani nel Centro dello Stato di New York. Strenna Nazionale. Utica,

N.Y.: Tipografia della "Luce," 1912. Pp. 103.

Includes brief biographies of prominent Italians and histories of churches.

519. Frangini, A.
Italiani in Los Angeles, Cal. Strenna Nazionale. Cenni Biografici. Los Angeles: Tipografia dell'*Italo-Americano*, G. Spini, 1913. Pp. 109.

Sketches of Italian churches and religious personnel involved with them.

520. Frangini, A.
Colonie Italiche in California. Strenna Nazionale. Cenni Biografici. Stockton, Cal.: L. Stamper e L.N. Ciari, 1914. Pp. 98.

Brief accounts of churches and of Italian priests serving Italian immigrants in California.

521. Frangini, A.
Italiani in San Francisco e Oakland, Cenni Biografici. San Francisco: 1914. Pp. 135.

Includes brief description of the founding of the Chiesa del Corpus Domini in 1898 by the Salesian priest, Rev. Cassinis.

522. Frankling, Laurence.
"The Italian in America: What He Has Been, What He Shall Be." *The Catholic World*, LXXI (April, 1900), 67-80.

In this article the author discusses the beneficial role played by Catholic settlements in protecting the Catholic faith of Italian immigrants in New York City.

523. Frasca, Michael.
"Why I am Entering the Ministry." *The Assembly Herald*, (December, 1913), 687-688.

An Italian immigrant's personal experience, including his decision to become a Protestant minister.

524. Frisco Lines.
"Colonia Italiana: Tontitown, Arkansas, Stati Uniti d'America." *Italians in the United States. A Repository of Rare Tracts and Miscellanea.* New York: Arno Press, 1975. Pp. 25.

A brief history of the development of Tontitown and the key role of Fr. Peter Bandini. Italian text, St. Louis, Missouri, 1899.

525. Fusco, Nicola.
"San Pietro Italiano di Pittsburgh." *Il Carroccio*, XII (November, 1920), 519-522.

The author rejects the charge that Italian immigrants built their churches and schools with subsidies from Irish and German-American Catholics. Rather, Italians had to overcome the discrimination of their fellow Catholics.

526. Fusco, Nicola.
"The Italian Racial Strain." *Catholic Builders of the Nation*. 5 Vols. Edited by C.E. McGuire. Boston: Continental Press, Inc., 1923. II, 111-126.

In this article, the author lists outstanding Italian Catholics and their contributions to American life in these areas: exploration, missionary activity, art, the military, letters, inventions, colonizing work, and labor.

527. Fusco, Nicola.
"A Catholic Priest's Work." *Il Carroccio*, XX (September, 1924), 281-284.

Fr. Fusco's work on behalf of Italian immigrants.

528. Fusco, Nicola.
"Eusebio Chino, l'italiano scopritore della Penisola Californiana, 1644-1711." *Il Carroccio*, XXIX (Gennaio, 1929), 33-41.

On the achievements and Italian origin of Fr. Kino.

529. Gallagher, John P.
A Century of History. The Diocese of Scranton: 1868-1968. Scranton: The Diocese of Scranton, 1968. Pp. xiv-615.

History of the Diocese of Scranton with special mention of Bishop Michael J. Hoban who established many territorial parishes for European immigrants: Poles, Slovaks, Italians, Lithuanians, and Germans.

530. Gallo, Patrick J.
Ethnic Alienation. The Italian-Americans. Rutherford: Fairleigh Dickinson University Press, 1974. Pp. 254.

A study of the political behavior of a small sample of three generations of Italian-Americans in an attempt to uncover the causes of alienation of ethnic groups in American society. Gallo finds that political alienation is proportionately correlated to lack of identification and practice of Italian-Americans. The book is an edited version of Patrick J. Gallo, "Political Alienation Among Italians of the New York Metropolitan Region." Unpublished Ph.D. dissertation, New York University, 1971.

531. Gambera.
"Il Clero Italiano in America e l'Assistenza degli Emigrati Italiani."
Italica Gens, II (Maggio, 1911), 217-225.

Reproduction of a letter sent by Fr. Giacomo Gambera to *The New World*,
Chicago's Catholic newspaper, on February 25, 1911. In this letter, Gambera,
basing himself on his pastoral experience among Italian immigrants, defends
the Italian clergy and the religiosity of the immigrants against those who
would view the Italians as a "problem" for the church.

532. Gambino, Richard.
Blood of My Blood. The Dilemma of the Italian-Americans. Garden
City, New York: Doubleday & Co., Inc., 1974. Pp. viii-350.

Interpretative reflection on the Italian-American experience, based on personal
experience. Includes a chapter titled "Religion, Magic and the Church," pp.
193-222.

533. Garraghan, Gilbert J.
"John Anthony Grassi, S.J., 1775-1849." *The Catholic Historical
Review*, XXIII (October, 1937), 273-292.

Summary sketch of the highlights of Father Grassi's career as a Jesuit
missionary in the United States.

534. Garraghan, Gilbert J.
The Jesuits of the Middle United States. 3 vols. New York: America
Press, 1938. Pp. xi-660, iv-699, v-666. Reprinted, New York: Arno
Press, 1978.

This 3-volume study contains much information on the work of Italian
Jesuits in the West.

535. Garraghan, Gilbert J.
"Samuel Charles Mazzuchelli, Dominican of the Frontier." *Mid-
America*, N.S., IX (October, 1938), 253-262.

Text of an address delivered at Rosary College, River Forest, Illinois, on
Mazzuchelli Day, November 4, 1936.

536. Gavazzi, Alessandro.
*Father Gavazzi's Lectures in New York, Reported in Full by T.C.
Leland, Phonographer; Also, the Life of Father Gavazzi, Corrected
and Authorized by Himself. Together with Reports of His Addresses
in Italian, to his Countrymen in New York*. Translated and Revised
by Madame Julie de Marguerittes. New York: DeWitt and Davenport,
Publishers, 1853. Pp. 299.

The Introduction notes: "The first edition of the 'Life' of Father Gavazzi, which was published by itself, met a most favorable reception, and was sold in immense numbers, at all the Father's lectures, and by the trade throughout the country. This little memoir has been extended, and the events brought down to the present time, and the whole is now incorporated in the present volume, as a suitable introduction to the Lectures. Besides the regular course of ten Lectures, this volume contains a brief sketch of the Addresses in the Italian language, made by Father Gavazzi to his countrymen in New York, every Sunday evening, during the course of his English lectures." In his lectures, Gavazzi spoke "against the power of the Pope, because Popery is inimical to the liberty of the people."

537. Gavazzi, Alessandro.
The Lectures Complete of Father Gavazzi, As Delivered in New York. Reported by an Eminent Stenographer, and Revised and Corrected by Gavazzi Himself. Including Translations of His Italian Addresses With Which the Greater Part of the Lectures Were Prefaced. To Which is Prefixed, Under His Authority and Revision, The Life of Gavazzi, Continued to the Time of His Visit to America, by G.B. Nicolini, His Friend and Fellow Exile, Author of a History of the Late Roman Republic. New York: Published by M.W. Dodd, 1854. Pp. xxiv-393.

538. "Gavazzi Versus the See of S. Peter." *The Catholic World*, XVI (October, 1872), 55-61.

This article, written "By a Protestant Doctor of Philosophy," takes issue with "Father Gavazzi" and his arguments against the papacy. The author gives historical proof that St. Peter had been in Rome.

539. Genna, G.
"Letters from Alaska. Letter from Fr. G. Genna to Rev. Fr. Cataldo. St. Michael's, Alaska, July 1, 1888." *Woodstock Letters*, XVII (1888), 325-326.

A description of the missions in Alaska.

540. Gentile, Luigi.
"Mexico, Letter of Fr. Gentile to the members of the Mission of New Mexico at Woodstock." *Woodstock Letters*, XIV (1885), 391-396.

A visit to the missions and missionary stations in New Mexico and Texas by Italian missionary Jesuits.

541. Genzmer, George Harvey.
"Finotti, Joseph Maria." *Dictionary of American Biography*, VI (1931), 396.

Brief biography of Finotti, born at Ferrara, Italy, in 1817. He entered the Society of Jesus in 1833 and went to America in 1845 to work in the Jesuits' Maryland Province. Ordained in 1847, he left the Jesuits in 1852. He went to Boston where he did parochial work and became literary editor of the Boston *Pilot*. His most valuable contribution was the compiling of the *Bibliographia Catholica Americana: A List of Works Written by Catholic Authors and Published in the United States: Pt. I, 1784-1820* (1872), which he did not live to complete.

542. Gertrude, M. Agnes.
"Italian Immigration into Philadelphia." *Records of the American Catholic Historical Society of Philadelphia*, LVIII (June-September-December, 1947), 133-143, 189-208, 256-267.

This is a general study on Italians in Philadelphia. It deals with "Religious Aspects of Italian Life in Philadelphia" on pages 194-207. The entire study is based on secondary sources.

543. G.G.
"In Onore di un Apostolo." *Italica Gens*, III (Ottobre-Novembre, 1912), 324-328.

Regarding Fr. Giovanni Vogel, pastor of an Italian parish in Brooklyn, New York.

544. Giambastiani, Louis M.
"In the Melting Pot: The Italians." *Extension*, VII (September, 1912), 9-10, 20-21.

A concise, but important article written after years of experience within the Italian immigrant community of Chicago. The variety of regional backgrounds of the Italian immigrants impedes social unity. The family is "essentially religious," but there is little church attendance. Marriage takes place at a very young age; American-born assimilate quickly. Protestant proselytizing has little success. Indifference to religion is the greatest danger. Author feels that when Italian immigrants join the middle class, their religious behavior will be comparable to that of other Catholics.

545. Giardina, G.
Il P. Cataldo, S.J. Apostolo dei Pellirosse. Palermo: Ed. Regina Apostolorum, 1928. Pp. 82.

Cataldo was one of the principal missionaries in the Northwest.

546. Gil.
"L'Ufficio Regionale dell'*Italica Gens* in New Orleans (Luisiana-Stati Uniti N.A.)." *Italica Gens*, V (Gennaio-Febbraio, 1914), 13-23.

Describes the founding and work of the *Italica Gens* in New Orleans. Started by Fr. Vincenzo Scramuzza and incorporated on June 18, 1913, it had 650 cases of assistance in the first year.

547. Gillis, James M.
Common Sense of Immigration. New York: The Paulist Press, 1924. Pp. 23.

This pamphlet is a response by the Paulist Father J. Gillis to Gino Speranza's later writings on assimilation. Gillis rejects Anglo-Saxon supremacy and the need of Protestantism as the dominant religion. He attacks Speranza's advocacy of extra-legal methods to perpetuate Anglo-Saxon Protestant power.

548. Giorda, F.
"Washington Territory. Extract of a Letter from Father F. Giorda. DeSmet, Pine Creek P.O., W.T., October 21st, 1879." *Woodstock Letters*, IX (1880), 27-28.

Describes the beginning of the new mission which replaced the Coeur D'Alêne Station and was named after Fr. DeSmet.

549. Giorda, Joseph.
"Il Missionario Gesuita Tra i Selvaggi Nasoforati." *Museo delle missioni cattoliche*, 15 (1872), 593-603.

Father Giorda's work with American Indians.

550. Goering, John M.
"The Structure and Processes of Ethnicity: Catholic Family Size in Providence, Rhode Island." *Sociological Analysis*, 26 (Fall, 1965), 129-136.

Discusses influence of Catholic belief on family size among Italian-Americans in Providence, Rhode Island.

551. *Golden Crown to Honor Mary Help of Christians*. New York: The Salesians of Don Bosco, 1928. Pp. 131.

A souvenir journal reporting, in English and Italian, the history of the institutions and activities of the Salesian Fathers and Sisters on behalf of Italian immigrants in the eastern part of the United States. Scattered but informative.

552. Gould, Charles F.
"Portland Italians, 1880-1920." *Oregon Historical Quarterly*, LXXVII (September, 1976), 239-260.

A brief history of the Portland Italians within the framework of the Italian-American migration and the specific conditions of Portland, Oregon. Review of activities and accomplishments of prominent Italian-Americans. Description of the Italian neighborhoods in Portland. Study based on documentation and personal interviews. It lists churches built by Italians in the city.

553. Grassi, John.
"The Catholic Religion in the United States in 1818." *Woodstock Letters*, XI (1882), 229-246.

Grassi describes the first diocese in the United States, the religious orders and congregations, church buildings, the legal status of church property, the need for missionaries and the bright hopes for the future. A translation from the Italian: *Notizie Varie sullo stato presente della Repubblica degli Stati Uniti dell'America Settentrionale, scritte al principio del 1818, dal P. Giovanni Grassi, della Compagnia di Gesù.* Milano: 1819. Edizione Seconda.

554. Grassi, John.
"The Catholic Religion in the United States in 1818." *The American Catholic Historical Researches*, VIII (July, 1891), 98-112.

This is one of the earliest historical accounts of the Catholic Church in America. Grassi, an Italian Jesuit, was President of Georgetown College from 1812 to 1817.

555. Grassi, U.
"A Visit to the Kootenais. Extracts from a Letter of Fr. U. Grassi to Fr. Valente. Attaham, Jakima Co., Wash. Territory, December 14, 1872." *Woodstock Letters*, II (1873), 157-161.

Description of progress of the missionary work and the outstanding physical strength and moral qualities of the Indians.

556. Grassi, U.
"Indian Missions. The Sinpesquensi. Washington Territory, Yokama Co., October 4th, 1873." *Woodstock Letters*, III (1874), 68-73.

Describes the influence of the chief of the Sinpesquensi Indians, the work of the Oblate Fathers among them, and the value of prayer for the Indians.

557. Grassi, U.
"Indian Missions — Fort Colville, Wash. Ty., Letter of Fr. Grassi, April 23rd, 1878." *Woodstock Letters*, VII (1878), 174-178.

Describes efforts among the Spokane River Indians to bring some of their tribes back to the Catholic faith. No date given, but the letter refers to 1881.

558. Grassi, U.
"Indian Missions. Washington Territory. Letter of Father U. Grassi to Father Cataldo." *Woodstock Letters*, XI (1882), 65-70.

Work among the Spokane River Indians to bring back to the Catholic faith some fallen away tribes. No date given, but the letter refers to 1881.

559. Grasso, Pier Giovanni.
Personalità Giovanile in Transizione. Zürich: Pas-Verlag, 1964. Pp. 489.

A sociological study of young Italian immigrants in Boston with reference to their religious values and adaptation.

560. Graves, W.W.
Life and Letters of Fathers Ponziglione, Schoenmakers and Other Early Jesuits at Osage Mission. St. Paul, Kansas: The Author, 1916. Pp. 287.

Fr. Paul M. Ponziglione was a Jesuit missionary who worked among the Indians of the American West during the second half of the nineteenth century. This volume contains biographical information as well as some correspondence relating to Ponziglione.

561. Greco, Emilio.
Il Padre degli Emigrati Italiani in America e l'Apostolo dei Suoi Missionari. New York: Polyglot Publishing House, 1916. Pp. 24.
Brief biography of Scalabrini.

562. Greeley, Andrew M. and Peter H. Rossi.
The Education of Catholic Americans. Chicago: Aldine, 1966. Pp. xxii-368.
This sociological study includes data on Italian-Americans.

563. Greeley, Andrew M.
The American Catholic. A Social Portrait. New York: Basic Books, Inc., 1977. Pp. 280.

In this portrait of American Catholicism, Greeley provides a scholarly and factual description of the ethnic groups that constitute the American Church. One of the key ethnic groups he constantly refers to are the Italian-Americans, about whom he gives a significant amount of information.

564. Gregori, Francesco.
La Vita e l'Opera di un Grande Vescovo, Mons. Giov. Battista Scalabrini (1830-1905). Torino: L.I.C.E.-Roberto Berrutti & C., 1934. Pp. 615.

This is an old but still valuable biography of the Bishop of Piacenza, Giovanni Battista Scalabrini (1839-1905).

565. Grieco, Rose.
The Listening Heart. The Life of John Baptist Scalabrini Father to the Immigrants. New York: Society of St. Charles, 1965. Pp. 95.

A popularly written biography of Bishop Scalabrini.

566. Grivetti, Giuseppe.
"*L'Italica Gens* Negli Stati Uniti e Canadà al 31 Dicembre 1910." *Italica Gens*, II (Aprile, 1911), 145-169.

A detailed report on the services offered by the *Italica Gens* to Italian immigrants in the United States and Canada. Gives statistics.

567. Grivetti, Giuseppe.
"La missione dei Padri Scalabriniani a Boston." *Italica Gens*, II (Agosto-Settembre, 1911), 308-313.

Account of Scalabrinian activities in Boston.

568. Grivetti, Giuseppe.
"Il Nostro Segretariato Centrale di New York. Resoconto del Primo Anno di Attività." *Italica Gens*, III (Marzo-Aprile, 1912), 65-75.

Report on the work done on behalf of Italian immigrants by the New York office of the *Italica Gens*. Report covers the first 15 months of operation.

569. Grivetti, Giuseppe.
"Il Segretariato Centrale di New York Durante l'Anno 1912." *Italica Gens*, IV (Marzo-Aprile, 1913), 78-87.

Report on the activities for 1912 of the New York office of the *Italica Gens*.

570. Guglielmi, Francesco.
The Italian Methodist Mission in the Little Italy of Baltimore, Md. Seven Years of Evangelical Christian Work. Baltimore, Md.: W.V. Guthrie, 1912. Pp. 208.

A former priest, Guglielmi emigrated to Baltimore in 1904 and worked among Italian immigrants as a Methodist minister. He writes in an emotional style about his conversion and experience, his missionary activities, and the beginnings of the first Italian Methodist Episcopal Church in Baltimore.

571. "La Guida del Clero Italiano di New York." *Il Carroccio*, II (December, 1915), 76-77.

A report on Msgr. Gherardo Ferrante, named Vicar General for Italians by Cardinal J. Farley, Archbishop of New York. The role of Msgr. Ferrante is seen as one of coordination of the Italian parishes for greater religious and social awareness within the framework of acceptance of Italian and American values.

572. Guidi, J.
"V. Letter of Father J. Guidi to Father J. Cataldo. Pend'Oreilles, St. Ignatius' Mission, December 27, 1881." *Woodstock Letters*, XII (1883), 51-53.

Care for the sick Indians on the part of the missionaries.

573. Guidi, P.G.
"Washington Territory. Letter of Fr. P.G. Guidi to Fr. A. Romano, S.J. Colville, W.T., January 22nd, 1875." *Woodstock Letters*, IV (1875), 178-180.

Describes pastoral work among Indians, and the Indians' devotion to the Virgin Mary.

574. Guidi, P.G.
"Indian Mission-Washington Territory. From a Letter of Fr. P.G. Guidi, S.J., Colville, W.T., August 17th, 1875." *Woodstock Letters*, V (1876), 65-66.

Celebration of "Corpus Domini" feast among the Indians.

575. Guilday, Peter.
The Life and Times of John Carroll, Archbishop of Baltimore, 1735-1815. Westminister, Md.: Newman Press, 1922. Pp. 864.

This study of early days of Church in America has been updated by Melville's biography, *John Carroll of Baltimore, Founder of the American Hierarchy.* New York: Charles Scribner's Sons. 1955.

576. Guilday, Peter.
"Gaetano Bedini." United States Catholic Historical Society, *Historical Records and Studies*, XXIII (1933), 87-170.

Subtitled "An Episode in the Life of Archbishop John Hughes," this article focuses on Bedini, sent by Pope Pius IX to visit the United States for the purpose of investigating domestic church problems. The visit lasted from June 30, 1853 to February 4, 1854.

577. H.
"New Mexico." *Woodstock Letters*, XIII (1884), 42-50.

Refers to the increase in vocations, the need for English-speaking priests, and the work of the Italian Fathers. Includes a sketch of the life of Fr. Gasparri, founder of the Florissant mission in New Mexico.

578. Hallenbeck, Cleve, ed.
The Journey of Fray Marcos de Niza. Dallas: Southern Methodist University Press, 1949. Pp. 115.

On early exploration of New Mexico by an Italian Franciscan.

579. Hammon, Walter.
The First Bonaventure Men. The Early History of St. Bonaventure University and the Allegheny Franciscans. St. Bonaventure: St. Bonaventure University, 1958. Pp. 249.

A popular narrative on the arrival and activities of Italian Franciscans who established St. Bonaventure University, and other missions.

580. Harkness, Georgia E.
The Church and the Immigrant. New York: George H. Doran Company, 1921. Pp. 110.

This book examines how the church may aid in americanization. It gives the background of some major immigrant groups, including the Italians, describes the status of the immigrant and comments on such topics as teaching English and Citizenship, americanization courses and the "Agencies of Racial Progress."

581. Harrison, Margaret Hayne.
"The Lost Manuscript of Father Kino." *The Catholic World*, CX (February, 1920), 653-660.

This article deals with the discovery by Dr. Herbert Bolton of the University of California of the original historical memoir of Father Eusebio Kino, Jesuit missionary in the Southwest. The manuscript deals with the period 1683 to 1711.

582. Hayes, Patrick J.
"The Immigrant Problem." *Extension Magazine*, XVII (April, 1923), 13-14, 57.

In this article, Hayes describes the efforts made by the Archdiocese of New York, as well as the National Catholic Welfare Council, to help the incoming immigrants. Hayes, the Archbishop of New York from 1919 to 1938, was influential in centralizing the various agencies involved in emigrant aid work at the port of New York.

583. H.B.G.
"The Italian Work in New York." *The Baptist Home Mission Monthly*, XXVII (February, 1905), 80.

Brief description of "the exercises at the Christmas gathering of the First Italian Baptist Church in Mariner's Temple." The Rev. Agostino Dassori was the pastor, assisted by the Rev. Alfio Minutilla.

584. "Hear the Voice of the Children from Sunny Italy. Ages from Nine to Eighteen." The New York Mission and Tract Society, *Annual Report*, January, 1907, 7-11.

Quotations from young Italians on the benefits they have derived from attendance at the Protestant Church and Sunday School.

585. Heil, B.M.
"Servites." *The Catholic Church in the United States of America*. 3 vols. New York: The Catholic Editing Company, 1912-1914. I, 390-395.

Brief account of the founding and establishment of the Servants of Mary, or Servites, introduced in the United States in 1870.

586. Hill, Walter.
"Father Paul Mary Ponziglione: A Sketch." *Woodstock Letters*, XXX (1901), 50-56.

Ponziglione (1817-1900), an outstanding Italian priest and missionary among the Osage and other Indians, left an interesting "Memoir" of his work. Instrumental in the opening of over 40 parishes and missions in South Kansas, he spent most of his life thereafter arriving from his native Piedmont in the 1850s. He died in Chicago.

587. Hillenbrand, M.J.
"Has the Immigrant Kept the Faith?" *America*, LIV (November 23, 1935), 153-155.

Basing himself on his experience on a construction gang in Camden, New Jersey, where many of his co-workers were Italian, the author reflects on the religiosity of Italian immigrants. He observes that among these Italians, religion was taken seriously only by women and old men, and concludes that many Italian immigrants have abandoned the Church.

588. *A History of the Italian Catholic Federation, 1924-1974: The First Fifty Years.* New York: Kenedy, 1974. Pp. 112.

An illustrated narrative of the activities and achievements of a Federation of groups of laymen in parishes, mostly in California, where the Federation is based, and in some areas of the Midwest. The Federation is concerned with the spiritual care of Italian immigrants and ethnics.

589. Hodges, Leroy.
"The Church and the Immigrants: A Record of Failure and the Remedy." *The Missionary Review of the World*, n.s., XXV (March, 1912), 167-172.

Author contends that ethnic churches are too oriented to church life and forget social needs. These churches were founded because American Catholics did not care for immigrants. The proposed remedy is to educate and jointly lift up working masses of Catholics and Protestants.

590. Hoffman, M.M.
"Mazzuchelli, Samuel Charles." *Dictionary of American Biography*, XI (1933), 470-471.

Brief biography of Mazzuchelli, born in Milan, Italy, in 1806. He entered the Dominican Order in 1823, left for the American missions in 1828, and was ordained to the priesthood in Cincinnati in 1830. He worked as a missionary among the Indians in the Midwest. He described his missionary experiences in his *Memoirs*, written in Italian and printed in Milan in 1844. He died in 1864.

591. Hopcraft, M.L.
"Blandina Segale, Sister of Charity." *The Ave Maria*, LXXIX (May 8, 1954), 8-11.

This is a brief sketch of the work of Sister Blandina Segale in the frontier southwest of the 1870s.

592. Houtart, François.
Aspects sociologiques du Catholicisme Américain. Vie Urbain et Institutions Religieuses. Paris: Les Éditions Ouvrières, 1957. Pp. 340.

This volume reviews the evolution of the Catholic group in the United States and then focuses on the city of Chicago as a model of American urban Catholicism. The twelve Italian national parishes established in Chicago between 1885 and 1950 are briefly studied in relation to the geographical distribution of the Italian population.

593. Howard, Helen A.
"Padre Ravalli: Versatile Missionary." *The Historical Bulletin*, XVIII
(January, 1940), 33-35.

Brief article on an important figure in the Jesuit Missions in Montana.

594. Hughes, M.J.
"Lenten Mission in Old Mexico. By Fr. Gentile and Fr. Tomassini.
Old Albuquerque, N.M., May 23, 1898." *Woodstock Letters*, XXVII
(1898), 216-218.

Preaching at San Pablo de Meoquis and devotion to Our Lady of Mt.
Carmel. Rewarding response by the people of the efforts of these Jesuit
missionaries from the Neapolitan Province.

595. Ibarra de Anda, F.
El Padre Kino. Misionero y Gobernante. Mexico: Ediciones Xochitl,
1945, Pp. 188.

This is a popularly written biography in Spanish of the famous missionary in
the American Southwest.

596. "Indicibili Difficoltà per i Missionari di Evangelizzare gli Immigrati."
La Civiltà Cattolica, LI (July 23, 1900), 375-376.

A short statement on the difficulties of evangelizing immigrants in the United
States.

597. "Institute of the Sisters of St. Dorothy." *The Catholic Church in the
United States of America*. 3 vols. New York: The Catholic Editing
Company, 1912-1914. II, 153-154.

Very brief account of an institute founded in Italy in 1834 and introduced
into the United States in 1911.

598. Iorizzo, Luciano J. and Salvatore Mondello.
The Italian-Americans. New York: Twayne Publishers, Inc., 1971.
Pp. 273.

This general study of the Italian experience in the United States is a volume in
The Immigrant Heritage of America Series, edited by Cecyle S. Neidle.
Chapter X, pp. 179-192, is titled "The Religious Encounter."

599. Isoleri, A.
*Un Ricordo delle Feste Colombiane celebrate in Philadelphia, Stati
Uniti d'America, nell'Ottobre del 1892.* Philadelphia, Penna.: Printing
House, 1893. Pp. 64.

Speeches and programs held in Philadelphia to celebrate the 4th centennial of the discovery of America by Columbus. The pamphlet also prints the Encyclical Letter of Leo XIII for the occasion.

600. Istituto delle Missionarie del Sacro Cuore di Gesù.
Un decennio di opere (1930-1940). Roma: Scalia Editor, 1942.

Review of a decade of activity by the Cabrini Sisters, including work with Italian-Americans.

601. Istituto delle Missionarie del S.C. Di Gesù.
75 Anni Di Attività Cabriniana, 1880-1955. Roma: Tipografia "S. Giuseppe," 1956. Pp. 278.

This volume includes photos of the houses of formation, hospitals, and schools of the Cabrini Sisters and descriptions of their missions around the world, with some short notes on the lives of the sisters. For other anniversary publications useful for the understanding of the development of Cabrini's work see: Le Missionarie del Sacro Cuore negli Stati Uniti d'America. *Alla Reverendissima Fondatrice Dell'Istituto Delle Missionarie Del Sacro Cuore, Madre Francesca Saverio Cabrini Nella Fausta Occasione Del Giubileo D'Argento Della Sua Fondazione Offrono Questi Brevissimi Cenni Sulle Opere da lei Fondate negli Stati Uniti d'America*. Pp. 48; l'Istituto Delle Missionarie del Sacro Cuore. *Cinquant'Anni Di Vita, 1880-1930*. Milano: Arti-Grafiche Bertarelli, 1931. Pp. 225.

602. *Italian-American Who's Who*. 21 Vols. New York: The Vigo Press, 1935-1967.

A biographical dictionary of outstanding Italo-Americans and Italian residents of the United States. Includes biographies of clergymen.

603. "The Italian-Americans and the Irish-Americans." *The Catholic Review*, XXXI (April 16, 1887), 248-249.

An editorial which points out that the prejudice shown to newly arrived Italians is the same as the prejudice previously shown to the Irish. It advocates unity between these two groups, since both will be important to America.

604. Italian Baptist Association of America.
Fiftieth Anniversary, 1898-1948. Mount Vernon, N.Y.: 1948. Pp. 64.

Review of the achievements of the Italian Baptist Association.

605. "Italian Baptist Mission, Newark, N.J." *The Baptist Home Mission Monthly*, XXV (May, 1903), 122-123.

Brief account of Baptist mission work among the Italians in Newark.

606. Italian Catholic Federation.
Branch By-Laws, including Articles of Incorporation. San Francsico, California: 678 Green Street, 1963. Pp. 40.

Text of the Articles of Incorporation of the Central Council of the Italian Catholic Federation of California and of the Branch By-Laws. The Federation, open to Italian Catholics, aims "to uphold and develop the religious spirit among its members and to spread that spirit among the Italian people outside of the organization." This organization is especially active in the western part of the United States.

607. "Italian Festivals in New York." *The Chautauquan*, XXXIV (December, 1901), 228-229.

Description of popular Italian feasts.

608. "An Italian Martyr in New York." *The Vigo Review*, II (February, 1938), 11.

This is a letter written by Fr. Francesco Bressani (1612-1672) to the Father Provincial in Rome. It's a report of tortures which he suffered at the hands of Iroquois in 1644. He was made prisoner by the Indians while on his way to the Huron Mission.

609. "Italian Mission at Monson, Mass." *The Baptist Home Mission Monthly*, XXVII (April, 1905), 141.

Brief account of the establishment of an Italian Baptist church at Monson, Massachusetts. The Rev. Alfred Barrone was pastor. Includes a photograph of the church, with the inscription "Chiesa Apostolica Battista."

610. *The Italian Mission in the Heart of America now Christ Presbyterian Church and Northeast Community Center. A Report in Stewardship During Dr. Bisceglia's Ministry, June 1, 1918-May 31, 1965.* Kansas City: By the Author, 1965.

A pamphlet describing the pastoral and social activities of Dr. Bisceglia in Kansas City until his retirement from active duties.

611. "Italian Missionary Convention." *The Baptist Home Mission Monthly*, XXX (July, 1908), 302-303.

Account of the Tenth Annual Convention of the Italian Baptist Missionary
Society, held on June 9-11, 1908, at the Italian Baptist Church in New Haven.

612. "An Italian Missionary's Account of His Work." *The Baptist Home
Mission Monthly*, XXXI (February, 1909), 82-83.

Description of his work by the Rev. Mimi Marseglia, pastor of an Italian
Baptist church in Providence, Rhode Island.

613. "Italian Presbyterians." *The Missionary Review of the World*, N.S.,
XXX (August, 1917), 635.

"At the beginning of 1916 the Presbyterian Church in the U.S. had 103
churches and missions using the Italian language with 4,800 members and
more than 8,000 enrolled in its Italian Sunday schools. Last year over 1,100
Italians were received into these churches on profession of faith. Sixty Italian
speaking pastors are employed, 23 lay workers, 32 visitors and over 350
American volunteers. At least $100,000 is annually contributed by the
Presbyterian Church in the U.S. for this work of evangelization among
Italians over and above the amounts which Italian Presbyterians themselves
contribute."

614. "The Italian Theological School." *The Baptist Home Mission Monthly*,
XXIX (December, 1907), 447.

Description of services opening the Italian Department of Colgate Theological
Seminary, located at 79 Hewes Street, Brooklyn. The Rev. Antonio Mangano
was put in charge of the school.

615. "Italian West Side Work." The New York City Mission and Tract
Society, *Annual Report*, January, 1904, p. 19.

Notes the need for an organized evangelical church on the West Side due to
the large number of Italians who need religious services in that area.

616. "Italian Work In and Near Newark, N.J." *The Assembly Herald*, V
(August, 1901), 306-307.

A short article on the ten-year history of the First Presbyterian Church of
Newark, New Jersey, citing the various lay organizations in the parish.

617. "The Italian Young People and Their Church." The New York Mission
and Tract Society, *Annual Report*, January, 1907, pp. 21-22.

Account by a young Italian of how he joined the Protestant Church on
Broome Street in New York City.

618. "Gli Italiani negli Stati Uniti." *Il Carroccio*, II (January, 1916), 55-60.

     This regular feature of *Il Carroccio* includes reports on the activities of the Italian-American clergy on behalf of Italy and within the various immigrant communities in the United States.

619. "The Italians and Evening Mass." *The Ecclesiastical Review*, XLV (September, 1911), 340-342.

     In this article, the author argues in favor of the introduction of evening Mass for groups, such as the Italians, that often find it difficult to attend morning Mass because of other obligations.

620. "Italians in Gloversville." *The Baptist Home Mission Monthly*, XXIX (October, 1907), 360.

     Account, taken from a Gloversville, New York, paper describing a reception given by the Italian members of the First Baptist Church to the officers of the church.

621. "*L'Italica Gens*. Federazione per l'assistanza degli emigranti italiani in paesi transoceanici." *Le Missioni Italiane*. Bollettino trimestrale dell'Associazione Nazionale per soccorrere i Missionari Cattolici Italiani, XIII (December, 1909), 55-59.

     A description of the beginning and first activities of the *Italica Gens*, an association for assistance to overseas emigrants.

622. "*L'Italica Gens*." *Italica Gens*, I (Febbraio, 1910), 3-16.

     Article introducing the *Italica Gens*, a federation for the assistance of overseas emigrants, established and directed by the National Association for Italian Catholic Missionaries. It published a bulletin, *Italica Gens*, which reported on the activities on behalf of Italian immigrants carried out by its network of secretariats, usually located in the Italian national parishes. The bulletin was issued from February, 1910, to December, 1916. A complete set of the bulletin is available at the Centro Studi Emigrazione in Rome, the Center for Migration Studies in New York, and the Immigration History Research Center of the University of Minnesota in St. Paul, Minnesota.

623. "La *Italica Gens* nel Terzo Anno dalla sua Fondazione." *Italica Gens*, III (Dicembre, 1912), 353-358.

     Report of the work of the *Italica Gens* during 1912.

624. Ives, Ronald L.
"Father Kino's 1697 Entrada to the Casa Grande Ruin in Arizona: A Reconstruction." *Arizona and the West*, XV (Winter, 1973), 345-370.

Restudy, undertaken during the years 1968-1972, of the route to and from Casa Grande taken by Fr. Eusebio Francisco Kino, S.J., in 1697.

625. Jaluna, Agrippino.
Conquiste di Apostoli: Profili missionari. Catania: ed. Pia Società S. Paolo, 1938. Unpaged.

Includes biographies of Jesuit missionaries in North America.

626. Jemolo, Arturo C.
Church and State in Italy, 1850-1950. English Revised and Translated Edition. Tr. by David Moore. Oxford: Basil Blackwell, 1960. Pp. vii-344.

This is a comprehensive study of Church-State relations in Italy from the Risorgimento to the post-World War II period. It is a translation of *Chiesa e Stato in Italia dal Risorgimento ad Oggi*, published in 1955. It gives the background of religious conditions in Italy at the time of mass emigration.

627. "The Jesuit Missions of California." *Woodstock Letters*, XX (1891), 347-368.

Ample reference to Italian missionaries, from Fr. Salvatierra until 1891.

628. Jones, Henry D.
The Evangelical Movement Among Italians in New York City. A Study. New York: For the Comity Committee of the Federation of Churches of Greater New York and the Brooklyn Church and Mission Federation, 1933-1934. Pp. 39. Tables. Reprinted, *Protestant Evangelism Among Italians in America*. New York: Arno Press, 1975.

Important study with useful and extensive statistical information on Evangelical missionary work covering Italian immigrants from the 1870s to the 1930s.

629. Juliani, Richard N.
"Italians and Other Americans: The Parish, The Union, and The Settlement House." *Perspectives in Italian Immigration and Ethnicity*. Edited by Silvano M. Tomasi. New York: Center for Migration Studies, 1977. Pp. 179-186.

The author uses the *Consultors' Minutes* to examine the formation of Italian parishes in Philadelphia and, in particular, to explore the development of formal church policy in the archdiocese toward Italian Catholic immigrants.

630. Kansas City & Memphis Railway Company.
"Tontitown, Ark.: The World's Ideal Vineyard. Rogers, Arkansas." *Italians in the United States. A Repository of Rare Tracts and Miscellanea.* New York: Arno Press, 1975. Pp. 15.

Illustrated promotional brochure on Tontitown, Arkansas, "The Gem of the Ozarks in the Center of the Great Southwest" used by the Kansas City and Memphis Railway Company.

631. Kavanagh, Dennis J.
The Holy Family Sisters of St. Francis. San Francisco: Gilmartin Co., 1922. Pp. 328.

This work contains a description of the order and of the activities of the Sisters and the Salesian Fathers among the Italians in North Beach, San Francisco.

632. Kelley, Francis C.
"The Church and the Immigrants." *The Catholic Mind*, XIII (September 8, 1915), 471-484.

The author classifies the Italian immigrants as a "missionary group," but sees their situation as hopeful since they will send their children to Catholic schools and since their emotional religious approach provides a foundation on which to build.

633. Kelley, W.
"Salesians." *New Catholic Encyclopedia*, XII (1967), 982-983.

Account of founding and growth of the Society of St. Francis de Sales, also known as Salesians or Salesians of Don Bosco. The Salesians first arrived in the United States in 1898.

634. Kelly, Mary Gilbert.
"Italian Immigrants as They Really Are." *La Voce dell'Emigrato*, IV (October-November, 1927), 13-14.

A sympathetic view of Italian immigrants as a positive addition to both church and country.

635. Kelly, Mary Gilbert.
"The Catholic Charities and the Italian Auxiliary." *La Voce dell'Emigrato*, VI (April, 1929), 11-12.

This short article points out the on-going cooperation between the Catholic Charities of the Archdiocese of New York and the Italian Auxiliary.

636. Kelly, Mary Gilbert.
"The Work of the Italian Auxiliary Inc. for 1930." *La Voce del-l'Emigrato*, VIII (February-March, 1931), 35.

A review of the assistential activities of the Italian Auxiliary, a New York Catholic voluntary agency directed by Msgr. Germano Formica for the care of arriving Italian immigrants.

637. King, Henry M.
"An Italian's Confession of Faith." *The Baptist Home Mission Monthly*, XXVI (February, 1904), 46-47.

King, pastor of the First Baptist Church of Providence, Rhode Island, reports on "a confession of faith by a converted Italian."

638. Kino, Eusebio Francisco.
Kino's Historical Memoir of Pimería Alta. Translated by Herbert Bolton. 2 vols. Cleveland: The Arthur H. Clark Co., 1919. Pp. 379, 329.

Memoirs of the first great missionary, explorer and geographer of Pimería Alta, the name applied to Southern Arizona and Northern Sonora. Republished in offset by the University of California Press in 1948.

639. Kino, Eusebio Francisco.
Kino Reports to Headquarters. Translated and edited by Ernest J. Burrus. Rome: Institutum Historicum Societatis Jesu, 1954. Pp. 135.

Text of fourteen letters and reports, in both the original Spanish and English translation, sent by Kino to his superiors in Rome between February 14, 1682, and February 2, 1702.

640. Kino, Eusebio Francisco.
Correspondencia del P. Kino con los Generales de la Compañía de Jesús, 1682-1707. Edited by Ernest J. Burrus. Mexico: Editorial Jus, S.A., 1961. Pp. 96.

Compilation of the correspondence of Kino with the Generals of the Society of Jesus from the time of his arrival in Mexico to 1707.

641. Kino, Eusebio Francisco.
Kino's Plan for the Development of Pimería Alta, Arizona and Upper California; a Report to the Mexican Viceroy. Translated and annotated

by Ernest J. Burrus. Tucson: Arizona Pioneers' Historical Society, 1961. Pp. 70.

A report written by the Italian Jesuit Kino to the Mexican Viceroy in 1703 in which he describes his work and the needs of the Pimería province.

642. Kino, Eusebio Francisco.
Vida del P. Francisco J. Saeta, S.J., Sangre Misionera en Sonora. Prólogo y notas de Ernest J. Burrus. México: Editorial Jus, S.A., 1961. Pp. 214.

Account of the Sicilian Jesuit missionary and companion of Kino, martyred by Pimas Indians in 1695.

643. Kino, Eusebio Francisco.
Kino Writes to the Duchess. Letters of Eusebio Francisco Kino, S.J., to the Duchess of Aveiro. Sources and Studies for the History of the Americas: Volume I. Edited by Ernest J. Burrus. St. Louis, Mo.: St. Louis University, 1965, Pp. xii-290.

The Introduction to this volume notes that it "offers in translation the letters written by Frather Kino to the Duchess of Aveiro and by others to her concerning the renowned missionary of northern Mexico and southern Arizona. In the general introduction some 200 letters of other correspondents are briefly summarized. The Portuguese Duchess residing in Madrid was the most generous benefactress in colonial times of the foreign missions throughout the world." The title page says: "An Annotated English Translation and the Text of the Non-Spanish Documents Edited by Ernest J. Burrus, S.J."

644. Kunkle, Edward C.
"The Italian Mission in Scottdale, Pa." *The Baptist Home Mission Monthly*, XXX (September, 1908), 353-354.

Description of the establishment and work of the Italian Baptist Mission in Scottdale, Pennsylvania. Page 353 has a photograph of Rev. Hector Schisa and five Scottdale Italian Baptists.

645. Kuppens, Francis X.
"Christmas Day, 1865, in Virginia City, Montana." *Illinois Catholic Historical Review*, X(July, 1927), 48-53.

In this sketch, found among the unpublished papers of Fr. Francis Xavier Kuppens, S.J. (1838-1916), now preserved in the Archives of St. Louis University, mention is made of Father Giorda, who arrived in Virginia City a few days before Christmas, 1865, and "took up his lodging at the cabin of a good pious Catholic miner."

646. Lagnese, Joseph G.
"The Italian Catholic." *America*, XLIV (February 21, 1931), 475-476.

In this article the author argues that, in spite of lax religious practices, the average Italian immigrant "has the Catholic Faith deeply rooted in him" (p. 475). For two replies to this article, see F.J. Franchi, S.J., Letter to the Editor of *America*, XLIV (March 21, 1931), 583-584, and (Rev.) Paul I. Wursch, Letter to the Editor of *America*, XLIV (March 21, 1931), 584.

647. LaGumina, Salvatore J., ed.
Wop! A Documentary History of Anti-Italian Discrimination in the United States. Ethnic Prejudice in America Series. San Francisco, CA.: Straight Arrow Books, 1973. Pp. 319.

Documents anti-Italian sentiment in the United States. Chapter IV, pp. 163-180, is titled "Roman Catholicism as an Obstacle to Assimilation (1890-1914)."

648. Lalli, Franco.
La Prima Santa d'America. Brooklyn: Casa Editrice Fortuna Publishing Co., 1944. Pp. 140.

Biography of Frances Xavier Cabrini, the first American saint.

649. LaMartinella.
"Italian Catholics in America. Apropos of Archbishop Canevin's Pamphlet." *Il Carroccio*, XVIII (Ottobre, 1923), 355-356.

A response to Canevin's pamphlet, *Catholic Growth in the United States*, where the Latin race and the Italians in particular are blamed as stifling the growth of the Church because they are not as good as the Irish and Germans. Author points out that Italians show practically no leakage to Protestantism, support their institutions, but are discriminated against in the Church.

650. "Il Lavoro di Assistenza degli Emigrati svolto dal nostro Segretariato di New York dal Gennaio 1913 al Giugno 1915." *Italica Gens*, VI (Luglio-Settembre, 1915), 207-209.

Statistics on the social services offered to the Italian emigrants by the *Italica Gens* of New York from 1913-1915.

651. Lawson, Albert G.
"Italian Department of Colgate Theological Seminary." *The Examiner*, LXXXV (February 21, 1907), 234-235.

Announces the decision by the trustees of Colgate University to establish an Italian Department of the Theological Seminary for the purpose of educating ministers for Italian Baptist churches.

652. LeBerthon, Ted.
"Apostolate to Italo-Americans." *The Catholic Mind*, LI (April, 1953), 211-219.

Describes founding and work of the Italian Catholic Federation (ICF), "a family apostolate, uniting husband, wife and children in a common sacred enthusiasm." The ICF was established by Luigi Providenza in San Francisco in 1924. The article was reprinted from *The Marianist*, January, 1953.

653. LeBerthon, Ted.
"The Life of Luigi." *Catholic Digest*, XIX (January, 1955), 93-96.

Description of the Italian Catholic Federation (ICF), founded by Luigi Providenza in San Francisco in 1924. Condensed from *Jubilee*, November, 1954.

654. Lee, Samuel H.
"Italian Characteristics." *The Baptist Home Mission Monthly*, XXVII (May, 1905), 183-185.

Lee, President of the French-American College, Springfield, Massachusetts, describes a few Italian characteristics. This is part of a section titled "The Italians in America."

655. Lemke, W.J., ed.
The Story of Tontitown, Arkansas. Fayetteville, Arkansas: Washington County Historical Society, 1963. Pp. 36.

History of Father Pietro Bandini and of St. Joseph's Church in Tontitown.

656. Lenza, Antonio Giulio.
Critiche e Processi ai responsabili delle colpe. New York: Bagnasco Press, 1919. Pp. 144.

A wordy defense of the author's position as an Italian Independent Roman Catholic priest with particularly vehement criticism of the Irish-American clergy as anti-Italian.

657. "Leo XIII and the Italian Catholics in the United States." *The American Ecclesiastical Review*, I (February, 1889), 41-48.

This article includes the Latin text of a letter sent to the American hierarchy by Pope Leo XIII on December 10, 1888, dealing with the problematic question of the Italian immigrants in the United States. The Latin text of the letter, *Quam aerumnosa*, is introduced by five pages of commentary in English. An English translation of the papal letter can be found in John Tracy Ellis, ed. *Documents of American Catholic History*, Revised Logos Edition, Vol. II, 466-470.

658. "Letters from Bishop Benedict Joseph Flaget to Bishop Joseph Rosati, St. Louis, Mo." *Social Justice Review*, LXII (September, October, November, December, 1969; January, March, 1970), 169-172, 206-208, 241-244, 278-280, 314-318, 419-422; LXIII (April, May, June, July-August, 1970), 28-30, 61-63, 97-99, 136-138.

In ten separate installments, the magazine publishes correspondence between Bishops Flaget and Rosati that spans the years 1816-1840.

659. Linkh, Richard M.
American Catholicism and European Immigrants (1900-1924). Staten Island, N.Y.: Center for Migration Studies, 1975. Pp. 200.

An attempt at a broad review of the policies of the Catholic Church toward the immigrants. Linkh concludes that Church leaders rejected hasty americanization and opted for gradual assimilation into a "melting pot with an extremely low flame." He describes Catholic social settlements, Catholic participation in the post-war "Americanization drive and Catholic attitudes toward immigration restriction. Immigrants inlcuding the Italians, were mostly helped by Catholics of their own nationality."

660. Lockwood, Francis C.
"Father Eusebio Francisco Kino." *Arizona Historical Review*, I (April, 1928), 69-79.

Account of Jesuit Fr. Kino's explorations and missionary work among the Pima Indians and in Southern California and Arizona.

661. Lockwood, Francis C.
With Padre Kino on the Trail. Social Science Bulletin No. 5. Tucson: University of Arizona, 1934. Pp. 142.

A biography of a Jesuit missionary and explorer in the Southwest.

662. LoGatto-Perry, Joseph J.
An Italian Pioneer in America. Paterson, N.J.: The Rocco Press, 1969. Pp. 110.

A filiopietistic biography of Carlo Cianci (1881-1968), a leading Italian priest in Paterson, New Jersey, who organized three parishes, two parochial schools, a day nursery, an orphanage and other institutions for the Italians.

663. Lopreato, Joseph.
Italian Americans. Ethnic Groups in Comparative Perspective. New York: Random House, 1970. Pp. xiv-204.

Study of Italian immigration and immigrants' adjustment to American society.

Chapter 4, titled "Social Institutions and Change," pp. 56-99, deals also with religion.

664. Lord, Robert H., John E. Sexton, and Edward T. Harrington.
History of the Archdiocese of Boston in the Various Stages of Its Development, 1604 to 1943. 3 vols. New York: Sheed & Ward, 1944. Pp. xix-812, vi-766, vi-808.

This is the standard history of the Archdiocese of Boston. It contains some references to Italians in the archdiocese.

665. Lorit, Sergio C.
Frances Cabrini. New York: New City Press, 1970. Pp. 204.

A translation from the Italian of a popular biography, *La Cabrini*. Roma: Città Nuova Edtrice, 1965. Pp. 199.

666. Luchetti, Antonio.
Missionari genovesi gesuiti in Alasca. Memorie dei Padri Gian Luca Lucchesi e Crispino Rossi. Genova: Ed. Scuola Tipografica Derelitti, 1940. Pp. 172.

Detailed information regarding the activities of Italian Jesuit missionaries in Alaska.

667. Lying, Edward J.
"Catholic Missionary Society of Philadelphia." *Catholic Charities Review*, VI (September, 1922), 236-239.

On Catholic settlements designed primarily to serve Italians in Philadelphia.

668. Lynch, Bernard J.
"The Italians in New York." *The Catholic World*, XLVII (April, 1888), 67-73.

In this article Lynch describes the Italian immigrants coming in ever greater number into New York City. The author claims that these Italians constitute a problem for the American Catholic Church, especially because of the shortage of Italian clergy and the difference between Italian Catholicism and that found in the United States. He urges the formation of duplex parishes, where Italian priests can assist the Italian immigrants.

669. Lynch, D.
"In the Italian Quarter of New York." *The Messenger of the Sacred Heart of Jesus*, XXXVI (February, 1901), 115-126.

This is a valuable description of the Italian colony in New York and of the various religious institutions caring for the needs of the immigrants in the colony.

670. Lynch, D.
"The Religious Conditions of Italians in New York." *America*, X (March 21, 1914), 558-559.

In this brief article, the author takes issue with "Our Biggest Catholic Question," an editorial printed in *The Catholic Citizen* (Milwaukee), November 8, 1913. Lynch claims that the statistics given in the Milwaukee newspaper article are exaggerated, though he does admit that much work needs to be done if the great majority of Italian Catholics are to be kept within the Church.

671. McAstocker, John C.
"Father Cataldo and the Golden Jubilee of St. Michael's Mission." *Woodstock Letters*, XLV (1916), 167-181.

Description of the work of a pioneer Italian priest in the Rocky Mountains since 1865, among the Spokane and the Nez-Percé Indians, in Alaska, and a founder of Gonzaga University.

672. McAvoy, Thomas T.
A History of the Catholic Church in the United States. Notre Dame: University of Notre Dame Press, 1969. Pp. 504.

A popular history of the Catholic Church in the United States, strictly traditional in approach and interpretation and with little awareness of the ethnic and cultural complexity of the Catholic population.

673. McCarty, Mary E.
The Sinsinawa Dominicans. Outlines of Twentieth Century Development, 1901-1949. Dubuque: The Hoermann Press, 1952. Pp. 591.

History of the Sisters of the Order of St. Dominic, Sinsinawa, Wisconsin, a religious community of Sisters founded by Fr. Samuel Mazzuchelli, O.P., in the nineteenth century.

674. McCulloch, M.
"California-Rocky Mountain Mission." *The Catholic Church in the United States of America.* 3 vols. New York: The Catholic Editing Company, 1912-1914. I, 286-302.

Account of founding and development of the California-Rocky Mountain Mission of the Society of Jesus. It includes references to several Italian Jesuit missionaries from the province of Turin.

675. McGarvey, Cyprian.
"Passionists." *The Catholic Church in the United States of America*. 3 vols. New York: The Catholic Editing Company, 1912-1914. I, 330-337.

Account of founding and development of the Passionist Order in the United States. It includes references to several Italian Passionists.

676. McGloin, John Bernard.
"Michael Accolti, Gold Rush Padre and Founder of the California Jesuits." *Archivum Historicum Societatis Jesu*, XX (July-December, 1951), 306-315.

Account of Fr. Accolti's life and work in California (1849-1878). Accolti came from Italy, was superior of the Oregon mission and a founder of the University of San Francisco.

677. McGloin, John Bernard.
"John B. deNobili,S.J., Founder of California's Santa Clara College." *British Columbia Historical Quarterly*, 17 (July-October, 1953), 215-222.

Fr. deNobili, a Jesuit from Rome, labored in British Columbia and California as a missionary and started the University of Santa Clara.

678. McGloin, John.
Jesuits by the Golden Gate. The Society of Jesus in San Francisco, 1849-1969. San Francisco: University of San Francisco, 1972. Pp. 309.

This commemorative volume gives biographical information on Frs. Michele Accolti and John Nobili, the founding fathers of St. Ignatius Church in San Francisco. It also describes the beginning of a "Seminary of Learning" which gradually became the University of San Francisco.

679. McGreal, Mary Nona.
Samuel Mazzuchelli, O.P. A Kaleidoscope of Scenes from His Life. Madison, Wisc.: n.d. Pp. 58.

A pictorial presentation of Fr. Mazzuchelli's life and achievements, with special reference to the founding of a new Congregation of Sisters.

680. McKevitt, Gerald.
"The Jesuit Arrival in California and the Founding of Santa Clara College." *Records of the American Catholic Historical Society of Philadelphia*, 85 (September-December, 1974), 185-197.

This is a brief account of the founding in 1851 of Santa Clara College in San Francisco by the Italian Jesuit missionary Michael Accolti.

681. McKevitt, Gerald.
"From Franciscan Mission to Jesuit College: A Troubled Transition at Mission Santa Clara." *Southern California Quarterly*, LVIII (Summer, 1976), 241-254.

Tells the story of the transition of Santa Clara, at Fr. John Nobili's hands, from a Franciscan mission to a Jesuit college.

682. McLanahan, Samuel.
Our People of Foreign Speech. A Handbook distinguishing and describing those in the United States whose native tongue is other than English. With Particular Reference to Religious Work Among Them. Literature Department. Presbyterian Home Missions. New York: Fleming H. Revell Company, 1904. Pp. 105.

Contains some information on Italian Protestant ministers and Evangelical work among Italian immigrants.

683. McNicholas, John T.
"The Need of American Priests for the Italian Missions." *The Ecclesiastical Review*, XXXIX (December, 1908), 677-687. Reprinted, Moquin, Wayne, ed. *A Documentary History of the Italian Americans.* New York: Praeger Publishers, 1974.

McNicholas, a Dominican priest, argues that the needed pastoral work among Italian immigrants in the United States can best be accomplished by American diocesan and religious priests who have undergone preparation for such work in Italy. He puts little faith in Italian priests who come to the United States to work among the immigrants.

684. McSorley, Joseph.
"The Church and the Italian Child. The Situation in New York." *The Ecclesiastical Review*, XLVIII (March, 1913), 268-282.

The author says that his intention in this article is "to sum up and contribute to the general fund the most important information," gathered from a variety of sources, on the religious conditions of Italian children in New York. His aim is to "direct the light of experience upon the question of the Italian child's attendance at religious exercises" (p. 268).

685. Mackey, U.L.
"A Venture in Co-operation: How They Built the Italian Branch of

the Webb Horton Church, Middletown, N.Y." *The Missionary Review of the World,* XL (August, 1917), 595-597.

Description of the establishment of the Italian Evangelical Church, Middletown, New York.

686. *La Madre Francesca Saverio Cabrini.* Torino: Società Editrice Internazionale, 1928. Pp. 386.

Thorough biography of Mother Frances Xavier Cabrini.

687. Maffei, Gioacchino.
"Il Dovere degl' Italiani d'America." *Italica Gens,* VII (Luglio-Dicembre, 1916), 134-148.

Maffei, a priest from Worcester, Massachusetts, discusses Italians in America and points out certain things they must do to improve their position in America. Describes Italian attitudes toward religion.

688. Maffei, Gioacchino.
L'Italia nell'America del Nord. Rilievi e Suggerimenti per la grandezza e l'onore d'Italia. Valle di Pompei: Tipografia di Francesco Sicignano & F., 1924. Pp. 164.

Maffei starts with the peopling and progress of America and the arrival of the first Italian immigrants. He observes that Northern Italians assimilate faster because they settle outside the ethnic ghetto. Southern Italian immigration is more temporary and unskilled. He describes the arrival of the immigrants, the Little Italys and their organization, especially the church. He relies on his long experience as pastor of an Italian immigrant community in Worcester, Massachusetts.

689. Maffi, Pietro.
La Madre Francesca S. Cabrini. Commemorazione. Torino: Libreria Editrice Internazionale, 1919. Pp. 20.

Text of a speech by Cardinal Maffi on the occasion of the anniversary of the death of Frances X. Cabrini.

690. Magnani, F.
La Città di Buffalo, N.Y. e paesi circonvicini e le colonie Italiane. Buffalo: Tipografia Editrice Italiana, 1908. Pp. 60.

This booklet is an historical account of the beginning of the Italian community of Buffalo, the regional origin of the immigrants in Italy and their achievements in America. A few pages describe the Italian parishes and priests of Buffalo.

691. Magnani, F.
Bressani — Tonti — Busti. Three Italians in the History of Niagara Frontier. Buffalo, N.Y.: The Author, 1931. Pp. 15.

Brief account of life and activities of three Italians in the Niagara Valley: Francesco Giuseppe Bressani, S.J. (1612-1672), Henri deTonti (d. 1704), and Paul Busti (1749-1824). Fr. Bressani worked among the Indians in Canada and western New York in the 1640s.

692. Mainiero, Joseph, ed.
History of the Italians in Trenton. Trenton, N.J.: Commercial Printing Co., 1929. Pp. 137.

Describes the colonization, the share of the Italian immigrants in the city's development, their social and commercial interests. A chapter is dedicated to the Italian churches and schools.

693. Maldotti, Pietro.
"Relazione sull'Operato della Missione del Porto di Genova dal 1894 al 1898 e sui due Viaggi al Brasile." *Studi Emigrazione,* V (Febbraio-Giugno, 1968), 417-480.

This report by the missionary Pietro Maldotti, written in 1898, deals with his activities both at the port of Genoa and in Brazil. The report is divided into three parts: the first part deals with Maldotti's work at the port of Genoa, 1894-1898; the second part gives his description of Brazil as a result of two visits there, one from April 12 to August 2, 1896 and the other from May 18 to December 12, 1897; and the third part describes the condition of the Italian immigrants in Brazil.

694. Manci, V.L.
"The Texas Cyclone. Letter from Fr. Manci. Cuero, DeWitt Co., Texas, November 30th, 1875." *Woodstock Letters,* V (1876), 67-79.

The disaster caused by a hurricane at Indianola and effort of the missionary to help. Manci points out the many nationalities of his congregation.

695. Mandalari, A.N.
"New Mexico Mission." *The Catholic Church in the United States of America.* 3 vols. New York: The Catholic Editing Company, 1912-1914. I, 302-307.

Brief account of the New Mexico Mission of the Society of Jesus, founded in 1867 at Archbishop John Baptist Lamy's request by the Society's Neapolitan Province.

696. Mangano, Antonio.
      Training Men for Foreign Work in America. n.p., n.d.

      8 page pamphlet, available at the library at the Union Theological Seminary,
      New York in which Mangano discusses the need to prepare Protestant
      ministers to work among the immigrants.

697. Mangano, Antonio.
      "The Associated Life of the Italians in New York City." *Charities*, XII
      (May 7, 1904), 476-482. Reprinted, Francesco Cordasco and Eugene
      Bucchioni, eds. *The Italians: Social Backgrounds of An American
      Group*. Clifton, New Jersey: Augustus M. Kelley, Publishers, 1974.

      In this essay Mangano describes some of the more important institutions in
      the Italian colony of New York City at the beginning of the twentieth century.
      The author gives some information on the various Italian churches in
      Manhattan. The entire issue of *Charities* for May 7, 1904, was devoted to the
      Italians in the United States. See Lydio F. Tomasi, ed. *The Italian in America:
      The Progressive View, 1891-1914*. New York: Center for Migration Studies,
      1972. Pp. xii-221, and the 1978 second ed., which reproduces 39 selections on
      the Italians originally published in *Charities*.

698. Mangano, Antonio.
      "Evangelism Among the Italians." *The Baptist Home Mission Monthly*,
      XXVII (October, 1905), 374-375.

      Mangano, Missionary Pastor of the First Italian Baptist Church in Brooklyn,
      reports on the previous summer's work among the Italians of Williamsburg
      in Brooklyn, New York.

699. Mangano, Antonio.
      "Italian Tent Work in Brooklyn." *The Baptist Home Mission Monthly*,
      XXVIII (October, 1906), 370-371.

      Description of summer Vocation Bible School, in a "Gospel Tent," in
      Brooklyn's Italian section.

700. Mangano, Antonio.
      "A Successful Mission for Italians." *The Baptist Home Mission
      Monthly*, XXXI (July, 1909), 338-340.

      Account of Italian Protestant work in Orange, New Jersey.

701. Mangano, Antonio.
      "Italian Evangelization in Brooklyn." *The Baptist Home Mission
      Monthly*, XXXI (November, 1909), 465-467.

Description of "A Two Months' Campaign in a Tent" among Brooklyn's Italians.

702. Mangano, Antonio.
"Italian Work in Barre, Vermont." *Missions*, VII (June, 1916), 476-477.

Describes work of Baptists among Italians in Barre, Vermont.

703. Mangano, Antonio.
Religious Work Among Italians in America. A Survey For the Home Missions Council. Philadelphia: The Board of the Home Missions and Church Extension of the Methodist Episcopal Church, 1917. Pp. 51. Reprinted, *Protestant Evangelism Among Italians in America.* New York: Arno Press, 1975.

Survey of the Italian communities in the United States done in 1916-17 by the Rev. Antonio Mangano, of the Italian Department of Colgate Theological Seminary, Brooklyn. The survey, sponsored by the Immigrant Work Committee of the Home Missions Council, representing the interests of thirteen evangelical denominations, was especially concerned with the Italians' religious needs and the work of the churches among them.

704. Mangano, Antonio.
Sons of Italy: A Social and Religious Study of the Italians in America. New York: Missionary Education Movement of the United States and Canada, 1917. Pp. 234. Reprinted, New York: Russell & Russell, 1972.

In this volume, Antonio Mangano, Professor-in-charge of the Italian Department of Colgate Theological Seminary, Brooklyn, deals with the following topics: chapter I, Italian Colonies in America; chapter II, Italian Life in Italy; chapter III, Religious Backgrounds; chapter IV, The Italians as a Citizen; chapter V, Assimilating the Italian; chapter VI, Protestant Churches; and chapter VII, The Italian's Contribution to the America of Tomorrow.

705. Mangano, Antonio.
"Thirty Years of Work with the Italians of Buffalo." *The Baptist*, VI (December 28, 1925), 1318-1319.

Mangano, a leading Italian Protestant minister among Italian immigrants, reviews Baptist missionary activity among them in Buffalo.

706. Manzotti, Fernando.
La polemica sull'emigrazione nell'Italia unita. Seconda edizione riveduta e accresciuta. Milano: Società Editrice Dante Alighieri, 1969. Pp. 203.

One of the best monographs published in Italy on Italian mass emigration and the state and church policies affecting it.

707. Marchione, M.
"Religious Teachers Filippini." *New Catholic Encyclopedia*, XII (1967), 332.

Brief account of a teaching community of sisters founded in Italy by St. Lucy Filippini. In 1910, Pope Pius X sent some of these sisters to the United States to work among Italian immigrants.

708. Marchisio, Juvenal.
"The Italian Catholic Immigrant." *Roman Catholicism and the American Way of Life*. Edited by Thomas T. McAvoy. Notre Dame: University of Notre Dame Press, 1960. Pp. 172-178.

This brief essay on Italians in the United States offers some general comments, with some reference to the Italian immigrants and the Catholic Church.

709. Mariano, John Horace.
The Second Generation of Italians in New York City. Boston: The Christopher Publishing House, 1921. Pp. x-317.

This study on the second generation of Italians in New York City includes some information on the *Italica Gens*, a free federation of the Italian Catholic clergy in the United States supported by the Italian National Association for Catholic Missionaries.

710. Marinacci, Barbara.
They Came from Italy. The Stories of Famous Italian-Americans. New York: Dodd, Mead & Company, 1967. Pp. viii-246.

Biographies of prominent Italians in America. Includes: "A Saint Among the Immigrants: Francesca Xavier Cabrini," pp. 95-114.

711. Marino, Anthony I.
The Catholics in America. New York: Vantage Press, 1960. Pp. 300.

This is a popularly written account of Catholics in America. It includes comments on a variety of Catholic Italian-Americans.

712. Marinoni, Antonio.
"L'Uomo e l'Opera." *Il Carroccio*, V (Febbraio, 1917), 105-108.

This is a tribute to Fr. Pietro Bandini at the time of his death. Professor Marinoni, of the University of Arkansas, gives here a sketch of Bandini's life, with emphasis on his involvement in the Italian colony of Tontitown, Arkansas. Bandini lived from 1852 to 1917.

713. Marolla, Edoardo.
"The First Bishop of St. Louis." *Atlantica*, (July, 1930), 10-11.

Brief biographical sketch of Giuseppe Rosati, the first bishop of St. Louis, Missouri.

714. Marolla, Edoardo.
"Father Giovanni Nobili." *Atlantica*, (August, 1930), 23-26.

Biographical sketch of an Italian Jesuit missionary, founder of the University of Santa Clara, California.

715. Marolla, Edoardo.
"Sister Justina. An Apostle of the Italians. Co-Founder of the Santa Maria Institute of Cincinnati." *Atlantica*, (May, 1931), 221-222, 230.

Brief biographical sketch of Sister Justina Segale, a Sister of Charity, who helped organize the "Santa Maria Italian Educational and Industrial Home," incorporated in December, 1890, in Cincinnati, Ohio.

716. Marolla, Edoardo.
"Father Giuseppe Maria Finotti. Pioneer Priest, Bibliographer, Writer." *Atlantica* (January, 1932), 259-260.

Biographical sketch of Fr. Finotti, Jesuit, editor of the *Boston Pilot*, and author of various books, including the *Bibliographia Catholica Americana* (1872), a "list of all the works written by Catholic authors between 1784 and 1820 published in the United States." The book was reprinted by Burt Franklin, New York, 1971.

717. Marolla, Edoardo.
"The Bentivoglio Sisters. Founders of the Order of the Poor Clares in the United States." *The Vigo Review*, I (July, 1938), 10-11.

Account of the establishment in the early 1880s, at Omaha, Nebraska, of the first convent of the Order of the Poor Clares by two daughters of the distinguished Italian family of Bentivoglio, Mothers Maria Maddalena del Sacro Cuore di Gesù and Maria Costanza di Gesù.

718. Marraro, Howard R.
American Opinion on the Unification of Italy, 1846-1861. New York: Columbia University Press, 1932. Pp. xii-345.

Marraro's important study touches on the Roman Question and its impact on American Catholics and Italian refugees in the United States and the incidents related to the visit by Archbishop Bedini and Fr. Alessandro Gavazzi, a critic of the papacy.

719. Marraro, Howard R.
"The Closing of the American Diplomatic Mission to the Vatican and the Efforts to Revive It, 1868-1870." *The Catholic Historical Review*, XXXIII (January, 1948), 423-447.

Account of the events surrounding the closing of the American diplomatic mission at the Vatican, based largely on newspaper articles.

720. Marraro, Howard R.
"Italians in New York in the Eighteen Fifties. Part II." *New York History*, XXX (July, 1949), 276-303.

This is the second of two articles by Marraro on New York's Italians in the 1850s. See the same journal for April, pp. 181-203. This article contains information on Fr. Alessandro Gavazzi, a former Catholic priest who came to New York on March 20, 1853 and, through speeches and lectures against the church and the papacy, stirred up much public sentiment both for and against him, see pp. 276-279. The article also recounts public reaction to the visit of Monsignor Gaetano Bedini, in 1853 and 1854, see pp. 279-285. Pp. 285-288 give some information on the Italian school at the Five Points, a school started in 1855 by the Children's Aid Society, a Protestant agency, to care for needy Italian children.

721. Marraro, Howard R.
"American Opinion on the Occupation of Rome in 1870." *The South Atlantic Quarterly*, LIV (April, 1955), 221-242.

The Roman question was regarded as a problem for the civilized world. The newspapers favored the Italian government, but the Catholic population followed events in Rome with anxiety. Catholics of the United States stood in favor of papal temporal powers and demonstrated against the invasion of Rome by the Italians and their King.

722. Marraro, Howard R.
"Il Problema Religioso del Risorgimento Italiano Visto dagli Americani." *Rassegna Storica del Risorgimento*, XLIII (Luglio-Settembre, 1956), 463-472.

Rome's invasion by the Italian army was seen differently by Catholics and Protestants in the United States. Newspaper opinion reflected this fact.

723. Martignoni, Angela.
My Mission is the World: The Life of Mother Cabrini. Translated by Clarence Tschippert. New York: Vatican City Religious Book Co., 1949. Pp. 285.

This is a translation of the Italian: *Madre Cabrini, la Santa delle Americhe. La vita, i viaggi, le opere.* New York: Vatican City Religious Book Company, 1945. Pp. 249. Not much of a biography, but good on chronology.

724. Martindale, C.C.
Mother Francesca Saverio Cabrini: Foundress of the Missionary Sisters of the Sacred Heart. London: Burns, Oates and Washburne Ltd., 1931. Pp. xv-76.

Life of Frances Xavier Cabrini "based on her biography by a member of her congregation."

725. Martire, Egilberto.
"Notizie sul P. Bressani, S.J., esploratore al Canada." *Atti del I Congresso Nazionale di studi romani.* Roma: Istituto di Studi Romani, 1929. I, 613-623.

Deals with the explorations of the Jesuit missionary Bressani in Canada and upstate New York.

726. Mastrogiovanni, Salv.
Le Prime Società di Patronato per gli Emigranti negli Stati Uniti ed in Italia. Venezia: Tip. Dell'Istituto Industriale, 1906. Pp. 31.

This pamphlet describes various societies established in the United States to give protection to the Italian immigrants. The author focuses on Protestant societies established in Boston, New York and Palermo at the turn of the nineteenth century.

727. Matthews, John L.
"Tontitown. A Story of the Conservation of Men." *Everybody's Magazine,* X (January, 1909), 3-13.

This is an account of the founding and successful development of the Italian agricultural colony of Tontitown, Arkansas. The author emphasizes the fact that agricultural colonies such as this one preserved the skills and values of the immigrants, most of whom came from a peasant background. The article is not too accurate on Fr. Bandini's background in Italy and New York, where he had been the founder of the Italian St. Raphael Society in 1891.

728. May, Ellen.
"Why Italians Need the Gospel." *The Missionary Review of the World*, N.S., XXII (November, 1909), 817-820.

The author argues that Protestant missionary activity among the Italians is needed because of their superstitious beliefs.

729. Maynard, Theodore.
The Story of American Catholicism. New York: The Macmillan Company, 1941. Pp. xv-694.

A popular history of the church in the United States. It briefly mentions the issue of Italian immigrants and their religious care. See Theodore Maynard. *The Catholic Church and the American Idea.* New York: Appleton-Century-Crofts, 1953. Pp. 309, where Maynard surveys the americanization of the Italian immigrants by the Church (pp. 141-153).

730. Maynard, Theodore.
Pillars of the Church. New York: Longman, Green & Co., 1945. Pp. 308.

Series of sketches on prominent American Catholics; includes a sketch of Mother Cabrini.

731. Maynard, Theodore.
Too Small a World: The Life of Mother Cabrini. Milwaukee: Bruce Publishing Co., 1945. Pp. xvi-335.

This is a popularly written biography of Frances Xavier Cabrini, who worked among the Italian immigrants at the turn of the century.

732. Maynard, Theodore.
Great Catholics in American History. New York: Doubleday, 1958. Pp. 261.

21 biographical sketches of prominent American Catholics, including Fr. Samuel Mazzuchelli and Mother Frances Cabrini.

733. Mazzuca, Marco.
"Italians — New Haven, Conn." *The Baptist Home Mission Monthly*, XXIV (October, 1902), 282.

The author, a Baptist missionary, describes his work among Italians in New Haven.

734. Mazzuchelli, Samuel.
Memoirs Historical and Edifying of a Missionary Apostolic of the

Order of Saint Dominic Among Various Indian Tribes and Among the Catholics and Protestants in the United States of America. Translated by Mary B. Kennedy. Chicago: W.F. Hall Printing Company, 1915. Pp. xxv-375.

The memoirs of Fr. Samuel Mazzuchelli, O.P., a missionary in the Midwest, originally published in Italian in 1844. A redaction of the English translation, by Maria M. Armato and Mary J. Finnegan, was published by The Priory Press in Chicago in 1967.

735. Meehan, Thomas F.
"Evangelizing the Italians." *The Messenger*, XXXIX (January, 1903), 16-32.

This is an informative summary of Protestant proselytizing among Italian immigrants in New York City at the turn of the nineteenth century. The author gives a list of Italian Catholic churches in New York City and vicinity and gives detailed information on the various ways in which Protestant missionary organizations have attempted to influence the immigrants. He calls for more effective efforts on the part of Catholics to offset this Protestant influence. See Editorial. "Our Duty to Our Fellow Catholic Italians." *The Messenger*, XXXIX (January, 1903), 89-92.

736. Meloni, Alberto C.
"Italy Invades the Bloody Third: The Early History of Milwaukee's Italians." The Milwaukee County Historical Society, *Historical Messenger*, XXV (March, 1969), 34-45.

Account of the coming of the Italians to Milwaukee and their replacing of the Irish in the city's third ward.

737. *In Memoria della Rev.ma Madre Francesca Saverio Cabrini Fondatrice e Superiora Generale delle Missionarie del S. Cuore di Gesù Volata al Cielo in Chicago il 22 Dicembre, 1917.* New York: A Bernasconi, 1918. Pp. 462.

Collection of eulogies and condolences from religious and civic leaders throughout the world on the occasion of the death of Mother Cabrini.

738. "In Memoriam. A Short Account of Fr. Vito Carozzini, S.J." *Woodstock Letters*, VI (1877), 124-129.

Work of Fr. Carozzini at San Miguel, Las Vegas, Las Animas, La Junta and Pueblo. Carozzini was born in Lecce in 1837 and studied in Spain, taught in Puerto Rico, and was sent to work in the United States in 1873.

739. Mengarini, Gregory.
"The Rocky Mountains. Memoirs of Fr. Gregory Mengarini." *Wood-stock Letters*, XVII (1888), 298-309; XVIII (1889), 25-43, 142-152.

Autobiographical account of Mengarini's life and missionary work among the Flathead and Coeur d'Alène Indians starting with his trip to the West on the invitation of Bishop Rosati and the beginning of his mission with Fr. DeSmet.

740. Mengarini, Gregory.
Recollections of the Flathead Mission: Containing Brief Observations Both Ancient and Contemporary Concerning This Particular Nation. Translated and edited by Gloria Ricci Lothrop. Glendale, Cal.: Clark, 1977. Pp. 256.

This is a translation of the recollections by the Italian Jesuit, Gregory Mengarini, of his work among the Flathead Indians at the mission of St. Mary's, Montana. The mission, begun in 1841 and initially promising, though under-financed, failed within a decade.

741. Mignacco, Filippo.
Lettera aperta a tutti gli Italiani in San Josè, Cal. San Francisco: Tipografia del giornale *L'Italia*, 1906. Pp. 8.

A letter written by Jesuit Fr. Mignacco inviting the Italians of San Jose, California, to build their own church.

742. "Milizia di Dio e della Patria." *Il Carroccio*, XXXV (April, July, and December, 1932), 130-132, 231-234, 310-314.

Brief biographical sketches of Italian-American priests and their activities in the Italian communities of the United States: E. Gianetto, B. Filitti, S. Zarrilli, N. Soriano, E. Longo, G. Congedo, F. deFrancesco, A. Idone, S. Neri, and I. Cirelli.

743. Minogue, Anna C.
The Story of the Santa Maria Institute with Preface by the Most Rev. Henry Moeller, D.D., Archbishop of Cincinnati. New York: The America Press, 1922. Pp. 174.

Record of religious work among Italians in Cincinnati done by the Sisters of Charity of Mother Seton. Describes in particular the work of two Sisters of Charity, Justina and Blandina Segale, and mentions their cooperation with the priests of the Church of Sacro Cuore, a national Italian parish.

744. Minogue, Anna C.
"Meeting the Italian Situation in Cincinnati." *N.C.W.C. Bulletin*, VIII (September, 1926), 21.

Catholic Settlement work for Italian immigrants in Cincinnati, started in 1897, developed into the Santa Maria Institute, which performed a variety of functions associated with a large settlement.

745. "The Mission in the Rocky Mountains in 1881." *Woodstock Letters*, XI (1882), 43-56.

A statistical description of the Italian Jesuit missions of Helena, St. Peter's, St. Ignatius, St. Mary's (Montana), Sacred Heart, St. Joseph (Idaho), Colville, Iakima (Washington Terr.).

746. "Le Missionarie del S. Cuore in America." *Italica Gens*, I (Aprile, 1910), 119-124.

Report on the activities of the sisters of Mother Frances Xavier Cabrini in various parts of the United States.

747. Missionary Fathers of St. Charles. The Province of St. John the Baptist. *75th Anniversary*. Chicago: 1962. Pp. 96.

History and description of activities of several Italian parishes staffed by the Scalabrinian Congregation in the Midwest.

748. "Missionary Sisters of the Sacred Heart." *The Catholic Church in the United States of America*. 3 vols. New York: The Catholic Editing Company, 1912-1914. II, 440-444.

Brief account of a religious institute founded by Frances Xavier Cabrini and introduced into the United States in 1889.

749. Missionary Zelatrices of the Sacred Heart.
Golden Jubilee [of the] Missionary Zelatrices of the Sacred Heart in the United States. New Haven, Conn.: The Author, 1953.

This community of sisters staffed several Italian schools in the United States.

750. *La Missione dell'Alaska. Memoria del R.P. Pasquale Tosi D.C. D.G. Superiore della Missione*. Roma: Tipografia A. Befani, 1893. Pp. 74.

Reprint of articles dealing with Fr. Pasquale Tosi and the Jesuit mission in Alaska taken from *Civiltà Cattolica*, Serie XV, V (1893), 503-512, 627-640; VI, 502-512; VII, 376-384.

751. *Missione Della Provincia Torinese Della Compagnia Di Gesù Nelle Montagne Rocciose Della America Settentrionale.* Turin, Italy: Giulio Spierani e Figli, 1863 and 1887. Pp. 97.

Useful for the work of Italian Jesuits in the Northwest. Letters of missionaries.

752. "Missioni di San Carlo dell'Istituto Cristoforo Colombo Istitute negli Stati del Nord America." *Bollettino dell'Emigrazione*, 1 (1903), 59-60.

Reports statistics on the activity and distribution of the Scalabrini Fathers in the United States to 1903.

753. "Missioni Religiose." *Bollettino dell'Emigrazione*, 18 (1907), 354-407.

Review of Catholic work among Italian immigrants in the United States.

754. "A Model Italian Colony in Arkansas." *The American Monthly Review of Reviews*, XXXIV (September, 1906), 361-362.

This brief article refers to the fact that two Italian magazines, the *Nuova Antologia* of Rome and the *Rassegna Nazionale* of Florence have given considerable space to the story of the Italian agricultrual colony at Tontitown, Arkansas. The article goes on to relate aspects of that story.

755. Molinari, Paolo.
"Madre Cabrini e gli emigranti." *La Civiltà Cattolica*, II (1968), 555-564.

Cabrini and the immigrants in America.

756. Mondello, Salvatore.
"Protestant Proselytism among the Italians in the U.S.A. as Reported in American Magazines." *Social Sciences*, XLI (April, 1966), 84-90.

The author reports and analyzes Protestant America's attitudes toward the Italian Catholic community in the United States from the 1880s to the mid-1930s as reflected in periodical literature. Protestant writers, especially during the World War I period believed that the Catholic faith of the Italian immigrants retarded their assimilation in American society.

757. Mondello, Salvatore.
"Baptist Churches and Italian-Americans." *Foundations*, XVI (July-September, 1973), 222-238.

An important study, based on excellent bibliographical references, on the role of Baptist Churches for Italian immigrants. The author concludes: "Tied to the considerable organized strength of the Baptist community and encouraged to retain their ethnic identity as long as they needed it, Italian

American Baptists enjoyed the best of both worlds. In their churches, Italian Baptists found spiritual comfort and Old World companions; in the organized structure of the Baptist community, they found a vital channel of economic and political upward mobility. In contrast to the Catholic Irish, Anglo-American and other Baptists had never viewed their church as the exclusive domain of their ethnic group. Rather, they were willing, indeed eager, to open their doors to all who accepted their spiritual message" (pp. 236-237).

758. Montclair Italian Evangelical Missionary Society.
First Annual Report of the Montclair Italian Evangelical Missionary Society Combined with an Address by Mr. Alberto Pecorini on the Italian Immigration Problem Delivered at Annual Meeting November Thirty, 1903. Montclair, N.J.: 1904. Pp. 16.

Reports on the activities of Protestant evangelists. In his address, Pecorini argues that Americanization is the best way for Italian immigrants to succeed in the United States.

759. Monti, Alessandro.
La Compagnia di Gesù nel Territorio della Provincia Torinese. Memorie Storiche Compilate in Occasione del Primo Centenario della Restaurazione di Essa Compagnia. Vol. V: *La Provincia Dispersa e Ristabilita.* Chieri: Stabilimento Tipografico M. Ghirardi, 1920.

This is volume five of a five-volume series published between 1914 and 1920. Pages 572-602 contain an appendix which summarizes the American missions of the Jesuits of the Province of Turin, Italy.

760. Moore, Anita.
"A Safe Way to Get on the Soil. The Work of Father Bandini at Tontitown — A New Hope for Our Newest Citizens and for the Small Seekers for Land." *World's Work*, XXIV (June, 1912), 215-219. Reprinted, Moquin, Wayne, ed. *A Documentary History of the Italian Americans.* New York: Praeger Publishers, 1974.

This is a sympathetic account of the work of Fr. Pietro Bandini in the Italian colony of Tontitown, Arkansas. The colony was established in 1898 by Fr. Bandini and a band of twenty-six hardy but poor Italian families. By 1912 this group had developed a self-supporting town that provided a model of a successful Italian agricultural colony in the United States.

761. Morrillo, A.
"VII. Nez-Percè Mission. Extract from a Letter to Father Cataldo." *Woodstock Letters*, XII (1883), 56-58.

Letter written by A. Morrillo, S.J., describing relations between Catholic and Protestant Indians.

762. Morrillo, A.
"Letter from Father Morrillo. Lapwai, Idaho Ty., January 2nd, 1883."
Woodstock Letters, XII (1883), 330-332.

Refers to the danger of indifference toward Catholicism resulting from
Protestant proselytism among the Indians.

763. Morrillo, A.
"Indian Mission, The Nez-Percés. Letter of Father Morrillo to Father
Cataldo. Lapawi, Idaho Territory, January, 1883." *Woodstock Letters*,
XIII (1884), 14-16.

Christmas novena among the Indians.

764. Morse, W.H.
"Our Missionaries to Italy." *The Baptist Home Mission Monthly*,
XXIX (September, 1907), 318-320.

Morse, Superintendent of the Bible Mission Society, argues that every "Italian
Protestant returning to Italy from America is a constituted missionary, and it
is not to our credit that we permit any to return without a supply of the
Scriptures."

765. Moseley, Daisy H.
"The Catholic Social Worker in an Italian District." *The Catholic
World*, CXIV (February, 1922), 618-628. Reprinted, Francesco Cordasco
and Eugene Bucchioni, eds. *The Italians: Social Backgrounds of An
American Group*. Clifton, New Jersey: Augustus M. Kelley, Publishers,
1974.

In this article, the author offers advice to Catholic social workers on how
they can best help Italians in urban areas deal with such matters as raising
children, health, religion, etc.

766. Muldoon, Peter J.
"Immigration to and Immigrants in the United States." *The Second
American Catholic Missionary Congress*. Edited by Francis C. Kelley.
Chicago: J.S. Hyland and Co., 1913.

Reference to Catholic settlement work among Italians.

767. Mullen, J.E.
"Stigmatine Fathers." *New Catholic Encyclopedia*, XIII (1967), 710-
711.

Account of founding and development of the Congregation of the Priests of
the Sacred Stigmata of Our Lord, established in Italy by Gaspare Bertoni in

1816. The Stigmatines first arrived in the United States in 1905, caring for Italian parishes in Massachusetts and New York.

768. Muredach, Myles.
"An Experiment in City Home Missions." *Extension Magazine*, XVII (April, 1923), 35-36, 62.

This article deals with the work of the Maestre Pie Filippini, a religious community of teaching sisters that came to the United States to establish parochial schools among the Italians at the request of the Bishop of Trenton, New Jersey, Thomas J. Walsh. Reprinted, John Zarrilli. *A Prayerful Appeal to the American Hierarchy in Behalf of the Italian Catholic Cause in the United States.* Two Harbors, Minnesota: 1924. Pp. 19-26.

769. Musmanno, Michael A.
The Story of the Italians in America. Your Ancestor Series. Garden City, New York: Doubleday & Company, Inc., 1965. Pp. x-300.

Survey of Italians in the United States. Includes references to Italians and religion.

770. Nardi, Michael.
"The West Side Italian Church. 34-36 Charlton Street." The New York City Mission and Tract Society, *Annual Report*, January, 1909, 12-13.

Account of work of the evangelical church at 34-36 Charlton Street, New York City.

771. Nasalli, Giovanni Battista.
Commemorazione di Mons. Giovanni Battista Scalabrini. Piacenza: Tip. F. Solari di G. Tononi, 1909, Pp. 27.

A commemorative booklet on the life and work of Scalabrini.

772. Nava, Cesare.
Monsignor Giovanni Battista Scalabrini Vescovo di Piacenza. Roma: Tip. Pont. dell'Istituto Pio IX, 1916. Pp. 23.

Short biography of Scalabrini and his work for immigrants.

773. *Nel XXV Anniversario dell'arrivo negli Stati Uniti d'America delle Missionarie del S. Cuore de Gesù.* Roma: Stabilimento Tipografia Befani, 1914. Pp. 17.

Commemorative booklet for the 25th anniversary of the arrival in the United States of the Missionary Sisters of Frances Xavier Cabrini.

774. *Nel XXV Anniversario dell'Istituto dei Missionari di S. Carlo per gli Italiani Emigrati Fondato da Mons. Giovanni Battista Scalabrini Vescovo di Piacenza (1887-1912).* Roma: Tipografia Pontificia Istituto Pio IX, 1912. Pp. xxvii-80.

Testimonal letters of the Catholic Hierarchy and pictorial history of the main achievements of the Missionaries of St. Charles among Italian migrants in the Americas. Very useful information concerning parish activities, statistical data, and social works carried out in favor of migrants.

775. Nelli, Humbert S.
Italians in Chicago, 1880-1930. A Study in Ethnic Mobility. New York: Oxford University Press, 1970. Pp. xx-300.

This is a good study of the Italians in Chicago during the period of greatest Italian influx into the city. The author gives a brief account of the growth and role of the Catholic Church among the Chicago Italians on pp. 181-200.

776. Nichols, Floyd B.
"Making an Immigrants' Paradise." *Technical World Magazine*, XIX (August, 1913), 894-897.

This brief article on the Italian agricultural colony of Tontitown, Arkansas, describes the founding of the colony and argues that such efforts provide "the real solution of the problem of the immigration of the people from southern Europe into the United States."

777. Noa, Thomas L.
"Religion and Good Citizenship. The Family is the Basic Social Unit." *Vital Speeches of the Day*, XIX (October 15, 1952), 29-32.

Text of speech delivered by Bishop Noa of Marquette, Michigan, to the Federation of Italian-American Societies of the Upper Peninsula, Sault Ste. Marie, Michigan, August 17, 1952.

778. Nobili, John.
"Two Old Letters. II. Fr. John Nobili to Fr. Goetz. En route. June 6, 1848." *Woodstock Letters*, XVIII (1889), 78-79.

Nobili describes his knowledge of the Indian language and the start of a new mission-house.

779. *Note di Cronaca sull'origine e progresso della Chiesa di S. Antonio, 151 Sullivan St., New York.* Napoli: Tipografia Pontificia M. D'Auria, 1925. Unpaged.

An Italian and English language sketch of the founding and growth of the parish of St. Anthony's in lower Manhattan. The parish, established by Italian Franciscans, was committed mainly to the care of Italian immigrants.

780. "Notes and Remarks." *The Ave Maria*, LXVIII (January 9, 1909), 53-57.

On Fr. Peter Bandini of Tontitown, Arkansas.

781. *Notizie Storiche e Descrittive delle Missioni della Provincia Torinese della Compagnia di Gesù nell'America del Nord con Appendice sulle Antiche Missioni D.C.D.G. nel Territorio degli Stati Uniti e Breve Memoria della Vita ;del V.P. Giovanni Antonio Rubino S.J. Martire del Giappone.* Torino: Tipografia G. Derossi, 1898. Pp. xii-v.p.

This book contains the following: I. "Missione della California," pp. 1-47; II. "Missione delle Montagne Rocciose," pp. 1-51; III. "Missione dell'Alaska," pp. 1-46; Amalia Capello, "I Padri della Compagnia di Gesù in Alaska, California, Montagne Rocciose," pp. 1-71; Amalia Capello, "Credenze religiose degli Indiani d'America prima della scoperta di Colombo," pp. 1-11; IV. Appendice. 'Antiche Missioni dei PP. della Compagnia di Gesù nell'America Settentrionale e Territorio degli Stati Uniti 1613-1892," pp. 1-27; "Breve Memoria della Vita del V.P. Giovanni Antonio Rubino Martire del Giappone," pp. 1-48.

782. Nugent, F.V.
"Vincentians." *The Catholic Church in the United States of America.* 3 vols. New York: The Catholic Editing Company, 1912-1914. I, 433-452.

Account of the founding and growth of the Congregation of the Mission, or Vincentians, introduced into the United States in 1816. The Congregation included many priests of Italian origin.

783. O'Brien, Grace.
"Catholic Social Settlements." National Conference of Catholic Charities, *Proceedings.* Washington, D.C.: Catholic University of America, 1910. Pp. 138-145.

This is a description of Catholic settlement houses in the United States. The author argues that "the preservation of the faith of Catholic immigrants has been the fundamental reason for the adoption of settlement methods." The article lists settlements for Italians.

784. O'Brien, Grace.
"Catholic Settlement Work in Brooklyn." *Survey*, XVII (May 7, 1910),
203-204.

Assistance to Italians through settlement work.

785. O'Connor, Mary P.
*Five Decades. History of the Congregation of the Most Holy Rosary,
Sinsinawa, Wisconsin, 1849-1899*. Sinsinawa, Wis.: The Sinsinawa
Press, 1954. Pp. 370.

A history of the first fifty years of a religious community of women founded
by Fr. Samuel Mazzuchelli, O.P.

786. O'Connor, Mary P.
"Some Mazzuchellian 'Firsts.' " *The Salesianum*, XLIX (October, 1954),
161-169.

This article, adapted from the author's *Five Decades: A History of the
Congregation of the Most Holy Rosary, Sinsinawa, Wisconsin, 1849-1899*
(The Sinsinawa Press, Sinsinawa, Wisconsin, 1954), deals with the work of
Dominican Father Samuel Mazzuchelli in Wisconsin in the first half of the
nineteenth century.

787. O'Connor, Thomas F.
"Documents — Letters of John Grassi, S.J. to Simon Bruté de Rémur,
1812-1832." *Mid-America*, N.S., IV (April, 1933), 245-265.

In his brief introduction to the letters, O'Connor notes: "The following letters
written by Father John Grassi, S.J., to Father Simon Bruté de Rémur,
afterwards first Bishop of Vincennes, were found in the Canon Bruté de
Rémur Collection, Rennes, Frances [sic], by Sister Mary Salesia Godecker,
O.S.B., while in prosecution of researches preparatory to writing her life of
Bishop Bruté."

788. O'Connor, Thomas F., ed.
"Joseph Rosati, C.M., Apostolic Delegate to Haiti, 1842 — Two Letters
to Bishop John Hughes." *The Americas*, I (April, 1945), 490-494.

O'Connor prints two letters dated February 3 and 15, 1842, written by
Bishop Joseph Rosati of St. Louis, Missouri, to Bishop John Hughes, Coadjutor
of the Archdiocese of New York. Rosati had been appointed Apostolic
Delegate to Haiti to settle local ecclesiastical matters. The original letters are
in the Archives of the Archdiocese of New York.

789. An Old Missionary.
"Priests for Italian Immigrants." *The American Ecclesiastical Review,*
XX (May, 1899), 513-516.

In this article, the author sketches his experiences with Italian immigrants in
Marseilles, France in mid-nineteenth century, and his later experiences with
Italian and other immigrants in the Rocky Mountains region of the United
States.

790. Olivieri, Angelo.
"Protestantism and Italian Immigration in Boston in Late 19th
Century: The Mission of G. Conte." *The Religious Experience of
Italian Americans.* Edited by Silvano M. Tomasi. Staten Island, New
York: The American Italian Historical Association, 1975. Pp. 71-103.

Detailed account of the work of the Rev. Gaetano Conte, a minister of the
Methodist Episcopal Church, among the Italians of Boston's North End, from
1893 to 1903.

791. "L'opera delle nostre missioni negli Stati Uniti nel 1922." *L'Emigrato
Italiano,* XVII (Aprile, Maggio, Giugno, 1923), 10-53.

Scalabrinian activity in the United States among Italians in 1922.

792. "L'opera di Don Bosco per le missioni salesiane." *Il Carroccio,* XXIX
(Maggio, 1929), 425.

A listing of the parishes and other activities of the Salesian Fathers among
Italian immigrants in the United States.

793. "Le Opere Cattoliche a Nuova York." *La Civiltà Cattolica,* Serie
XVII, X (1900), 712-718.

This is a useful summary of a pastoral letter issued by Archbishop Michael
A. Corrigan of New York on the occasion of his *ad limina* visit to the Holy
See in 1900. It contains some information on the activities of the church in
New York among the immigrants at this time.

794. "Un Orfanotrofio Italiano a Denver." *Italica Gens,* VI (Gennaio-
Febbraio, 1915), 62-64.

A description of the Italian orphanage and school directed by the Missionary
Sisters of the Sacred Heart in Denver.

795. "The Organization of the 'Italian Presbyterian Church' of New York."
The Assembly Herald, XVI (January, 1910), 8-10.

Describes the organization of the "Presbyterian Church of the Ascension of New York, under the care and jurisdiction of the Presbytery of New York." The new church, with an Italian congregation, was located in New York's "Little Italy."

796. O'Sullivan, Donald.
"St. Frances Xavier Cabrini." *Studies*, XXXV (September, 1946), 351-356.

This is a brief biographical sketch of Cabrini's life and work.

797. Ottolini, Pietro.
Storia dell'Opera Italiana di Pietro Ottolini. Trenton, N.J.: Merlo's Publishing Co., 1945. Pp. 20.

Ottolini, an evangelist, describes his missionary work among Italians in America.

798. Owens, M. Lilliana.
"Frances Xavier Cabrini." *Colorado Magazine*, XXII (July, 1945), 171-178.

Deals with Cabrini's founding of Queen of Heaven Institute in Denver, Colorado.

799. Owens, M. Lilliana.
Jesuit Beginnings in New Mexico. Jesuit Studies — Southwest, Number One. El Paso, Texas: Revista Catolica Press, 1950. Pp. 176.

This volume, which deals extensively with Italian Jesuit missionaries in New Mexico, includes: I. Jesuit Beginnings in New Mexico; II. The First Jesuit Trek to New Mexico — 1867; and III. The Diary of the Mission to New Mexico.

800. Owens, M. Lilliana.
Reverend Carlos M. Pinto, S.J., Apostle of El Paso 1892-1919. Jesuit Studies — Southwest, Number Two. El Paso, Texas: Revista Catolica Press, 1951. Pp. xxi-228.

Scholarly biography of Fr. Carlos M. Pinto, born in Salerno, Italy, a member of the Naples Province of the Society of Jesus, who in 1892 was sent to El Paso, Texas, to spread the Gospel and minister to the scattered Catholics in the area.

801. Palladino, L. B.
"The Catholic Church in Montana." *Woodstock Letters*, IX (1880), 95-106.

Description of beginning and progress of church in Montana from 1840 to 1880s.

802. Palladino, L.B.
Anthony Ravalli, S.J., Forty Years A Missionary in the Rocky Mountains. Memoir. Helena, Mont.: Geo. E. Boos & Co. Printers, 1884. Pp. 11.

This memoir on the life and work of Anthony Ravalli, S.J., was "sold for the benefit of the Indian Schools in Montana."

803. Palladino, Lawrence B.
Indian and White in the Northwest; or, A History of Catholicity in Montana. Baltimore: John Murphy & Company, 1894. Pp. xxv-411.

Fr. Lawrence B. Palladino was an Italian Jesuit missionary in the American West from 1863 to his death in 1927. This book describes the work of the Jesuit missionaries in the West, especially Montana, during the nineteenth century. A revised and enlarged edition of this book was published in 1922. See L.B. Palladino, *Indian and White in the Northwest. A History of Catholicity in Montana 1831 to 1891.* 2nd ed. revised and enlarged. Lancaster, Pa.: Wickersham Publishing Company, 1922. Pp. xx-512.

804. Palladino, Lawrence B.
"Historical Notes on the Flathead." *The Indian Sentinel,* I (October, 1919), 6-16.

The Flatheads were an Indian tribe in the West. Palladino was a Jesuit missionary among them.

805. "Pallottine Sisters of Charity." *The Catholic Church in the United States of America.* 3 vols. New York: The Catholic Editing Company, 1912-1914. II, 416.

Brief account of the Pallottine Sisters of Charity, or Sisters of the Pious Society of Missions, founded in Rome in 1838 and first introduced into the United States in 1889 to work among Italian immigrants.

806. Palmieri, F. Aurelio.
"Italian Protestantism in the United States." *The Catholic World,* CVII (May, 1918), 177-189. Reprinted, Francesco Cordasco and Eugene Bucchioni, eds. *The Italians: Social Backgrounds of An American Group.* Clifton, New Jersey: Augustus M. Kelley Publishers, 1974.

This is a detailed summary of Protestant proselytism among Italian immigrants in the United States. The author concludes that "the gains of Protestant proselytism after fifty years of hard work, are reduced to hardly more than six thousand souls" (p. 189).

807. Palmieri, F. Aurelio.
"L'Aspetto Economico del Problema Religioso Italiano negli Stati Uniti." *Rivista Internazionale di Scienze Sociali e Discipline Ausiliarie*, LXXVII (Luglio, 1918), 184-210.

The economic aspect of the Italian religious problem in the United States.

808. Palmieri, F. Aurelio.
"Il clero italiano negli Stati Uniti." *La Vita Italiana*, VIII (Febbraio 15, 1920), 113-127.

This is a useful study of the number and activities of Italian priests and nuns in the United States. The author concludes that the number of Italian clergy is not large enough to take care of the spiritual needs of the Italian immigrants. See Aurelio Palmieri. "The Contribution of the Italian Catholic Clergy to the United States." *Catholic Builders of the Nation*, 5 vols. Edited by C.E. McGuire. Boston: Continental Press, Inc., 1923. II, 127-149.

809. Palmieri, F. Aurelio.
Il Grave Problema Religioso Italiano Negli Stati Uniti. Firenze: Tipografia Sordomuti, 1921. Pp. 68.

This is an excellent summary of the "Italian problem" and the various suggestions made to resolve it. Palmieri's booklet is divided into the following chapters: ch. I, the Italian religious problem and the American clergy; ch. II, the necessity for Italian priests in America; and ch. III, present conditions regarding assistance to Italian immigrants in the United States and hopes for the future.

810. Palmieri, F. Aurelio.
"The Contribution of the Italian Catholic Clergy to the Unitd States." *Catholic Builders of the Nation.* 5 vols. Edited by C.E. McGuire. Boston: Continental Press, Inc., 1923. II, 127-149.

This is a study of the number and activities of Italian clergy and nuns in the United States. See Aurelio Palmieri. "Il Clero Italiano negli Stati Uniti." *La Vita Italiana*, VIII (Febbraio 15, 1920), 113-127.

811. Palmquist, A.E.
"A New Work Among the Italians." *The Baptist Home Mission Monthly*, XXX (October, 1908), 376.

Baptist work among Italians in Connellsville, Pennsylvania.

812. Panunzio, Constantine M.
The Soul of an Immigrant. New York: MacMillan, 1921. Pp. 329.

Biography of an immigrant who converted to Protestantism. Reprinted, New York: Arno Press, 1969.

813. Paoli Gumina, Deanna.
"SS. Peter and Paul's: The Church of the Fisherman." *Columbus.* Magazine for the 1972 Columbus Day Celebration. San Francisco: Columbus Day Celebration, Inc., 1972. Pp. 13-14, 31, 39.

History of an Italian parish in San Francisco which was founded as a Spanish church. *Columbus* is an annual publication.

814. Parkinson Keyes, Frances.
Mother Cabrini, Missionary to the World. New York: Vision Books, 1959. Pp. 190.

Popularly written biography of Cabrini.

815. Parodi, A.
"Two Letters from Fr. Parodi. Ounalska, June 16, 1892, St. Michael, July 15, 1892." *Woodstock Letters*, XXI (1892), 364-365.

Describes his travels with a Russian Orthodox bishop and a Protestant minister. Notes that the places are already taken by the Orthodox and the Protestants.

816. Parodi, L.
"Letter of Father L. Parodi to Father J. Cataldo. Yakima, Ellensburgh, June 11, 1882." *Woodstock Letters*, XII (1883), 53-56.

Describes care for the sick, and baptisms and conversions among the Indians.

817. Parsons, Anne.
"The Pentecostal Immigrants: A Study of an Ethnic Central City Church." *Journal for the Scientific Study of Religion*, IV (Spring, 1965), 183-197.

Description of an Italian immigrant sect, the Chiesa Evangelica Italiana or the Italian Evangelical Church. Located in the central city, it functioned both as a preserver of the traditional community and as a dynamic force in social change.

818. Parsons, Anne.
   Belief, Magic, and Anomiee: Essays in Psychological Anthropology.
   New York: The Free Press, 1969. Pp. 392.

   Reference is made to Italian immigrants who became Pentecostals.

819. Parsons, J. Wilfrid.
   "The Catholic Church in America in 1819. A Contemporary Account."
   The Catholic Historical Review, V (January, 1920), 301-310.

   Brief sketch of Jesuit Fr. Giovanni Grassi, named Superior of the Maryland
   Jesuits and Rector of Georgetown on October 16, 1811, and of his *Notizie
   varie sullo stato presente della Repubblica degli Stati Uniti d'America
   settentrionale, scritte al principio del 1818.* Ed. 2. Milano per Giovanni
   Silvestro, MDCCXIX. The *Notizie varie* is one of the first accounts of the
   history of the Catholic Church in the United States.

820. "Passionist Nuns." *The Catholic Church in the United States of
   America.* 3 vols. New York: The Catholic Editing Company, 1912-
   1914. II, 416-418.

   Brief account of the introduction and growth of the Passionist Nuns in the
   United States. The first five nuns arrived from Italy in Pittsburgh in 1910.

821. Pasteris, Emiliano.
   "Le scuole italiane agli Stati Uniti e al Canada." *Pro Emigranti,* III
   (1909), 21-22.

   Points out the limited success of Italian Catholic schools.

822. "Pastoral Care of Foreign Catholics in America." *The Ecclesiastical
   Review,* LXX (February, 1924), 176-181.

   This is a reply to the article by John Zarrilli, "A Suggestion for the Solution
   of the Italian Problem." *The Ecclesiastical Review,* LXX (January, 1924), 70-
   77. The author of this anonymously written article is critical of the proposals
   made by Zarrilli. Zarrilli replied to the article in "Pastoral Care of Foreign
   Catholics in America and the Italian Problem," printed in the brochure by
   John Zarrilli, *A Prayerful Appeal to the American Hierarchy in Behalf of the
   Italian Catholic Cause in the United States.* Two Harbors, Minnesota: 1924.
   Pp. 11-19.

823. "Pastoral Care of Italian Immigrants." *The Ecclesiastical Review,*
   LXVIII, No. 5 (May, 1923), 506.

This number of the *Review* published an Instruction from Cardinal DeLai, Secretary of the Concistorial Congregation, in which the Ordinaries and parish priests of Italy are advised to provide persons emigrating from Italy with a certificate of their Baptism, Confirmation, and "status." The document is editorially supported by the *Review*.

824. "Per gli Emigranti Italiani." *La Civiltà Cattolica*, 65, II (1914), 360-369.

This article has an introduction to and the text of two documents by the Holy See relating to Italian immigration: Pius PP. X. Motu Proprio, "De Italis ad Externa Emigrantibus" (pp. 363÷365) and S. Congregatio Consistorialis. Decretum, "De Sacerdotibus in Certas Quasdam Regiones Demigrantibus" (pp. 366-369).

825. Perotti, Antonio.
Il Pontificio Collegio per l'Emigrazione Italiana, 1920-1970. Roma: Tipografia Italo-Orientale S. Nilo, n.d.

This is a history of the Pontifical College for Italian Immigration, established at Rome in 1920 to train priests for pastoral work among Italian immigrants. The study is based largely on official documents of the Holy See and the archives of the Scalabrini Congregation, Rome.

826. Perotti, Antonio.
"Documentazione sul pensiero sociale di G.B. Scalabrini sui fenomeni migratori." *L'Emigrato Italiano*, (February, 1962), 3-12.

A review of the social thinking of Scalabrini on migration phenomena.

827. Perotti, Antonio.
"Contributo di G.B. Scalabrini e dei suoi Missionari alle prime leggi organiche sull'emigrazione." *L'Emigrato Italiano*, (June, July, September, October, 1962), 3-20, 3-20, 5-22, 5-28.

An important analysis of the impact on Italian emigration legislation by Bishop Giovanni Battista Scalabrini of Piacenza and the missionaries of the religious society he founded.

828. Perotti, Antonio.
"La società italiana di fronte alle prime migrazioni di massa. — Il contributo di Mons. Scalabrini e dei suoi primi collaboratori alla tutela degli emigranti." *Studi Emigrazione*, V (Febbraio-Giugno, 1968), 1-196. Reprinted, New York: Arno Press, 1975.

This is a detailed study of the problems facing Italian immigrants during the early stages of the period of mass migration that extended from the 1880s to the 1920s. The author outlines Bishop Scalabrini's efforts on behalf of the immigrants, such as his work to bring about government legislation favorable to the immigrants and his establishment of an emigrant aid society in Italy and in the Western Hemisphere. The study is based on primary sources.

829. Pesaturo, Ubaldo U.M.
Italo-Americans of Rhode Island. 2nd ed. Providence, R.I.: Visitor Printing Co., 1940. Pp. 193.

The author subtitles this work "An historical and biographical survey of the origin, rise and progress of Rhode Islanders of Italian birth or descent." Originally published in 1936, this book gives descriptions of churches, pastors, and religious schools on pp. 15-24.

830. Petty, A. Ray.
"120,000 Italians in the Back Yard." *The Baptist*, III (February 25, 1922), 107.

Describes work of Judson Memorial Church on Washington Square, in the lower west side of Manhattan, among Italian immigrants. Mentions the Judson Health Center and the Judson Neighborhood House.

831. Piccinni, Gaetano Michael.
Blessed Frances Xavier Cabrini in America. New York: The Missionary Sisters of the Sacred Heart, 1942. Pp. 46.

A short accurate biography with pertinent bibliography.

832. Pirazzini, Agide.
"Training an Italian Ministry for America." *The Assembly Herald*, XXIV (March, 1918), 152-153. Reprinted, *Protestant Evangelism Among Italians in America.* New York: Arno Press, 1975.

Suggestions for ministers going to work among Italian immigrants.

833. Pisani, Lawrence Frank.
The Italians in America. A Social Study and History. New York: Exposition Press, 1957. Pp. 293.

This is a popular account of the Italians in the United States. Chapter XI, pp. 163-172 is titled "Religion in America."

834. Pisani, Pietro.
L'Emigrazione. Avvertimenti e Consigli agli Emigranti. Firenze: Ufficio Centrale dell'Unione Popolare fra i Cattolici d'Italia, 1907. Pp. 82.

Pisani, a priest associated with *Italica Gens*, prepared this booklet to provide social and religious advice for emigrating Italians.

835. Pisani, Pietro.
"Un Pioniere della Colonnizzazione Italiana negli Stati Uniti d'America." *Italica Gens*, I (Febbraio, 1910), 31-37.

Account of Fr. Pietro Bandini and the Italian agricultural colony at Tontitown, Arkansas.

836. Pisani, Pietro.
"La Colonia Italiana di Chicago, Ill. e la nuova iniziativa di Marconiville." *Italica Gens*, I (Maggio, 1910), 155-178.

Report on the Italian colony of Chicago and its churches. Describes the founding of Marconiville, an experimental agricultural settlement.

837. Pisani, Pietro.
"Asili Infantili e Orfanotrofi pei Figli di Italiani a New York." *Italica Gens*, I (Agosto-Settembre, 1910), 307-315.

Account of several kindergartens and orphanages for the children of Italian immigrants in New York established by Italian religious communities.

838. Pisani, Pietro.
"La Colonia Italiana di Providence." *Italica Gens*, I (Ottobre-Novembre, 1910), 349-369.

Gives valuable information on the Italian community in Providence, Rhode Island. Includes information on Catholic and Protestant churches.

839. Pisani, Pietro.
"Gli Italiani a Rochester, N.Y." *Italica Gens*, II (Gennaio, 1911), 25-31.

Account of Italians in Rochester, New York, including information on schools and churches.

840. Pisani, Pietro.
L'Immigrazione Italiana nell'America del Nord. Note e Proposte. Roma: Ufficio della Rivista Internazionale, 1911.

Pisani, later a bishop in Italy, offers suggestions for the care of Italian immigrants in the United States and Canada.

841. Pistella, Domenico.
     The Crowning of a Queen. Translated by Peter Rofrano. New York: Shrine of Our Lady of Mt. Carmel, 1954. Pp. 167.

     History of Pallottine work among Italian immigrants in the United States, especially devotion to Our Lady of Mt. Carmel and the development of Our Lady of Mt. Carmel parish in East Harlem, New York City.

842. Pius PP. X.
     "Epistola Qua Pius PP. X Archiepiscopum Neo-Eboracensium laudat of pastoralem diligentiam erga Italos illuc commigrantes." *Acta Sanctae Sedis*, XXXIX (1906), 21.

     Letter written by Pope Pius X to Archbishop John Farley of New York on February 26, 1904, praising him for his pastoral concern on behalf of the Italian immigrants in his archdiocese.

843. Pius PP. X.
     "Ad R.D. Dominicum Vicentini Sacerdotem, Moderatorem Instituti A S. Carolo Pro Italis Demigrantibus, Occasione Solemnitatum in Memoriam Joannis Baptistae Scalabrini, Eiusdem Operis Institutoris, Celebratarum." *Acta Apostolicae Sedis*, IV (September 16, 1912), 581-582.

     Letter written by Pope Pius X on September 4, 1912, to Fr. Domenico Vicentini, Superior General of the Congregation of St. Charles, on the occasion of the 25th anniversary of the foundation of the Congregation praising the work for Italian migrants.

844. Pius PP. X.
     "Motu Proprio De Catholicorum In Exteras Regiones Emigratione." *The Ecclesiastical Review*, XLVII (October, 1912), 451-452.

     Letter dated August 15, 1912, establishing a new department in the Congregation of the Consistory to direct the spiritual care of immigrants.

845. Pius PP. X.
     "Motu Proprio: De Italis ad Externa Emigrantibus." *The Ecclesiastical Review*, L (June, 1914), 719-722.

     With this document, dated March 19, 1914, Pope Pius X institutes an ecclesiastical college in Rome to give a special course of two years' training to Italian priests who wish to dedicate themselves to the spiritual assistance of Italian emigrants, especially in the United States.

846. Pius PP. XI.

"Venerabilis Dei Famula Francisca Xaveria Cabrini, Instituti Missionariarum A Sacro Corde Iesu Fundatrix, Beata Renuntiatur." *Acta Apostolicae Sedis*, XXXI (January 28, 1939), 10-15.

Letter of Pope Pius XI, dated November 13, 1938, declaring Frances Xavier Cabrini a blessed.

847. Pius PP. XII.

"In Sollemni Canonizatione Beatae Franciscae Xaveriae Cabrini, Virginis, In Basilica Vaticana Die VII Mensis Iulii A. MDCCCCXXXXVI Peracta." *Acta Apostolicae Sedis*, XXXVIII (August 1, 1946), 269-273.

Decree of canonization of St. Cabrini and homily of Pius XII, see *Acta Apostolicae Sedis*, XXXI (January, 1938), 10-15 for the document in which St. Cabrini was declared a blessed.

848. Pius PP. XII.

"Constitutio Apostolica de Spirituali Emigrantium Cura." *Acta Apostolicae Sedis*, XLIV (September 30, 1952), 649-704.

Apostolic Constitution by Pope Pius XII published August 1, 1952, on the pastoral care of migrants.

849. Plumley, G.S.

"Report of Calvary Church. Worth Street, Near Centre." New York City Mission and Tract Society, *55th Annual Report*. New York: 50 Bible House, 1882. Pp. 38-48.

This is the annual report for 1881 of Calvary Church, Worth Street, Near Centre, in New York City. Plumley was the pastor. Notes the introduction of Italian work by the church, due to the presence of so many Italian immigrants in its vicinity. In June, 1881, the Rev. Antonio Arrighi was engaged by the church to minister to the Italians. He was given the position of assistant pastor.

850. Plumley, G.S.

"Report of Calvary Church. Worth Street, Near Centre." The New York City Mission and Tract Society, *56th Annual Report*. New York: 50 Bible House, 1883. Pp. 20-24.

This is the annual report for 1882 of Calvary Church, Worth Street, Near

Centre. Includes activities of Rev. A. Arrighi, assistant pastor, who ministered to the Italians. Brief reports for 1883 and 1884 were filed by "The Secretary."

851. Polzer, Charles W.
"Kino — Peacemaker, Pathfinder, Pioneer." *Ave Maria*, XCVIII (December 14, 1932), 5-9, 30.

This is a brief account of the missionary work of Fr. Eusebio Kino in the American Southwest in the late seventeenth century. Fr. Kino was from the Italian Tyrol.

852. Ponziglione, Paul Mary.
"Letter from Fr. Ponziglione to Very Rev. Fr. O'Neil. Osage Missions, Neosho Co., Kansas, December 31, 1871." *Woodstock Letters*, I (1872), 111-121.

Spreading of Christianity in the Virdigris River Region and among the Osage Indians in Kansas. Ponziglione reports on his missionary trips and his apostolate among Catholic settlers and Indians.

853. Ponziglione, Paul Mary.
"New Catholic Stations in Kansas. From Two Letters of Fr. Ponziglione. Osage Mission, Neosho Co., Kansas. July 1, 1872; Dec. 31, 1872." *Woodstock Letters*, II (1873), 149-156.

Description of mission work among settlers and Indians in various counties of the Kansas Territory and along the Arkansas River. Description of lynching and frontier life.

854. Ponziglione, Paul Mary.
"Osage Missions, Neosho Co., Kansas, December 31, 1873." *Woodstock Letters*, III (1874), 126-132.

Historical development of the Jesuit missions in the Neosho Valley with reference to first Catholic immigrant families.

855. Ponziglione, Paul Mary.
"Osage Missions, Neosho County, Kansas, July 1st, 1874." *Woodstock Letters*, IV (1875), 64-71.

The beginning of the missions in 1854, when the Osage nation numbered about 7,000 souls. Describes the method of apostleship among the Indians of South Kansas, immigration to the territories ceded by the Indians, and request by the Indians for a Catholic mission and school house.

856. Ponziglione, Paul Mary.
"Brother John DeBruyn. Letter of Fr. P.M. Ponziglione to Fr. John Van Krevel. Osage Mission, Neosho Co., Kansas. February 8th, 1875." *Woodstock Letters*, IV (1875), 110-114.

A memoir of Brother John DeBruyn on the 10th anniversary of his death.

857. Ponziglione, Paul Mary.
"Osage Mission, Neosho County, Kansas. December 1, 1874." *Woodstock Letters*, IV (1875), 160-166.

Relates his activities in preaching, sacraments and conversions among the Indians who, he notes, were occasionally murdered by white settlers without cause.

858. Ponziglione, Paul Mary.
"St. Francis' Institution, Osage Mission, Neosho Co., Kansas, July 13, 1875." *Woodstock Letters*, V (1876), 54-59.

Describes the missionary work at Independence, Montgomery County, Kansas, and the organization of the Catholic Temperance Society. Points out discrimination of Catholic Indians by the Indian agent.

859. Ponziglione, Paul Mary.
"Residence of St. Francis Hieronymo, Osage Mission, Neosho Co., Kansas, January 1st, 1876." *Woodstock Letters*, V (1876), 144-148.

Report of the founding and progress of the new mission and the discrimination of the United States Agent against Indians and Catholics.

860. Ponziglione, Paul Mary.
"St. Francis' Institution, Osage Mission, Neosho Co., Kansas, July 1st, 1876." *Woodstock Letters*, V (1876), 223-229.

Description of the Jesuit missions' progress. Notes that the "mother church" is surrounded by 8 smaller churches and many other missionary stations and that some churches have been relinquished to secular clergy. Describes educational work among the Indian children.

861. Ponziglione, Paul Mary.
"Osage Mission, Neosho Co., Kansas, December 30th, 1876." *Woodstock Letters*, VI (1877), 100-105.

Describes the work in Wilson County and the obstacles to evangelization he has encountered. Notes that the Congregation of Propaganda Fide has created an Apostolic Prefecture and that the Missouri Province has lost the missions it had since 1824.

862. Ponziglione, Paul Mary.
"Origin of the Osage Mission." *Woodstock Letters*, VI (1877), 141-147.

Historical account written by Ponziglione in 1869, dealing with the period 1820 to the late 1860s.

863. Ponziglione, Paul Mary.
"Osage Mission, Neosho Co., Kansas. July 1st, 1877." *Woodstock Letters*, VI (1877), 194-199.

Author notes that the Jesuits will continue "ad interim" their work in the newly established Prefecture. He decries the little liberty given to the Indians.

864. Ponziglione, Paul Mary.
"Osage Missions, Neosho Co., Kansas, December 31st, 1877." *Woodstock Letters*, VII (1878), 99-105.

Ponziglione describes the customs of the "Medicine-Men" and his contacts with the Kansas (Kaw) Indians.

865. Ponziglione, Paul Mary.
"St. Francis' Institute, Osage Mission, Neosho Co., Kansas, July 1, 1878." *Woodstock Letters*, VII (1878), 184-187.

Reports the building of a stone school house, work among the Dacotahs, and tribal feuds.

866. Ponziglione, Paul Mary.
"Indian Missions. Neosho County, Kansas. December 15, 1878." *Woodstock Letters*, VIII (1879), 80-86.

Describes work among the Cherokees, now mostly Protestant, who were Catholic before moving west from Florida, Tennessee, and Georgia.

867. Ponziglione, Paul Mary.
"Indian Missions — Residence of St. Francis de Hieronymo, Osage Mission, Kansas, July 17th, 1879." *Woodstock Letters*, VIII (1879), 158-163.

Relates work among the Osage and other Indians in the Creek and Cherokee reservations.

868. Ponziglione, Paul Mary.
"Indian Missions. Letter of Fr. Ponziglione, Osage Mission, Kansas December 31st, 1879." *Woodstock Letters*, IX (1880), 118-124.

Discusses the rapid growth of the Catholic population, due to immigration and a petition for more Catholic missionaries and a Catholic school for the Indians. Notes that the United States Government instead sent the Indians to the reservation and gave them an Episcopalian minister.

869. Ponziglione, Paul Mary.
"Indian Missions. Letter from Fr. Ponziglione. Osage Mission, Kansas June 30th, 1880." *Woodstock Letters*, IX (1880), 213-226.

Describes his work among the Cherokees and his difficulties with the United States Agent and School Superintendent concerning administration of sacraments to children in school.

870. Ponziglione, Paul Mary.
"Letter of Father Ponziglione — Osage Mission, Neosho Co., Kansas. December 31st, 1880." *Woodstock Letters*, X (1881), 133-137.

A progress report for the year 1880, including a visit to San Francisco.

871. Ponziglione, Paul Mary.
"Letter from Father Ponziglione. Osage Mission, Neosho Co., Kansas, July 7th, 1881." *Woodstock Letters*, X (1881), 286-292.

Describes the life-style of the Osage and Kaw Indians.

872. Ponziglione, Paul Mary.
"Letter from Father P.M. Ponziglione. Osage Mission, Neosho Co., Kansas. December 31, 1881." *Woodstock Letters*, XI (1882), 163-169.

Progress report including a reference to the problem of alcohol among the Indians and the conversion of some Osage Indians.

873. Ponziglione, Paul Mary.
"Letter from Father Ponziglione. Osage Mission, Neosho Co., Kansas, July 1st, 1882." *Woodstock Letters*, XI (1882), 279-286.

The problem of education among Indian children. Settlement rights. Indians vs. United States Government.

874. Ponziglione, Paul Mary.
"Letter from Father P.M. Ponziglione. Osage Mission, Neosho Co., Kansas, December 31, 1882." *Woodstock Letters*, XII (1883), 112-116.

The tale of a strange navigator to Florida before Columbus. "An Historical Hypothesis."

875. Ponziglione, Paul Mary.
"Letter from Father Ponziglione. Osage Mission, Neosho County, Kansas, July 2, 1883." *Woodstock Letters*, XII (1883), 292-298.

Protestant proselytism among Catholic Indians. Epidemic among the Osages. Care for the sick.

876. Ponziglione, Paul Mary.
"History of the Society's Work in South Eastern Kansas." *Woodstock Letters*, XIII (1884), 19-32.

Gives a list of churches and missions established by the Jesuits, most of them by Fr. Ponziglione himself, and an account of their development since 1827. The historical notes are taken from the records of St. Francis Institute and the "History of the Catholic Church among the Indian Tribes" by J.G. Shea, New York, 1855. Includes a detailed resumé of the work of Fr. Ponziglione from 1851 to 1883.

877. Ponziglione, Paul Mary.
"Osage Mission, Kansas. June 6th, 1884." *Woodstock Letters*, XIII (1884), 309-320.

Describes the dedication of the new Church of St. Francis Hieronymo and includes some personal reminiscences by Ponziglione.

878. Ponziglione, Paul Mary.
"Osage Mission, Neosho County, December 31st, 1884." *Woodstock Letters*, XIV (1885), 230-242.

The story of the old St. Francis Church.

879. Ponziglione, Paul Mary.
"St. Francis' Institution. Osage Mission, Neosho County, Kansas. January 1st, 1884." *Woodstock Letters*, XIII (1886), 142-149.

Story of the mission starting in 1849 and dedication of the church's bell in memory of Fr. Shoenmakers.

880. Ponziglione, Paul Mary.
"St. Stephen's Mission. Shoshane Reservation, Wyoming Ter., September 20, 1886." *Woodstock Letters*, XV (1886), 278-284.

Author describes his transfer to the new mission, its organization and the building of the convent and residence.

881. Ponziglione, Paul Mary.
"Indian Traditions among the Osages." *Woodstock Letters*, XVIII (1889), 68-76.

Description of religion, family, organization and government within the Indian tribes.

882. Ponziglione, Paul Mary.
"The Arapahoe Indians, St. Stephen's Mission, Lander, Wyoming, April 14th, 1890." *Woodstock Letters*, XIX (1890), 312-316.

Describes winter in the mission and the devotion of the Indians to the Blessed Mother. Notes that feasts for the Indians are seen as signs of "goodwill" from the missionary.

883. Ponziglione, Paul Mary.
"The Arapahoes in Wyoming. A Letter from Fr. Ponziglione to the Editor. St. Stephen's Mission, Spokane Reservation, December 23, 1890." *Woodstock Letters*, XX (1891), 220-224.

Historical notes on St. Stephen's Mission.

884. Ponziglione, Paul Mary.
"The Arapahoes in Wyoming. A Letter from Fr. Ponziglione to the Editor. Wyoming, August 29, 1891." *Woodstock Letters*, XX (1891), 385-388.

Describes progress in education among Indian children.

885. Ponziglione, Paul Mary.
"Recollections of Father Van Quickenborne and the Osage Missions. A Letter from Fr. Ponziglione to the Editor. St. Ignatius College, Chicago, Ill. May 28, 1894." *Woodstock Letters*, XIV (1895), 37-42.

Notes on the work of Van Quickenborne, a pioneer in Kansas and Oklahoma.

886. Ponziglione, Paul Mary.
"Plan of a Reduction for our North American Indians." *Woodstock Letters*, XXV (1896), 353-361.

Ponziglione, who worked among the Indians for 50 years, describes the colonialist and aggressive attitude of the United States Government toward the Indians and why the "reduction" plan didn't materialize. The "reduction" was similar to the one adopted in Paraguay. The Act was signed by President Andrew Jackson and Jesuit Father General Roothmaan.

887. Ponziglione, Paul Mary.
"Reminiscences of Half a Century. A Last Letter from Father Ponziglione. St. Ignatius College, Chicago, November 28, 1899." *Woodstock Letters*, XXIX (1900), 267-272.

Describes how he first met the Jesuits from Missouri in Genoa, his trip to Rome under trying circumstances in 1848 and his voyage to the United States.

888. Porcelli, Clemente.
"I Francescani Italiani negli Stati Uniti e gli Emigrati." *Il Carroccio*, XXI (April, 1925), 432-434.

Twelve Franciscan parishes among Italian immigrants are sources of *italianità* and of a variety of social and religious services.

889. Power, Francis.
A Woman of the Bentivoglio. Notre Dame, 1930. Pp. 30.

Account of the saintly sisters, Annette and Constance Bentivoglio, known respectively as Sr. Mary Maddalelena and Sr. Mary Constance in the Order of the Poor Clares, who came to America in 1875 and established the Order in New Orleans and Omaha, where they worked with poor Italian immigrants.

890. P. P.
"La scuola del Buon Consiglio di Philadelphia." *Italica Gens*, I (Marzo, 1910), 49-58.

Description of establishment of Good Counsel School in Philadelphia by Fr. Angelo Caruso.

891. P. P.
"La Parrochia di S. Francesco e la Colonia Italiana di Hoboken, N.J." *Italica Gens*, II (Marzo, 1911), 137-140.

A history of the parish of St. Francis and the Italian community of Hoboken, New Jersey.

892. Prando, P.
"Montana Territory. Letter from Father Prando to Father Cataldo. St. Peter's Mission, M.T., January 13, 1881." *Woodstock Letters*, X (1881), 144-148.

Notes the cooperation of Protestants and the great number of conversions among the Indians.

893. Prando, P.

"Indian Missions. Mission of the Rocky Mountains. I. The Black-Feet Indians. Letter of Father P. Prando to Father J. Cataldo. Mission of St. Peter, July 28, 1881." *Woodstock Letters*, XII (1883), 34-37.

Relates the appreciation of the Indian chief for the love shown by the missionary toward the Indians.

894. Prando, P.

"II. Father Prando to Father Cataldo." *Woodstock Letters*, XII (1883), 37-43.

Description of the customs among the "Medicine-Men."

895. Prando, P.

"Rocky Mountains Missions. Letter from Father Prando to Rev. Fr. Cataldo, St. Peter's Mission." *Woodstock Letters*, XII (1883), 305-316.

Refers to the Christian cemetery, the fact that poligamy among Indians raises difficulties regarding Baptism, superstition, the fact that hunting privileges have been taken away by the United States Government, the situation of slavery in the reservation, and the expulsion of Fr. Prando from the mission-reservation by the United States Government.

896. Prando, P.

"Another Letter from Fr. Prando." *Woodstock Letters*, XII (1883), 317-326.

Fr. Prando notes that he has defied expulsion and gone back to his Indians, and describes his work at Birch Creek.

897. Prando, P.

"From the same to his Superior." *Woodstock Letters*, XII (1883), 326-330.

A letter written by Fr. Prando from Black Rock Camp describing his activities and noting that poligamy among the Indians raises difficulties regarding Baptism.

898. Pratt, W.W.

"Our Italian Mission in Passaic." *The Baptist Home Mission Monthly*, XXVI (September, 1904), 343.

Report on the new mission work among Italians in Passaic, New Jersey, with Rev. Bruno Bruni and Mrs. Eugenia E. Bruni, of Milan, Italy, as missionaries.

899. "Un Prete Italiano Primo Sindaco di un Comune degli Stati Uniti del Nord-America." *Italica Gens,* I (Marzo, 1910), 86-87.

Brief report on Fr. Pietro Bandini's election as mayor of Tontitown, Arkansas, taken from *The St. Louis Republic.*

900. Preziosi, Giovanni.
"Le Scuole Italiane negli Stati Uniti del Nord e la Scuola Parrocchiale del Buon Consiglio di Philadelphia." *Rivista Internazionale* (September, 1906).

Discusses Italian Catholic schools and specifically the parochial school of Our Lady of Good Counsel parish in Philadelphia.

901. Preziosi, Giovanni.
"Congregation of St. Charles Borromeo." *The Catholic Church in the United States of America.* 3 vols. New York: The Catholic Editing Company, 1912-1914. I, 186-192.

Brief account of the founding and work of the Congregation of St. Charles Borromeo. Founded by Bishop Giovanni Battista Scalabrini of Piacenza in 1887, the Congregation soon established itself in the most important Italian communities in the United States.

902. Prindiville, Kate Gertrude.
"Italy in Chicago." *The Catholic World,* LXXVII (July, 1903), 452-461.

This article deals with the work of the Rev. Edward M. Dunne among the Italian immigrants in Chicago's Holy Guardian Angels parish at the turn of the century. It gives details on the Sunday school established there.

903. *Pro Deo et Patria. Il Dono Inestimabile dell'Italia all'America. I Figli degli Italiani che Entrano nella Vita Americana — Attraverso la Porta della Cultura e della Religione.* New York: Società Fondatori della Scuola Italo-Americana della Chiesa dei SS. Cuori, 1926. Pp. 16.

Education and religion are described as the gates through which Italian immigrants enter American life.

904. "Il Problema dell'Emigrazione d'Innanzi al Parlamento." *La Civiltà Cattolica,* Serie XVII, V (1899), 129-145.

This article summarizes the pamphlet by Fr. Pietro Maldotti, "Relazione sull'Operato della Missione del Porto di Genova dal 1894 al 1898 e sui due viaggi al Brasile," originally published in Genoa in 1898 and reprinted in

Studi Emigrazione, V (Febbraio-Giugno, 1968), 417-480. The pamphlet describes Maldotti's work at the Port of Genoa among the immigrants during the years 1894-98 and his two trips to Brazil to survey the condition of the immigrants.

905. Properzi, Nazareno.
"Uno Nuova Missione Italiana tra le colonie del Massachusetts."
Italica Gens, VII (Gennaio-Giugno, 1916), 78-82.

Regarding the establishment of the Church of St. Anthony of Padua in Somerville, Massachusetts.

906. *Prospetto di Alcuni Regolamenti per il Bene Spirituale e Temporale della Congregazione del SS. Sacramento esistente nella Chiesa della Madonna del Rosario in Kumbuldt* [sic] *Street, Brooklyn, N.Y. Stabilita nel 1° Gennaio del'anno 1901.* Brooklyn, N.Y.: 1902. Pp. 35.

An example of a church-related voluntary organization's statutes.

907. Protestant Episcopal Church in the U.S.A. — Province of New England: Committee on the Various Races. *Report.* Boston: 1915. Pp. 14.

A contemporary view of Italian immigrants: "The Italians are lapsed or lapsing by the thousands from the Church of their ancestors, and we have the means of saving them. We have several Italian priests in our orders in New England. We need more. Here is a great opportunity. But in many of our ordinary parishes our clergy should seek out the Italians. A devoted woman visitor is invaluable. Work among the children is especially important...Italians understand the English Eucharist, when celebrated with lights, and simple Catholic ceremonial. Of course our Morning and Evening Prayers are meaningless to them. The word 'Protestant' signifies to them no faith, no sacraments, almost no God" (p. 7).

908. Provincia Minoritica dell'Immacolata Concezione del Nord America. *L'Opera dei Francescani Italiani a Favore degli Emigrati negli Stati Uniti d'America, 1855-1925.* Roma: Stabilimento d'Arti Fotomeccaniche Grimaldi & Mercandetti, 1925. Pp. 96.

Pictorial book prepared for the Vatican Missionary Exhibit of the 1925 Holy Year. It presents the history of the Italian Franciscans in the United States from their beginning in the diocese of Buffalo. It lists all priests and parishes entrusted to the Order for the care of Italian immigrants, gives statistics from the "Status Animarum" reports, and describes buildings and parish activities.

909. Pucci, Paolo.
"Scoperta e Riconosciuta la Tomba di Padre Eusebio Chini." *Italiani nel Mondo*, XXII (25 November, 1966), 20-23.

News item on the discovery of the tomb of Fr. Chini (Kino).

910. Purcell, Richard J.
"Mengarini, Gregory." *Dictionary of American Biography*, XI (1933), 535-536.

Brief biography of Mengarini, born in Rome in 1811. He entered the Society of Jesus in 1828, was ordained a priest in 1840, and volunteered for the Indian missions in America. He worked in several Jesuit Indian missions, became fluent in Indian dialects, and wrote several Indian grammars and dictionaries. He died in 1886.

911. Purcell, Richard J.
"Morini, Austin John." *Dictionary of American Biography*, XIII (1934), 190.

Brief biography of Morini, born in Florence, Italy, in 1826. He entered the Servite Order in 1844 and was ordained a priest in 1850. Invited by Bishop Joseph Melchior of Green Bay, Wisconsin, to establish a foundation in his diocese, the Servites sent Morini with a group of religious to the United States in 1870. Morini took charge of a congregation at Menasha, Wisconsin, and later established Our Lady of Sorrows Church in Chicago as a mother house. Subsequently, the Servites spread to other parts of the United States. Morini died in 1909.

912. Purcell, Richard J.
"Nobili, John." *Dictionary of American Biography*, XIII (1934), 536.

Brief biography of Nobili, born in Rome in 1812. He entered the Society of Jesus in 1826, was ordained a priest in 1843, volunteered for the American missions, and accompanied Fr. Pierre-Jean DeSmet to the Rocky Mountains. In 1849 he was sent to San Francisco where he soon established the College of Santa Clara, becoming its first president. He died in 1856.

913. Purcell, Richard J.
"Palladino, Lawrence Benedict." *Dictionary of American Biography*, XIV (1934), 170-171.

Brief biography of Palladino, born in Dilecto, Italy, in 1837. He entered the Society of Jesus in 1855 and was ordained a priest in 1863. Volunteering for the California missions, he taught at St. Ignatius College in San Francisco and at Santa Clara and was afterwards assigned to the Indian missions in the Rocky Mountains. In 1894 he published *Indian and White in theNorthwest; or a History of Catholicity in Montana*, a primary source of information for the state. He died in 1927.

914. Purcell, Richard J.
"Ravalli, Antonio." *Dictionary of American Biography*, XV (1935), 393-394.

Brief biography of Ravalli, born in Ferrara, Italy, in 1811. He entered the Society of Jesus in 1827 and was ordained a priest in 1843. In 1844 he went to the Indian missions in the Rocky Mountains. He died in 1884.

915. Ragaru, L.
"Extract from a letter of Fr. Ragaru to Fr. Cataldo. St. Michael's, Alaska, June 30th, 1888." *Woodstock Letters*, XVII (1888), 328-329.

Description of work among the Indians of the Yukon River.

916. Rahill, Peter J.
"New Orleans Under Bishop Rosati." *Social Justice Review*, LX (November, 1967), 244-250.

This article deals with Rosati's work in New Orleans in the 1820s.

917. Rahill, Peter J.
"St. Louis Under Bishop Rosati." *Misouri Historical Review*, LXVI (July, 1972), 495-519.

Brief account of Rosati's work as Bishop of St. Louis.

918. Rappagliosi, Carlo.
Memorie del P. Filippo Rappagliosi, D.C.D.G., missionario apostolico nelle Montagne Rocciose. Roma: Tipografia di Bernardo Morini, 1879. Pp. 152.

This volume, in the Western Americana collection of Yale University, gives descriptive information on the Jesuit missions in the Rocky Mountains, the customs of the Indians and their religion. It contains a diary of Fr. Rappagliosi, a Jesuit missionary born in 1841 in Rome, who came to work among the Indians in 1873 and died in 1878, leaving a great impact because of his holy life.

919. *Rapporto della Società di San Raffaele Arcangelo per la Protezione degli Italiani Immigranti, Boston, Mass., 1902-1904*. Boston: Stamperia Marino & Freda, 1905. Pp. 17.

Report of activities on behalf of Italian immigrants by the Boston Branch of
the St. Raphael's Society for Italian immigrants.

920. Reagan, Nicholas J.
"The Italian Custody of the Immaculate Conception." *The Catholic
Church in the United States of America*. 3 vols. New York: The
Catholic Editing Company, 1912-1914. I, 236-239.

Brief account of the founding and work of the Franciscan Italian Custody of
the Immaculate Conception. Erected on March 1, 1861, the Custody includes
various parishes in several American cities. Its task is the care of Italian
immigrants in the United States.

921. Reilly, Louis W.
"Father Ravalli, Pioneer Indian Missionary." *The Catholic World*,
CXXV (April, 1927), 67-73.

This article deals with the work of Jesuit Fr. Anthony Ravalli at St. Mary's
Indian Mission in Montana, as well as other missions, during the period 1843
to 1884.

922. *Relatio Collationum quas Romae coram S.C. de P.F. Praefecto
habuerunt Archiepiscopi pluresque Episcopi Statum Foederatorum
Americae*. Baltimore: Foley Bros., 1883. Pp. 35.

Text of the minutes of the Roman meetings held during November-December,
1883, in preparation for the Third Plenary Council of Baltimore, between
officials of the Sacred Congregation for the Propagation of the Faith and
American Bishops. For an English translation, see *The Jurist*, XI (January to
October, 1951), 121-132; 302-312; 417-424; 538-547. Instruction to the American
Hierarchy from Propaganda Fide. Chapter XII deals with Italian migrants
and the Church's care for them.

923. "Relations of the 'Medicine-Men' with the Evil Spirit." *Woodstock
Letters*, III (1874), 213-216.

Includes a letter by Fr. Urbano Grassi from Attanam, Washington Territory,
dated May 26, 1874, which relates magic practices among the Indians.

924. "Religion of Lucky Pieces, Witches and the Evil Eye." *World Outlook*,
III (October, 1917), 24-25.

Comments on popular religious practices of Italian immigrants.

925. *La Religiosità Meridionale. Selezione CSER* (6-7 Giugno-luglio, 1972).
Roma: Centro Studi Emigrazione, 1972. Pp. vii-159.

Analysis of the southern Italian religious mentality based on secondary sources.

926. *Report of the Committee on Americanization of the Italian Baptist Missionary Association.* New York: Americanization Committee, 1918. Pp. 22. Reprinted, *Protestant Evangelism Among Italians in America.* New York: Arno Press, 1975.

The report states that of all the means which are being used for the work of americanization that of evangelization is the cheapest for its prosecution, the quickest for its results, and the most fruitful for its achievements. Means are suggested for spreading americanization.

927. "Rev. John B. Guida." *Woodstock Letters*, XLIX (1920), 122-126.

Obituary of Fr. Guida (1828-1919) a Jesuit missionary born in Nola near Naples. He was the founder of St. Peter's Church in Denver, Colorado, taught at Georgetown College, and was briefly arrested in a case of mistaken identity in 1865 as assassin of Lincoln.

928. Reynolds, Minnie J.
"The Italian and His Church at Home." *The Missionary Review of the World*, N.S., XX (August, 1907), 607-610.

This article was originally written for *The Home Missionary*. The author, a Protestant, describes the attitude of the inhabitants of Trapani, Sicily toward the Catholic Church. She concludes that many Sicilians have lost respect for the Church and do not practice their religion.

929. Reynolds, Minnie J.
"The Religious Renaissance in Italy." *The Missionary Review of the World*, N.S., XXIV (August, 1911), 597-603.

Although focusing on the Italian religious scene, the author argues that Italian immigrants are open to evangelical work and states that a sign of Italian religious renaissance is the fact that over 100 of 220 Italian Protestant Churches in the United States were started by nuclei of Italian Waldensians.

930. *Riassunto del Convegno degli Anziani delle chiese inorganizzate tenuto nella chiesa Cristiana, 224 Hudson St., Buffalo, N.Y. nelle giornate 6 e 7 Settembre, 1942.* Pp. 6.

Summary report of a meeting of elders of Italian independent Christian Churches in the United States.

931. Ricci, Eugenia.
Il Padre Eugenio Chino, esploratore missionario della California e dell'Arizona. Milano: Ed. Alpes, 1930. Pp. 184.

Background and activities of Fr. Kino. Echo of his work in Europe. Bibliography on Kino's published and unpublished works in chronological order. Sixteen illustrations.

932. Ricciardelli, Raffaele.
Vita del Servo di Dio Felice de Andreis. Rome: 1923.

The most complete work on the early years of the Congregation of the Mission in the United States based entirely on primary sources in the Archives of the Procurator General of the Congregation of the Mission, Rome. Fr. Rosati figures prominently in this narrative which closes with the death of Felix deAndreis in 1820.

933. Riis, Jacob A.
"Feast-Days in Little Italy." *The Century,* LVIII (August, 1899), 491-499. Reprinted, Wayne Moquin, ed. *A Documentary History of the Italian Americans.* New York: Praeger Publishers, 1974.

Colorful description of feast-day celebrations in New York's "Little Italy" by the Danish-born journalist, Jacob Riis.

934. Riordan, Joseph W.
The First Half Century of St. Ignatius Church and College. San Francisco: H.S. Crocker, 1905. Pp. 389.

Indicates major role of Italian Jesuits in San Francisco.

935. Rizzato, Remo.
L'Apostolo degli Emigrati. Mons. Giovanni Battista Scalabrini. Providence: Service-Plus Press, 1946. Pp. 128.

Popular biography of Scalabrini.

936. Rizzato, Remo.
Figure di Missionari Scalabriniani. New York: D'Alteri's Press, 1948. Pp. 122.

Sketches of Scalabrinian missionaries among Italian immigrants, Filiopietistic.

937. Rizzatti, Ferruccio.
"L'Italiano Padre Eusebio Chini, Pionere, Esploratore, Civilizzatore." *L'Illustrazione Italiana,* VIII (Maggio 25, 1930), 911-913.

On Kino as explorer.

938. Robbins, Jane E.
"Italian Today, American To-Morrow." *The Outlook*, LXXX (June 10, 1905), 382-384.

In this article Robbins describes the Italian immigrants to the United States and generally praises their finer qualities. The author argues that in time the Italians will americanize.

939. Roberto, Maria Domenica.
Francesca Saverio Cabrini. La Santa degli Emigrati. Firenze: Casa Editrice Salani, 1939. Pp. 372.

Popularly written biography of Frances Xavier Cabrini.

940. Roemer, Theodore.
The Catholic Church in the United States. St. Louis, Mo.: B. Herder Book Co., 1950. Pp. viii-444.

A textbook on the history of the church in the United States for use in seminaries and colleges with a superficial reference to the Italian immigrants and the church.

941. Rolle, Andrew F.
"The Italian Moves Westward: Jesuit Missionaries Formed the Vanguard of Italy's Many-Sided Impact on the Frontier." *Montana, the Magazine of Western History*, XVI (January, 1966), 13-24.

Brief account of Italians, including missionaries, who migrated to Montana.

942. Rolle, Andrew F.
The Immigrant Upraised. Italian Adventurers and Colonists in an Expanding America. Norman, Oklahoma: University of Oklahoma Press, 1968. Pp. xvi-391.

This is a study of Italian immigrants to the United States who migrated westward, beyond the Atlantic seaboard. Rolle shows that these immigrants, unlike the majority who stayed in the eastern cities, suffered little discrimination, were readily assimilated, and rose rapidly in both the economic and social spheres. There are references to religion and the Catholic Church throughout the book. Appendix A, pp. 339-343 is titled "Italian Clerics in the Spanish Southwest."

943. Rolle, Andrew F.
The American Italians: Their History and Culture. Minorities in American Life Series. Belmont, California: Wadsworth Publishing Company, Inc., 1972. Pp. ix-130.

Useful, compact survey of Italians in the United States. Chapter 6, pp. 37-46, is titled "Missionaries," and chapter 11, pp. 95-107, is titled "The Professions, Culture, and the Spiritual Life."

944. Rosati, Joseph.
Life of the Very Rev. Felix De Andreis, C.M., First Superior of the Congregation of the Mission in the United States and Vicar General of Upper Louisiana. Chiefly from Sketches written by the Right Rev. Joseph Rosati, C.M., First Bishop of St. Louis, Mo. With an Introduction by The Most Rev. John J. Kain, D.D., Archbishop of St. Louis, Mo. St. Louis, Mo.: B. Herder, 1900. Pp. xiii-308.

Kain notes in his introduction: "The Rev. Francis Burlando, C.M., director of the Sisters of Charity in the United States, translated Bishop Rosati's manuscript into English and had it published in Baltimore in 1861. The present publication is Fr. Burlando's translation, with some corrections and additions."

945. Rose, Philip M.
The Italians in America. New York: George H. Doran Company, 1922. Pp. vii-155. Reprinted, New York: Arno Press, 1975.

P.M. Rose was the supervisor of Italian congregational work in Connecticut and pastor of the first Italian Congregational Church, Hartford, Connecticut. In this book he analyzes Italian immigration and makes recommendations for a more effective Protestant effort among the immigrants.

946. Roselli, Bruno.
"An Arkansas Epic." *The Century*, XCIX (January, 1920), 377-386.

This is an account of the founding and development of the Italian colonies of Sunnyside and Tontitown in Arkansas. These agricultural colonies were given attention both in the American and the Italian press.

947. Rosmini, Emilia de Sanctis.
La Beata Francesca Saverio Cabrini. Roma: Istituto Grafico Tiberino, 1938. Pp. 389.

Standard popular biography of Francis X. Cabrini and her social and educational activities.

948. Rossi, Jeremiah.
"The Rocky Mountains. Letter from the Mission of the Sacred Heart. December 5th, 1887." *Woodstock Letters*, XVII (1888), 73-81.

Report from the mission among the Coeur d'Alêne Indians with descriptions of Indian customs and mentality, their devotion to the Black-Robe ("They follow the Gospel of Fr. Cataldo"), the school program for the Indian children, and Christian feasts among the Indians.

949. Rossi, Peter H. and Alice S.
"Parochial School Education in America." *Daedalus*, 90 (Spring, 1961), 300-328.

Contains a few interesting observations concerning Italian attendance in Catholic parochial schools.

950. Rosso, Giuseppe.
Italiani esploratori d'America (1492-1706). Genova: ed. Super, 1950. Pp. 40.

Series of sketches of Italian explorers, including some missionaries in America.

951. Rothensteiner, John.
History of the Archdiocese of St. Louis In its Various States of Development from A.D. 1673 to A.D. 1928. 2 vols. St. Louis, Mo.: Press of Blackwell Wielandy Co., 1928. Pp. xviii-859, xii-840.

This is the standard history of the Archdiocese of St. Louis. Vol. 1, pp. 419-813, treats the period of Bishop Joseph Rosati, who was the first bishop of the St. Louis diocese. Good also for Jesuit activities out of St. Louis.

952. Rozewicz, A.J.
"Another Problem Like the Italian." *The Ecclesiastical Review*, LXX (April, 1924), 381-386.

The author refers to the article by John Zarrilli, "A Suggestion for the Solution of the Italian Problem," *The Ecclesiastical Review*, LXX (January, 1924), 70-77, and to an article entitled "Pastoral Care Among Poles in America," in the January, 1924 issue of the *Polish Ecclesiastical Review*. He notes the similarity between the Italian and the Polish problems.

953. Rummel, Leo.
History of the Catholic Church in Wisconsin. Madison, Wisconsin: Knights of Columbus, 1976. Pp. viii-261.

Contains a few superficial comments on Italians and religion on pp. 112-114. Mentions Fr. Mazzuchelli's work in chapter 2.

954. Russo, Nicholas.
"The Origin and Progress of our Italian Mission in New York. A Letter from Father Russo, 303 Elizabeth St., New York, January 29,

1896." *Woodstock Letters*, XXV (1896), 135-143.

Description of "Little Italy" in New York and of the frictions between the Italian immigrants and the local church. Mentions Protestant proselytism, the eviction of some Italian families in order to build Our Lady of Loreto Church, and the mentality, difficulties and response received in working with the Italians.

955. Russo, Nicholas J.
"Three Generations of Italians in New York City: Their Religious Acculturation." *The Italian Experience in the United States*. Edited by S.M. Tomasi and M.H. Engel. New York: The Center for Migration Studies of New York, Inc., 1970. Pp. 195-209.

The author says that the purpose of this study is "to reconcile apparently incompatible sociological findings with regards to immigrants and their children, by 1) isolating the religious factor in the assimilation process of the Italian-Americans; 2) evaluating the role of the Catholic Church in their acculturation to American life; and 3) delineating a before-and-after situation of the religious practices and attitudes of the Italian-Americans, who were contrasted with the Irish as the dominant Catholic group in New York City" (p. 195.).

956. Russo, Nicholas J.
"From Mezzogiorno to Metropolis: Brooklyn's New Italian Immigrants — A Sociological, Pastoral, Academic Approach." *Studies in Italian American Social History*. Edited by Francesco Cordasco. Totowa, N.J.: Rowman and Littlefield, 1975. Pp. 118-131.

Describes distribution of new Italian immigrants in New York and the pastoral response of the Diocese of Brooklyn.

957. Ryan, John.
"Reminiscences of Some Distinguished Men of Science Connected in the Past with Georgetown College." *Woodstock Letters*, XXX (1901), 94-103.

Personal sketches of Frs. A. Secchi, J. Curley, B. Sestini, J.B. Pianciani, and J.A. Grassi.

958. Ryska, Justin M.
"The Memoirs of Austin Morini and the Arrival of the Servites in the Middle Western United States." *Studi Storici dell'Ordine dei Servi di Maria*, 12 (1962), 294-313.

This article deals with the founding of the Servite Order in the United States as related in the memoirs of Fr. Austin Morini, father of the American Servites. Morini belonged to the Tuscan Province of the Servite Order, began his American missionary work in the Diocese of Green Bay in 1870, and established the first Italian parish in Chicago.

959. Sabetti, A.
"Father Aloysius Sabetti. An Autobiography with Reminiscences of his Former Students." *Woodstock Letters*, XXIX (1900), 208-233.

Sabetti, born in 1839 in Roseto (Foggia), arrived in New York in 1871 and for many years taught with distinction at Woodstock College where he died in 1898.

960. S. Congregatio Concilii.
"Epistula Circularis ad Episcopos Italos et Americanos, Relate ad Sacerdotes Italos, qui ad Americanas Regiones Emigrant." *American Ecclesiastical Review*, XVIII (February, 1898), 193-195.

This is the text of directives sent by the Holy See to Italian and American bishops regarding Italian priests who emigrate to America. The document is dated July 27, 1890.

961. S. Congregatio Consistorialis.
"Litterae Circulares ad R. Mos Ordinarios Dioecesum Italiae, De Spirituali Emigrantium Cura." *Acta Apostolicae Sedis*, VI (December 30, 1914), 699-701.

Letter written by Cardinal G. DeLai, Secretary of the Sacred Consistorial Congregation, on December 6, 1914, to the bishops of Italy asking them for financial support and the names of priests interested in working for Italian immigrants.

962. S. Congregatio Consistorialis.
"Notificatio Circa Missionarios Operis 'De Adsistentia Operariorum Italicorum Ad Exteras Europae Regiones Migrantium.'" *Acta Apostolicae Sedis*, VII (February 27, 1915), 95-96.

This is a memorandum issued by the Sacred Consistorial Congregation regarding the supervision of priests who are chosen to minister to Italian workmen who emigrate to countries outside Europe. It is dated January 31, 1915. Also reported in *The Ecclesiastical Review*, LII (May, 1915), 585-586.

963. S. Congregatio Consistorialis.
"Litterae Circulares Ad R. Mos Americae Ordinarios, De Emigrantium

Italorum Cura." *Acta Apostolicae Sedis*, VII (March 31, 1915), 145-146.

Letter written by Cardinal C. DeLai on February 22, 1915, to the American bishops relating to the care of Italian immigrants. Also reported in *The Ecclesiastical Review*, LII (June, 1915), 710-712.

964. Sacra Congregatio Consistorialis.
"Lettera Circolare Ai Rev. Mi Arcivescovi E Vescovi Di Calabria Sulla Costituzione Di Patronati Ecclesiastici In Pro Degli Emigranti." *Acta Apostolicae Sedis*, VIII (December 1, 1916), 437-438.

Letter written by Cardinal G. DeLai, Secretary of the Sacred Consistorial Congregation, on November 24, 1916, announcing the formation of a church organization to assist immigrants in Calabria.

965. Sacra Congregatio Consistorialis.
"Notificazione Circa la Costituzione di un Prelato per l'Emigrazione Italiana." *Acta Apostolicae Sedis*, XII (November 2, 1920), 534-535.

Letter written by Cardinal C. DeLai, Secretary of the Sacred Consistorial Congregation, on October 23, 1920, announcing the establishment of the office of Prelate for Italian Emigration and appointing Michele Cerrati to that position. The Prelate was to supervise the clergy working among Italian immigrants and be the superior of the college established in Rome to train priests to work among Italian immigrants.

966. Sacra Congregatio Consistorialis.
"De Pontificio Collegio Sacerdotum Pro Italis Ad Externa Emigrantibus." *Acta Apostolicae Sedis*, XIII (June 18, 1921), 309-311.

Letter written by Cardinal C. DeLai, Secretary of the Sacred Consistorial Congregation, on May 26, 1921, relating to the establishment of a pontifical college in Rome to train priests for work among Italian immigrants.

967. Sacra Congregatio Consistorialis.
"Communicatio De Commigrantibus Ex Italia Tessera Ecclesiastica Muniendis." *The Ecclesiastical Review*, LXVIII (May, 1923), 495-497.

This is the text of an Instruction from Cardinal DeLai, Secretary of the Consistorial Congregation, in which the Ordinaries and parish priests of Italy are advised to provide persons emigrating from Italy with a certificate of their Baptism, Confirmation, and "status." It is dated January 26, 1923.

968. Salesian Fathers of Ven. Don Bosco.
New Italian Church of SS. Peter and Paul, San Francisco, Cal. — *1924*. Pp. 63.

An illustrated history of the festivities for the dedication of the church with a useful article on the work of the Salesians in San Francisco among Italian immigrants.

969. Salvatierra, Juan María de.
Selected Letters about Lower California. Translated and annotated by Ernest J. Burrus. Los Angeles: Dawson's Book Shop, 1971. Pp. 279.

Twenty-two reports and letters written by Salvatierra and dealing with Baja, California. Salvatierra worked from 1697 to 1717 to establish and consolidate the missions of Baja, California. It is from the letters and reports he wrote during those years that the selection was made for this book.

970. Salvemini, Gaetano.
Italian Fascist Activities in the United States. Edited by Philip V. Cannistraro. New York: Center for Migration Studies, 1977. Pp. lii-267.

This previously unpublished study of the Italian Fascist movement in the United States from 1922 to 1936 contains a chapter on Roman Catholic priests and the Fascist movement in America, pp. 145-164.

971. Sanderlin, George.
"The Wide World of Francesca Cabrini." *The Ave Maria*, LXXVIII (October 17, 1953), 15, 17-19.

This is a popularly written biographical sketch of St. Frances Xavier Cabrini, who worked among the Italian immigrants during the period of mass migration to the United States.

972. "The Santa Maria Institute: Laymen's Missionary League and Italians in Cincinnati." *America*, XXVI (January 19, 1921), 118.

On the role of the Santa Maria Institute established by Sr. Blandina Segale for the children of Italian immigrants.

973. Sardone, Francesco G.
"Il Prelato per l'Emigrazione Italiana." *Il Carroccio*, XXI (Maggio, 1925), 544-546.

This article deals with Monsignor Rocco Beltrami, who was appointed Prelate for Italian Emigration in 1925. The author gives a brief account of the role of the Prelate for Italian Emigration, a position established by Pope Benedict XV in October, 1920.

974. Sartorio, Enrico C.
Social and Religious Life of Italians in America. Boston: The Christopher Publishing House, 1918. Pp. 149. Reprinted, Clifton, New Jersey: Augustus M. Kelley Publishers, 1974.

The author, a Protestant minister who came to the United States as a young man, deals with the following topics relating to Italian immigration: chapter I, Life in the Italian Colonies; chapter II, Americanization; chapter III, The Religion of Italians; chapter IV, Churches and Missions in America; and chapter V, American Leadership.

975. Sartorio, Henry C.
"Work Among Italians." *The Churchman* (September 1, 1917), 273.

Description of work among Italians by a noted author and Protestant minister.

976. Sassi, Costantino.
Parrocchia della Madonna di Pompei in New York. Notizie storiche dei primi cinquant' anni dalla sua fondazione: 1892-1942. Marino: Santa Lucia, 1946. Pp. 102.

This is a history of the church of Our Lady of Pompei in Greenwich Village, New York City, from its foundatin in 1892 to 1942. It is well written and useful for information on the Italian community in lower Manhattan during this period. See Michael A. Cosenza. "Our Lady of Pompei in Greenwich Village. History of the Parish, 1892-1967 and St. Frances Xavier Cabrini's Story." *75th Anniversary, Our Lady of Pompei in Greenwich Village, May 7th, 1967.* New York: The Tenny Press, 1967.

977. Sayno, A.
"Buffalo e la sua Colonia Italiana." *Italica Gens,* VII (Gennaio-Giugno, 1916), 82-86.

Description of the development of the Italian settlement in Buffalo, New York. Mentions churches and schools.

978. Scalabrini, Angelo, ed.
Mons. Giovanni Battista Scalabrini, Vescovo di Piacenza. Trent'Anni di Apostolato: Memorie e Documenti. Roma: Manuzio, 1909. Pp. 699.

This is an important collection of newspaper articles, speeches, and comments relating to the life and work of Bishop Giovanni Battista Scalabrini of Piacenza, Italy. Pages 314-379 and 380-515 give material relating to Scalabrini's work on behalf of the Italian immigrants.

979. Scalabrini, Giovanni Battista.
Prima Conferenza Sulla Emigrazione. Piacenza: Istituto Cristoforo Colombo, n.d. Pp. 18.

This is the text of a conference given at Rome, February 8, 1891. In it, Scalabrini discusses aspects of Italian immigration and describes some of his efforts on behalf of the Italian immigrants.

980. Scalabrini, Giovanni Battista.
Ai Missionari per gl'Italiani nelle Americhe. Piacenza: Tip. G. Tedeschi, 1892. Pp. 15.

An official letter of Bishop Scalabrini outlining the purpose of the work of his missionaries among Italian immigrants in the United States. It emphasizes social and religious assistance.

981. Scalabrini, Giovanni Battista.
"L'Emigrazione Italiana in America." *Studi Emigrazione*, V (Febbraio-Giugno, 1968), 199-230.

This pamphlet, written by Bishop Giovanni Battista Scalabrini of Piacenza in 1887, deals with the problems associated with increasing Italian emigration. The Bishop calls for the establishment of an association to assist the emigrants.

982. Scalabrini, Giovanni Battista.
"Il Disegno di Legge sull'Emigrazione Italiana." *Studi Emigrazione*, V (Febbraio-Giugno, 1968), 231-257.

This pamphlet, issued in 1888 in the form of an open letter to Paolo Carcano, a senator in the Italian Parliament, discusses the immigration bill then under consideration by the Italian Parliament.

983. Scalabrini, Giovanni Battista.
"Dell'Assistenza alla Emigrazione Nazionale e degli Statuti che ci Provvedono." *Studi Emigrazione*, V (Febbraio-Giugno, 1968), 259-269.

Published in 1891, this was a report made by Bishop Scalabrini at the Exposition of Palermo. The Bishop summarizes his efforts on behalf of the Italian immigrants both in Italy and the Americas.

984. Scalabrini, Giovanni Battista.
"L'Italia all'Estero." *Studi Emigrazione*, V (Febbraio-Giugno, 1968), 271-289.

This is the text of a conference given by Bishop Scalabrini of Piacenza at the Italian General Exposition held at Turin in 1898. In his conference, Scalabrini noted some of the weaknesses of the immigration law of 1888 and called for speedy passage in Parliament of a new, more comprehensive immigration law.

985. Scalabrini, Giovanni Battista.
"L'Emigrazione degli Operai Italiani." *Studi Emigrazione*, V (Febbraio-Giugno, 1968), 291-302.

This is the text of a conference given by Bishop Scalabrini of Piacenza at the 1899 Italian Catholic Congress held at Ferrara. In his conference, Scalabrini called for the passage by the Italian Parliament of a more comprehensive and effective law to regulate immigration.

986. *Schema Decretorum Concilii Plenarii Baltimoreasis Tertii.* Baltimore: 1884. Pp. 250.

In this summary of the decrees to be discussed at the Third Council of Baltimore, Italian immigration was to be considered in chapter 1 of Title VIII. It was proposed that Italian speaking priests be provided for the immigrants and that the latter be directed to agricultural colonies. See Frederick J. Zwierlein. *The Life and Letters of Bishop McQuaid, Prefaced with the History of Catholic Rochester Before His Episcopate.* 3 vols. Rochester, N.Y.: The Art Print Shop, 1925-1927. II, 333-335.

987. Schiavo, Giovanni E.
The Italians in Chicago: A Study in Americanization. Chicago, Ill.: Italian American Publishing Co., 1928. Pp. 207. Reprinted, New York: Arno Press, 1975.

Chapter X, pp. 75-81, is titled "Religious Activities."

988. Schiavo, Giovanni.
The Italians in Missouri. Chicago: Italian American Publishing Co., 1929. Pp. 216. Reprinted, New York: Arno Press, 1975.

Includes chapters on religious activities of Italians in Missouri.

989. Schiavo, Giovanni.
"Father Joseph M. Cataldo. Founder of Gonzaga University and Father of the City of Spokane." *Atlantica*, (May, 1930), 5-8.

Biographical sketch of Jesuit Father Cataldo, "the last of the great Italian pioneers in the United States."

990. Schiavo, Giovanni.
"Father Eusebio Francesco Chini. Scientist, Explorer and Civilizer of Arizona." *Atlantica* (October, 1930), 13-17.

Brief sketch of Father Chini, emphasizing the fact that Chini was an Italian.

991. Schiavo, Giovanni.
"Who Discovered Arizona? The Story of Fra Marco da Nizza." *Atlantica* (November, 1930), 112-114.

Schiavo argues that Friar Marco da Nizza "aroused the interest of the great Coronado in the country north of Mexico, and persuaded that explorer to extend his travels in that direction."

992. Schiavo, Giovanni.
"Father Giovanni Salvaterra. The Apostle of Lower California." *Atlantica* (December, 1930), 160-162.

Brief biographical sketch of Fr. Giovanni Salvaterra, Jesuit missionary in lower California in the late seventeenth and early eighteenth centuries.

993. Schiavo, Giovanni.
"Father Samuel C. Mazzuchelli." *Atlantica* (August-September, 1931), 60-61.

Brief biographical sketch of Fr. Mazzuchelli and his work as a Dominican missionary in the American Midwest from 1830 to 1864.

994. Schiavo, Giovanni.
The Italians in America Before the Civil War. New York: Vigo Press, 1934. Pp. 399. Reprinted, New York: Arno Press, 1975.

Includes descriptions of Fra Marco da Nizza, Fr. Eusebio Francesco Chino, the Waldenses, Fr. Angelo Inglesi, "Founder of the Society for the Propagation of the Faith," Bishops Giuseppe Rosati of St. Louis, Ignazio Persico of Savannah, and Francesco Porro of New Orleans, Fr. Samuel Mazzuchelli, Fr. Charles Constantine Pise, and Fr. Giuseppe Maria Finotti.

995. S[chiavo], G[iovanni].
"An Italian Martyr in New York. Father Francesco Bressani — 1612-1672." *The Vigo Review,* II (February, 1939), 11, 17.

Brief sketch of Fr. Bressani, early Jesuit missionary in North America. The author says that he was "the first man to describe Niagara Falls, thirty years before Hennepin, and the second Catholic priest to visit the present site of the city of New York, Jogues having been the first."

996. Schiavo, Giovanni E.
    Italian-American History. 2 vols. New York: Vigo Press, 1947-1949. Pp. 604, 1056. Reprinted, New York: Arno Press, 1975.

    Volume 2, *The Italian Contribution to the Catholic Church in America*, is a massive compilation of information on Italian priests and parishes in the United States. The presentation is along the line of brief biographical sketches of individuals and institutions with no effort at either synthetic unity or historical interpretation.

997. Schick, Robert.
    "Father Bandini: Missionary in the Ozarks." *The Ave Maria*, N.S., LXVI (December 20, 1947), 782-786.

    This is a brief account of the founding of the Italian settlement at Tontitown, Arkansas in 1898 and Fr. Pietro Bandini's role in it.

998. Schisa, Hector.
    "Italians and the Gospel." *The Baptist Home Mission Monthly*, XXX (March, 1908), 109-111.

    Schisa, missionary pastor at Uniontown, Pennsylvania, describes "the welcome which the Italians give to evangelical work, to the Gospel itself, to the manner of understanding it, of accepting it, and of the hopes there are in it."

999. Schoenberg, Wilfred P.
    Jesuits in Montana, 1840-1960. Portland, Oregon: The Oregon-Jesuit, 1960. Pp. 120.

    This booklet gives brief sketches of various Jesuit Indian missions in Montana during the period 1840-1960. It has some valuable information on the work of Italian Jesuit missionaries from the Turin Province in Italy.

1000. "La Scuola Parrocchiale dell'Assunta a Chicago." *Italica Gens*, I (Febbraio, 1910), 23-30.

    Report on the Italian parochial school of Assumption parish in Chicago.

1001. Segale, Blandina.
    At the End of the Santa Fe Trail. Milwaukee: The Bruce Publishing Company, 1948. Pp. xi-298.

    The journal of Sister Blandina, a Sister of Charity, dealing with her work in the American Southwest from 1872 to 1892. This is a reprint of a work originally published in 1932.

1002. Semeria, Giovanni.
"Che Cosa Fanno i Nostri Preti?" *Il Carroccio*, XIX (Maggio, 1924), 560-562.

Semeria praises the work of Italian priests in America as defenders of true *italianita* and refers in particular to Fr. Jannuzzi, a Scalabrinian pastor in New York.

1003. Senner, Joseph H.
"Immigration from Italy." *North American Review*, CLXII (June, 1896), 651-659.

Senner notes that Italian priests have to use English in their ministry to the second generation.

1004. Serafini, Vincent.
"Looking Forward. The Second Biennial Conference on Italian Evangelization." *The Assembly Herald*, XXIV (March, 1918), 156-157. Reprinted, *Protestant Evangelism Among Italians in America*. New York: Arno Press, 1975.

Plans for the development of evangelical work among Italians.

1005. "Settlement Work Among the Italians." *St. Vincent de Paul Quarterly*, XIII (May, 1908), 210.

Brief comment on "the increased interest shown in the welfare of the Italian immigrants by the Catholic prelates, pastors, press and people throughout the country."

1006. Sharp, John K.
History of the Diocese of Brooklyn, 1853-1953. The Catholic Church on Long Island. 2 vols. New York: Fordham University Press, 1954. Pp. xxiii-392, viii-394.

This is the standard history of the Diocese of Brooklyn, New York. Vol. I, pp. 173-175 and vol. II, pp. 80-81 give some information on the Italian immigrants in the Brooklyn Diocese.

1007. Shaughnessy, Gerald.
Has the Immigrant Kept the Faith? New York: The Macmillan Company, 1925 Pp. 289. Reprinted, New York: Arno Press, Inc., 1969.

This is the standard study of the numerical growth of the Catholic Church in the United States, from the beginning of colonization to 1920. The author takes issue with the traditional argument that millions of Catholic immigrants left the Catholic Church after arriving in the United States. He concludes that the great majority of Catholic immigrants stayed in the church.

1008. Shearer, Donald.
Ignatius Cardinal Persico, O.M. Cap. Spencer, Mass: The Heffernan Press, 1932. Pp. 234.

Sketchy biographical study of an Italian-born friar who came to the United States in 1866 and was Bishop of Savannah from 1870 to 1872. Originally, an M.A. thesis at the Catholic University of America, 1931.

1009. Shipman, Andrew J.
"Our Italian Greek Catholics. A Remnant of the Oriental Church in Italy and America." *The Messenger* (February, 1906), 152-168.

Brief history of Italian Greek Catholics in Italy and America. The author offers the opinion that there are 450,000 Italians in New York City, of which about 15 to 20,000 are Italian Greek Catholics. Other Italian Greek Catholics are scattered in Long Island, New Jersey, etc. Weekly paper of Italian Greek Catholics: *L'Operaio.* Italo-Albanese societies in Manhattan: Società S. Giorgio, Società Italo-Albanese, Società Uguaglianza, Soc. San Giuseppe, Soc. Gabriele Buccola, Soc. Cuore di Gesù, Società Civitese, Soc. Sicula-Albanese, Soc. San Bartolomeo, Soc. San Paolo, Soc. Stella Albanese. The author thinks that half of the Italian Greek population emigrated to the United States. They are still without a church of their own in New York City. Author advocates a church for their rite. Fr. Papas Ciro Pinnola of Mezzojuso, came to the United States to gather the scattered flock.

1010. Shipman, Andrew J.
"Greek Catholics in America." *The Catholic Encyclopedia*, VI (1909), 744-752.

This article on the Uniat churches of the Byzantine or Greek Rite includes a section on "Italian Greek Catholics." A large proportion of Italo-Greeks arrived in the United States during the period of mass migration. They settled chiefly in New York, Philadelphia, and Chicago.

1011. "A Short History of the Mission of Our Lady of Loreto, New York." *Woodstock Letters*, XLVI (1917), 172-187.

Historical notes written on the occasion of the silver jubilee of this Italian parish in the "Little Italy" of lower Manhattan, New York.

1012. "Sketch of the Nez Percé Indians." *Woodstock Letters*, IX (1880), 43-50, 191-199; X (1881), 71-77, 198-204.

Topics discussed include relations of the Indians with the Hudson Bay Company, evangelization by the French Canadians, persecution of the Indians, request by the Indians for a church and school, relationship with the United States Agent, conversions and rivalries among the Indians, account sent from the Colville Mission, November 28, 1880, and work of Italian Jesuits.

1013. Shriver, William P.
Immigrant Forces. Factors in the New Democracy. New York: Missionary Education Movement of the United States and Canada, 1913. Reprinted, New York: James S. Ozer Publisher, 1971. Pp. ix-277.

This is a study of the new immigration and Protestant missionary efforts among the new immigrants. There are many references to Italian immigrants and their relationship to Catholicism and various types of Protestantism.

1014. Shriver, William P.
At Work with the Italians. New York: Missionary Education Movement of the United States and Canada, 1917. Pp. 37.

A pamphlet reporting Shriver's Presbyterian missionary work among Italian immigrants.

1015. Shriver, William P.
"An Italian Year." *The Assembly Herald*, XXIV (March, 1918), 157-158. Reprinted, *Protestant Evangelism Among Italians in America*. New York: Arno Press, 1975.

Shriver, Director of City and Immigrant Work for the Board of Home Missions, gives a brief review of Protestant work with Italian immigrants and sees it as a great opportunity.

1016. Shriver, William P.
"Evangelical Movement Among Italians." *The Missionary Review of the World*, LVIII (January, 1935), 5.

Presbyterian activities among immigrants from Italy.

1017. Shriver, William P.
"Board of National Missions of the Presbyterian Church in the United States of America." *Il Rinnovamento*, April 11, 1936.

A letter in support of the Italian Evangelical Publication Society and its newspaper, *Il Rinnovamento*, inviting all churches to support it financially.

1018. Shriver, William P.
       Adventure in Missions. The Story of Presbyterian Work with Italians.
       5th ed. New York: Board of National Missions of the Presbyterian
       Church in the United States, Unit of City and Industrial Work, 1946.
       Pp. 93.

       Good documentation on the number and institutions of Italian-American
       Presbyterians, the problems of bilingual ministers and their need for
       administrative ability in America, and the crisis in ethnic identity with second
       generation.

1019. Simpson, A.B., comp.
       Michele Nardi, the Italian Evangelist: His Life and Work. New York:
       Mrs. Blanche P. Nardi, 1916. Pp. 143.

       Biography of the Italian-born M. Nardi, his conversions, ministry and
       proselytizing in the United States (Illinois, St. Louis, California), in Italy; and
       back in New York and New Jersey; back again in Italy, where he died. Added
       are comments of persons familiar with Nardi's activity. Good and typical
       example of the Protestant work among Italian immigrants.

1020. "Sisters of the Venerini Institute." *The Catholic Church in the United
       States of America.* 3 vols. New York: The Catholic Editing Company,
       1912-1914. II, 487-488.

       Brief account of the Venerini Institute, an Italian religious community devoted
       to teaching. It was introduced into the United States in 1909.

1021. *Sixteenth Annual Report of Columbus Hospital for the Italian
       Immigrants Year 1911.* New York: 1912. Pp. 61.

       Statistics on the activity of the hospital under the charge of the Missionary
       Sisters of the Sacred Heart in New York City.

1022. Skinner, Lilian M.
       "Our Italian Neighbors." *Neighbors. Studies in Immigration From the
       Standpoint of the Episcopal Church.* New York: Domestic and Foreign
       Missionary Society, 1920. Pp. 85-108.

       Describes Italian immigrants, their religious indifference, and ways of working
       with them.

1023. Smith, John Talbot.
       The Catholic Church in New York. 2 vols. New York: Hall & Locke
       Company, 1905. Pp. xviii-328, x-329-628.

This study is subtitled "A History of the New York Diocese From Its Establishment in 1808 To The Present Time." Vol. 2, pp. 447-449, 469-475, and 603-605, gives some information on the relationship between the Italian immigrants and the Archdiocese of New York from the start of mass migration to 1908.

1024. Società dei Missionari di Emigrazione di Sant'Antonio di Padova. *Relazione dell'Operato dalla Società dei Missionari di S. Antonio di Padova nell'anno 1914.* Presentata al Regio Commissariato dell'Emigrazione. Roma: Fava, 1915. Pp. 25.

Annual report for 1914 of the Society of the Missionaries for Migrants of St. Anthony of Padua, concerned with assisting immigrants on board ship and in the ports of departure and arrival. It publishes two bulletins for the information of migrants: *Pro emigrante* (8,000 copies) and *Amico dell'emigrante e dell'operaio* (10,000 copies).

1025. "La Società di S. Raffael per la Protezione degli Emigranti Cattolici." *La Civiltà Cattolica*, 60 (1909), 474-476.

This brief article summarizes the work of the various national branches of the St. Raphael Society.

1026. "La Società di San Raffaele Tedesca e l'Opera di Mons. Scalabrini per l'emigrazione italiana in America." *Italica Gens*, I (Marzo, 1910), 59-65.

Article points out the influence of the German St. Raphael Society in the establishment of similar Catholic emigrant aid societies in Europe. Gives a brief summary of the Italian St. Raphael Society and reprints the 1908 report of the New York branch of the Italian Society.

1027. Società di unione e fratellanza italiana, St. Louis, Mo. *Libro di letture graduate con le prime nozioni elementari, per uso della scuola di lingua italiana, con un sunto di elementi di arimetica, in Saint Louis, Missouri.* St. Louis: M. Seiffarth, printer, 1869. Pp. 218.

This book contains, most probably, the first Italian-language catechism used by Italian immigrants in the United States. This Catholic catechism was part of the indispensable education the Italians of St. Louis wanted to impart to their children.

1028. Society of St. Raphael for the Protection of Italian Immigrants.
Annual Report, 1902-1903. Boston: 1903. Pp. 12.

First annual report of the Boston branch of the Catholic St. Raphael Society
for the Protection of Italian Immigrants.

1029. Sofia, Giovanni, ed.
Missioni Scalabriniane in America. Roma: Tip. Poliglotta Cuore di
Maria, 1939. Pp. viii-223.

This is a popularly written account of the various parishes and institutions
established by the Congregation of St. Charles Borromeo in the United States
and Brazil.

1030. Sorrentino, Giuseppe M.
*Dalle Montagne Rocciose al Rio Bravo. Brevi appunti Storici circa la
missione gesuitica del Nuovo Messico e Colorado negli Stati Uniti di
America.* Napoli: Casa Editrice Federico & Ardia, 1919. Pp. 307.

Account of Italian Jesuits' work in New Mexico and Colorado from 1867 to
1919, when the schools, parishes, mission stations and other missionary
activities initiated and developed by Jesuit priests and brothers from the
Province of Naples became a part of the American Jesuit Provinces of Missouri
and New Orleans. The narrative is factual and chronological with brief
sketches of individual missionaries and is based on primary archival sources,
mostly letters and reports of missionaries. It touches briefly on the assistance
of Italians arriving in Colorado around 1890. Even though popular in style,
this book is valuable for the history of the Catholic Church in Colorado and
New Mexico.

1031. Sorrentino, Joseph M.
"Religious Conditions in Italy." *America*, XII (October 17, 1914), 6-7.

In this brief article, the author argues favorably about religious conditions
and practices in Italy. The article stirred some controversy. See ensuing
correspondence: *America*, XII (October 31, November 7, 14, 21, 28, December
5, 12, 19, 1914), 66, 92-93, 121, 144-145, 168-169, 193-196, 221, 243-245 and
editorial 246 (bottom, p. 36).

1032. Souvay, Charles L.
"Andreis, Andrew James Felix Bartholomew de." *Dictionary of
American Biography*, I (1928), 276-277.

Brief biography of DeAndreis, born in Piedmont in 1778 and ordained a priest
in 1801. In 1815 he was invited by Louis DuBourg, the administrator-apostolic
of the Diocese of Louisiana, to go there as a missionary. He died, probably of
typhoid, in 1820.

1033. Souvay, Charles L.
"Rosati, Joseph." *Dictionary of American Biography*, XVI (1935), 155-156.

Brief biography of Rosati, born at Sora in the Kingdom of Naples in 1789. He entered the Congregation of the Mission in Rome in 1807 and was ordained a priest in 1811. In 1815 he left for America to join Fr. Andrew deAndreis in the recently organized Louisiana Mission. In 1823 Pope Pius VII appointed him coadjutor to the Bishop of Louisiana and, when Louisiana was divided into the Diocese of New Orleans and St. Louis, he was appointed first bishop of the latter. He died in 1843.

1034. *Souvenir Notes of the Silver Jubilee or the 25th Anniversary of the Celebration of the First Mass of the Rev. Antonio Isoleri, Ap. Miss., Founder and Pastor of the New St. Mary Magdalen DePazzi's Italian Church.* Philadelphia, Pa.: 1894. Pp. 76.

Front page in Italian: Le Nozze d'Argento or "Silver Jubilee" of the Rev. Antonio Isoleri, Ap. Miss. — Souvenir Notes. Newspaper clippings, official talks and addresses on the occasion of the Silver Jubilee of Rev. A. Isoleri.

1035. St. John, G.B. and William P. Shriver.
"Church and Coke: At the Heart of Old Redstone." *The Assembly Herald* (March, 1913), 125-128.

Includes references to Presbyterian work among Italian immigrants.

1036. *Statuti della Pia Società dei Missionari di San Carlo per gli Italiani Emigranti.* Roma: Tipografia Poliglotta Vaticana, 1925. Pp. 34.

Rules of the Missionaries of St. Charles (Scalabrinians) for Italian emigrants.

1037. *Statuto dell'Unione del Clero Italiano nell'America del Nord, 1914.* New York: Catholic Polyglot Publishing House, 1914. Unpaged.

Text of statutes of the association of Italian priests working among Italian immigrants in the United States.

1038. *Statuto e Regolamento della Società S. Raffaele Arcangelo in Boston, Mass.* Boston: Stemperia Marino & Freda, 1905. Pp. 11.

Statutes of the Boston branch of the Society of St. Raphael for the protection of Italian immigrants.

1039. *Statuto, Regolamento della Società di Mutuo Soccorso Santa Febronia, Patti e Circondario in Hoboken, New Jersey.* Hoboken: Stamperia La Sentinella, 1923. Pp. 37.

An immigrant fraternal society's statutes limiting membership to persons from the same town of origin in Italy.

1040. Steiner, Edward A.
The Immigrant Tide: Its Ebb and Flow. 2d ed. New York: Fleming H. Revell Company, 1909. Pp. 370.

Steiner, a professor at Grinnelll College in Iowa, wrote several books on immigration. In this study, he devotes chapter XXII, pages 311-328, to the topic "The Protestant Church and the Immigrant," a summary of Protestant work among Italian immigrants.

1041. Sterlocchi, Lorenzo.
Cenni Biografici di Monsignor Giov. Battista Scalabrini, Vescovo di Piacenza. 2a Edizione riveduta e corretta con appendice sulle Opere di Don Luigi Guanella ed il suo viaggio in America e 18 illustrazioni. Como: Scuola Tip. Casa Divina Provvidenza, 1913. Pp. 127.

A popularly written biography of Bishop Scalabrini with reference to his friendship with Blessed Luigi Guanella.

1042. Stibili, Edward C.
"The Interest of Bishop Giovanni Battista Scalabrini of Piacenza in the 'Italian Problem.' " *The Religious Experience of Italian Americans.* Edited by Silvano M. Tomasi. Staten Island, New York: The American Italian Historical Association, 1975. Pp. 11-30.

Detailed account of the attitude of the Italian government toward mass Italian migration during the period 1865-1888 and Bishop Scalabrini's intervention in favor of greater government protection of the immigrants.

1043. Stone, Alfred Holt.
"Italian Cotton-Growers in Arkansas." *The American Monthly Review of Reviews*, XXXV (February, 1907), 209-213.

This is a description of the work done at the Italian agricultural colonies of Sunnyside and Tontitown, Arkansas. The author attempts to prove that Italian labor was superior to Negro labor at Tontitown. He uses this as an example to argue that "it is through immigration that the South is to realize the ultimate development of her almost untouched resources" (p. 209).

1044. Stone, George M.
"The Italian Mission in Hartford." *Watchman*, 89 (October 31, 1907), 21.

Evangelical mission among Italian immigrants.

1045. "Story of Vincenzo and Ariel Bellondi." *The Baptist Home Mission Monthly*, XXVII (August, 1905), 306-309.

Account of Bellondi's missionary work in Buffalo and Barre, Vermont.

1046. "Strayed Sheep and Unshepherded Lambs." *The Ave Maria*, N.S., VI (July 14, 1917), 53.

This brief article comments on the inadequate religious condition of Italian immigrants. It argues that many Italians are "unshepherded" and that it is important that priests go out of their way to welcome these immigrants into their churches. This is especially important in the case of the children, who otherwise might be lost to the faith.

1047. "A Suburban Church." *The Commonweal*, XL (August 11, 1944), 405.

Anonymously written brief article under the heading "The Inner Forum," which comments on an Italian parish in an American suburban community where both priest and people use English as their common language.

1048. Sullivan, James S.
One Hundred Years of Progress. A Graphic, Historical, and Pictorial Account of the Catholic Church of New England. Archdiocese of Boston. Boston and Portland: Illustrated Publishing Company, 1895. Pp. 842.

The author describes the initial organized pastoral care of Italian immigrants in Boston.

1049. Suttles, Gerald D.
The Social Order of the Slum: Ethnicity and Territory in the Inner City. Chicago: The University of Chicago Press, 1968. Pp. xxii-243.

This sociological study analyzes the behavior of several ethnic groups in Chicago's Near West Side. Pages 41-46 deal with the role of religion in the area and include some observations on Italian parishes there.

1050. Sylvain, Robert.
Clerc, Garibaldien Prédicant des Deux Mondes. Alessandro Gavazzi (1809-1889). 2 vols. Quebec: Le Centre Pédagogique, 1962. Pp. viii-280, 287-587.

This is an excellent biography, in French, of Gavazzi, with an extensive bibliography and annotation on unpublished sources. Chapter XVII describes Gavazzi's activities in New York.

1051. Syrius.
"Fede e Patria: L'opera di P. Alfonso da Serino." *Il Carroccio*, XXV (Giugno, 1927), 633-634.

Description of the ministry of this Franciscan among the Italians in Boston, Pittsburgh, and Brooklyn starting in 1902.

1052. Tacchi-Venturi, Pietro.
"Per la biografia del Padre Giammaria Salvaterra: Tre nuove lettere." *Archivum Historicum Societatis Jesu*, 5 (1936), 76-83.

Three new letters written by Fr. Salvaterra, Kino's co-worker.

1053. Tansey, Anne.
"Saint Among the Skyscrapers." *The Ave Maria*, LXXI (May 6, 1950), 559-563.

This is a brief, popular sketch of St. Frances Xavier Cabrini, who worked among the Italian immigrants at the turn of the century and was canonized the first American saint in 1946.

1054. Tedeschini, Federico.
Portrait of a Saint, Mother Cabrini. Chicago: Missionary Sisters of the Sacred Heart, 1948. Pp. 11.

Translation of the pamphlet issued for the inauguration of St. Frances Xavier Cabrini's statue in St. Peter's Basilica in 1947.

1055. Tendorf, Francis A.
"Bayma, Joseph." *Dictionary of American Biography*, II (1929), 79-80.

Brief biography of Bayma, born at Ciriè, near Turin, in 1816. He entered the Jesuit novitiate at Chiete in 1832 and was ordained to the priesthood in 1847. A mathematician and physicist, he published his chief work, *Elements of Molecular Mechanics*, in 1866. In 1869 he was sent to California to work in the newly established Jesuit mission there. He held various positions and died in 1892.

1056. Tendorf, Francis A.
"Sestini, Benedict." *Dictionary of American Biography*, XVI (1935), 594-595.

Brief biography of Sestini, born in Florence in 1816. In 1836 he entered the Society of Jesus at Rome and was ordained to the priesthood in 1844. Following the outbreak of revolution in Rome in 1848, he emigrated to the United States, where he became connected with Georgetown University.

There, he continued his researches in mathematics and astronomy. He published several works in these areas. In 1866 he began publication of the *Messenger of the Sacred Heart*, a periodical with a large circulation. He died in 1890.

1057. Tessarolo, Giulivo, ed.
Exsul Familia. The Church's Magna Charta for Migrants. Staten Island, N.Y.: St. Charles Seminary, 1962. Pp. 300.

An annotated edition of the papal document on the pastoral care of migrants by Pope Pius XII, *Exsul Familia*, where reference is made to Italian migrants. For text of this papal document, see Pius XII, "Constitutio Apostolica de Spirituali Emigrantium Cura." *Acta Apostolicae Sedis*, XLIV (September 30, 1952), 649-704.

1058. Tessarolo, Giulivo.
"Scalabrinians." *New Catholic Encyclopedia*, XII (1967), 1111.

Brief account of founding and work of the Pious Society of the Missionaries of St. Charles, also known as the Scalabrini Fathers, established in Piacenza, Italy, by Bishop Giovanni Battista Scalabrini in 1887. The society was established to work among Italian immigrants in America.

1059. Testa, Stefano L.
"Strangers from Rome in Greater New York." *The Missionary Review of the World*, XXXI (March, 1908), 216-218.

Author feels assimilation of Italians will result from attendance at public schools and conversion to evangelical Protestantism. Lists 14 Italian Protestant Churches and missions in the Bronx and Manhattan.

1060. Testa, Stefano L.
"For the Italian, A Ministry of Christian and Patriotic Appeal." *The Assembly Herald*, XVII (January, 1911), 11.

Testa, a Protestant minister in Brooklyn, New York, argues the need both to americanize and Christianize the Italian immigrants.

1061. Testore, Celestino.
Nella Terra del sole a mezzanotte. La fondazione della missione de Alasca: P. Pasquale Tosi, 25 aprile 1837-14 gennaio 1898. Venezia: Missioni. Pp. 48.

Brief sketch of Fr. Tosi, founder of the Alaska mission.

1062. Thaon diRevel, Vittorio.
"Delle condizioni del'emigrazione negli Stati Uniti nell'anno 1882."
Bollettino Consolare, XX (1884), 3-59.

Report of the Italian Vice-Consul in New York on the conditions of Italian
immigrants in the United States. Italian priests work among Italians and
other nationalities with zeal. Italian priests in America on their own without
assignment have problems.

1063. Thaon diRevel, Vittorio.
"Rapporto circa l'emigrazione italiana nel distretto vice-consolare di
Boston." *Bollettino Consolare*, I (1889), 245-265.

Reports on the Italian immigrants in Boston, their religiosity and the Society
of San Marco.

1064. Thomas, Norman M.
"Six Years in Little Italy." *The Assembly Herald*, XXIV (March, 1918),
149-151. Reprinted, *Protestant Evangelism Among Italians in America*.
New York: Arno Press, 1975.

Description of the author's work among Italians of New York's East Harlem
where he was then a Presbyterian pastor. Thomas sees the justification of
Protestant work in the Italian colony in the "higher ethical standards" it
brings and in the affirmation of social justice.

1065. Thompson, Erwin N.
"Joseph M. Cataldo, S.J., and Saint Joseph's Mission." *Idaho Yesterdays*,
XVIII (Summer, 1974), 19-29.

About Cataldo's missionary work in the Northwest.

1066. Tolino, John V.
"The Church in America and the Italian Problem." *The Ecclesiastical
Review*, C (January, 1933), 22-32.

Two-sevenths of the entire American Catholic population are Italians, but
the American church does not pay too much attention to them. The Italian
religious situation is becoming worse as the years go by. There are wrong
attitudes on the part of the American clergy to this problem either in good
faith or in bad faith. Tolino states that the church in America must adopt a
new program as it has been done in Philadelphia. The national Italian parish
must be transformed into a territorial parish.

1067. Tolino, John V.
"Solving the Italian Problem." *The Ecclesiastical Review*, XCIX
(September, 1938), 246-256.

The author, pastor of an Italian church in Philadelphia, wrote several articles dealing with the Italian problem. In these articles, Fr. Tolino argues for the americanization of the Italian parishes and their schools.

1068. Tolino, John V.
"The Future of the Italian-American Problem." *The Ecclesiastical Review*, CI (September, 1939), 221-232.

The church in America must be a missionary church. It has in its membership the descendants of numerous ethnic groups: one-third of American Catholics are immigrants. The future of the 6,000,000 Italian Catholics depends on the instruction they will have. According to Tolino, the answer to this problem is this: More, better, bigger Catholic schools.

1069. Tolino, John V.
"The Priest in the Italian Problem." *The Ecclesiastical Review*, CIX (November, 1943), 321-330.

Tolino writes about the pioneer movement of americanizing Italian priests working with immigrants. After a few years, the Italians follow American ways of life, and so they and their children must be cared for with the same pastoral methods used for other Americans. Processions and folkloristic expressions understandable in southern Italy should not be confirmed in the American cities. Italian-born clergy must learn English and adopt American methods for their personal advantage and for the prestige of a church without "foreign islands."

1070. Tomasi, Silvano M.
"The Ethnic Church and the Integration of Italian Immigrants in the United States." *The Italian Experience in the United States*. Edited by S.M. Tomasi and M.H. Engel. New York: The Center for Migration Studies of New York, Inc., 1970. Pp. 163-193.

This is an important interpretative study of the role of the ethnic parish in the life of the Italian immigrant colonies of the United States. The author concludes that "the ethnic parishes with their saints and festivals, novenas and processions, and their 'indifferent' congregations, held together the Italians in America" (p. 192). See Silvano M. Tomasi. "Assimilation and Religion: The Role of the Italian Ethnic Church in the New York Metropolitan Area, 1880-1930." Unpublished Ph.D. dissertation, Fordham University, Department of Sociology, 1972.

1071. Tomasi, Silvano M.
"Americanizzazione o Pluralismo? La Chiesa Etnica Italiana Come Istituzione Mediatrice nel Processo d'Integrazione degli Emigrati negli Stati Uniti d'America." *Gli Italiani negli Stati Uniti*. L'emigrazione e

l'opera degli Italiani negli Stati Uniti d'America Atti del III Symposium di Studi Americani, Firenze, 27-29 Maggio 1969. Firenze: Università degli Studi di Firenze, 1972. Pp. 389-422. Reprinted, New York: Arno Press, 1975.

Analysis of the attitude of the official Catholic Church toward Italian immigrants, and the development of the Italian parishes whose role was to mediate among the different viewpoints.

1072. Tomasi, Silvano M.
Piety and Power: The Role of the Italian Parishes in the New York Metropolitan Area. Staten Island, N.Y.: Center for Migration Studies, 1975. Pp. xi-201.

Through a very thorough research work the author's book, as Oscar Handlin writes *(Contemporary Sociology: A Journal of Reviews,* VI [January, 1977], 88-89) throws light on the experience of the Italian immigrants who have been far too long neglected, and it treats an aspect of American religious history that has long cried for attention. The author describes the activities of the Italian parishes in New York and proves the specific role of the Italian national parish as a unique strategy of the immigrant community in dealing with a new society. The research, based primarily on archival sources, offers new insight in the emergence and growth of Italian-American parishes oriented to strengthen the solidarity of the immigrant community, so that the process of assimilation be genuine.

1073. Tomasi, Silvano M.
"Italian Catholics in America." *Catholics in America, 1776-1976.* Edited by Robert Trisco. Washington, D.C.: National Conference of Catholic Bishops Committee for the Bicentennial, 1976. Pp. 93-97.

Brief account of Italian immigration to the United States.

1074. Tomassini, Francis X.
"Colorado. A Letter from Fr. Tomassini. St. Ignatius' Church, Pueblo, Colorado, January 19th, 1884." *Woodstock Letters,* XIII (1884), 50-53.

Letter to Fr. Piccirillo describing the building of the new church.

1075. "Tontitown, an Italian Farming Community." (Service Bur. for Intercultural E ducation, New York [Publ.] I. New York, 1937. No. 5, pp. 1-8.)

Unpublished manuscript on the Italian colony of Tontitown, Arkansas. Available at the New York Public Library.

1076. "Tontitown in Arkansas." *The Interpreter*, VIII (April, 1929), 56-58.

This is a brief account of the founding of the Italian colony of Tontitown, Arkansas in 1898. It relates the role of Fr. Pietro Bandini in the establishment of the colony.

1077. Tosi, P.
"Letter of Fr. Tosi to Fr. Cataldo. Alaska, July 1888." *Woodstock Letters*, XVIII (1889), 326-328.

Work among the Tanana Indians.

1078. Tosi, P.
"Alaska. Diary of a Trip to the Coast. Fr. Tosi to Rev. Fr. Cataldo. Cosiorefsky, May 20, 1889." *Woodstock Letters*, XVIII (1889), 333-351.

A travel log of a 3-month journey with description of old Russian settlements, white trading posts and Eskimo huts.

1079. Tosi, Pascal.
"Through an unexplored Part of Alaska." *Woodstock Letters*, XXV (1896), 222-229.

This letter, reprinted from the *New York Sun*, March 15, 1896, describes a 2,000 mile sleigh-journey through a "Terra Incognita." It describes the aborigenes of Kotzebne Sound and notes the similarity of the Greek and Eskimo languages, the hot springs in a frozen lake, and the relics of a mammoth discovered in the permafrost by the Eskimos.

1080. Tosi, Pasquale.
L'Alasca e i suoi primi esploratori. Nuova edizione con prefazione e appendice del P. Enrico Rosa. Roma: ed. Civiltà Cattolica, 1926. Pp. 140.
Account of Alaska and its earliest explorers by Tosi, a Jesuit missionary in Alaska.

1081. Tourn, N.
I Valdesi in America. Torino: Unione Tipografica-Editrice Torinese, 1906. Pp. 127.

Account of the Waldenses in America. Published for the 1906 Exposition of Milan.

1082. "The Training of Italian Youths for the American Missions." *The Pastor*, VI (January, 1888), 82.

This article reports the founding of an institute in Piacenza, Italy, for the training of Italian priests to work in the American missions. It gives the entire text of the apostolic brief, *Libenter agnovimus*, dated November 25, 1887, which established the institute officially at Piacenza.

1083. *Travels of Mother Frances Xavier Cabrini*. Chicago, Illinois: The Missionary Sisters of the Sacred Heart of Jesus, 1944. Pp. xviii-277.

This is a translation of various letters written by Frances Xavier Cabrini between 1890-1906 describing her travels to various parts of the world.

1084. Treca, J.M.

"Letters of Fr. Jos. M. Treca to Rev. Father Cataldo. St. Michael's, Alaska, July 7, 1889." *Woodstock Letters*, XVIII (1889), 351-354.

Description of work in the mission by the Italian priests Tosi and Ragaru, and difficulties among the Eskimos.

1085. Treca, J.M.

"Letter from Fr. .Treca to Rev. Fr. Cataldo. Tununagamute, Cape Vancouver, Alaska, June 2, 1890." *Woodstock Letters*, XIX (1890), 358-365.

The author describes his work with Fr. Tosi in building the new mission, the numerous conversions, the May devotions among the Eskimos, and Indian customs.

1086. Treca, J.M.

"A Letter from Fr. Treca to Fr. Cataldo. Tamunagamut, Cape Vancouver, June 6th, 1891." *Woodstock Letters*, XX (1891), 334-340.

The author describes the teaching of religion through song and poetry, Indian hunting and fishing customs, and how the Indians learn how to cultivate the land and other work from the missionary.

1087. Treca, J.M.

"A Letter from Fr. Treca to a Friend. Alaska, Cape Vancouver, January 11, 1891." *Woodstock Letters*, XX (1891), 340-345.

The author describes how he bought a little steam-boat to reach the far-away missions, Indian generosity toward him, how he visited the missions by sleigh, Indian migration during summer months, and Indian conversion to the Roman Catholic Church from Russian Orthodoxy.

1088. Treca, J.M.

"Letters from Alaska. A Letter from Fr. Treca to Fr. Cataldo, Cape Vancouver, May 29, 1892." *Woodstock Letters*, XXI (1892), 356-359.

Description of Fr. Tosi's and writer's missionary activities, and the difficulties of the land and climate.

1089. Trione, Stefano.
L'Emigrazione e l'Opera di Don Bosco Nelle Americhe. San Benigno Canav.: Scuola tipografica Don Bosco, 1914. Pp. 24.

In this conference, given in Rome on February 5, 1914, the author describes the Salesian missions in North and South America with sketchy references to work among Italian immigrants in New York City, Paterson, New Jersey, Port Chester, New York, and California. The immigrant parish is seen as the center of educational, social and religious activities.

1090. Turchi, Ottavio.
Parole di Elogio — Nelle Funebri Onoranze Solenni di Trigesima rese dalle Missionarie del S. Cuore di Gesù alla loro Amatissima Fondatrice e Superiora Generale M. Francesca Saverio Cabrini il 24 Gennaio 1918. Roma: Scuola Tipografica Salesiana, 1918. Pp. 18.

Homily given in Rome on the 30th day of the death of Mother Cabrini.

1091. Turco, Luigi.
"The Spiritual Autobiography of Luigi Turco." St. Paul: Center for Immigration Studies, the University of Minnesota, 1969. Pp. 230.

Activities of this Italian Baptist minister born in Riesi, Sicily in 1890, educated at the Waldensian Seminary in Rome and at Colgate, and steady contributor to *The New Aurora.* Available only on microfilm.

1092. "Two Italian Women Workers." *The Baptist Home Mission Monthly,* XXVII (August, 1905), 309-310.

Brief autobiographies by Signorina Eleanora Vaccaneo, a missionary at the First Italian Church in New York City, and Signora Concetta Pezzano, bible reader of the First Italian Church in New York City.

1093. "Two Woodstock's Founders." *Woodstock Letters,* XXIX (1900), 298-315.

Sketches of Cardinal Mazzella and Fr. DeAugustinis, Italian Jesuits who for many years taught at Woodstock.

1094. United States Bureau of the Census.
Religious Bodies: 1916. 2 parts. Washington: Government Printing Office, 1919. Pp. 594, 727.

Useful for statistics on Italian Protestant churches and missions.

1095. United States Bureau of the Census.
Religious Bodies: 1926. 2 Vols. Washington: United States Government Printing Office, 1929-1930. Pp. 769, xiii-1405.

Useful for statistics on Italian Protestant churches and missions.

1096. U.S. Congress. House.
Acceptance of the Statue of Eusebio Francisco Kino Presented by the State of Arizona. Proceedings in the Rotunda, United States Capitol, February 14, 1965. 89th Congress, 1st Session. H. Doc. No. 158. Washington: United States Government Printing Office, 1965. Pp. 47.

Documents and description of ceremony relating to the placing in the Statuary Hall collection of the United States Capitol of the statue of Eusebio Francisco Kino as one of the two statues furnished and provided by the State of Arizona.

1097. U.S. Department of Commerce. Bureau of the Census.
Census of Religious Bodies, 1936. Bulletin No. 64. Italian Bodies: Statistics, Denominational History, Doctrine, and Organization. Washington: Government Printing Office, 1940. Pp. iv-9.

Gives information on these two denominations: the General Council of the Italian Pentecostal Assemblies of God and the Unorganized Italian Christian Churches of North America.

1098. Valletta, Clement L.
"The Settlement of Roseto: World View and Promise." *The Ethnic Experience in Pennsylvania.* Edited with an Introduction by John E. Bodnar. Lewisburg: Bucknell University Press, 1973. Pp. 120-143.

It shows the important role of the churches, the priest and religion in the growth of this Italian settlement of Pennsylvania.

1099. Van Ree, L.
"The Spokane Indians: Sketch of the Work of Our Fathers." *Woodstock Letters*, XVIII (1889), 354-364.

Origin and development of the missions. Reports on the activities of Frs. DeSmet and the Italian pioneers Caruana, Giorda, Cataldo, Diomedi, and Folchi.

1100. Varbero, Richard A.
"Philadelphia's South Italians and the Irish Church: A History of Cultural Conflict." *The Religious Experience of Italian Americans.*

Edited by Silvano M. Tomasi. Staten Island, New York: The American Italian Historical Association, 1975. Pp. 31-52.

Argues that "the Irish-American experience was intrinsically related to the Italo-American experience as a broader acculturative development, encompassing not only church, but also school, work, and political behavior. Accepting this assertion as a tool of analysis, I will first orchestrate some familiar themes on the Irish in America and in a tentative way enlarge the base for understanding the cultural rift between Irishmen and *Mezzogiorno* peasants. Secondly, I will deal with my initial findings on the approach and the consequences of Church policies in Philadelphia."

1101. Vasta, Achilles.
"The Arapahoes and Their Amusements. A Letter from Fr. Vasta. St. Stephen's Mission, Wyoming, April 26, 1892." *Woodstock Letters*, XXI (1892), 185-189.

Description of these Indians, their customs and ritual dances.

1102. Vasta, Achilles.
"A Baptism Among the Arapahoes. A Letter from Father Vasta. St. Stephen's Mission, Fremont Co., Wyoming, February 8, 1893." *Woodstock Letters*, XXII (1893), 227-230.

Refers to the Sioux Indians, their customs, and some conversions.

1103. Vavolo, J.W.
"Training an Italian Congregation in the Support of the Church." *The Assembly Herald*, XXIV (March, 1918), 154-155. Reprinted, *Protestant Evangelism Among Italians in America*. New York: Arno Press, 1975.

Evangelical efforts to teach Italian immigrants to support their church.

1104. Vecoli, Rudolph J.
"Prelates and Peasants, Italian Immigrants and the Catholic Church." *Journal of Social History*, II (Spring, 1969), 217-268.

The author refers to this lengthy article as "an initial reconnaisance into the history of the Italian immigration in its relations to the American Catholic Church" (p. 220). He discusses the Italian "problem" and concludes that the contadini by and large failed to identify both with American Catholicism and American Protestantism. Rather, they retained their peasant religiosity and were not americanized by their contact with the American Church.

1105. Vecoli, Rudolph J.
"Cult and Occult in Italian-American Culture. The Persistence of a

Religious Heritage." *Immigrants and Religion in Urban America.* Edited by R.M. Miller and T.D. Marzik. Philadelphia: Temple University Press, 1977. Pp. 25-47.

Utilizing a variety of sources, the author attempts to delineate the religious culture of the Italians and its encounter with American Catholicism. He concludes that the "Italian immigrants brought with them an ancient religious culture, a Mediterranean sensibility prevaded by mysticism and passion. The American Church rejected this gift, to its and their great loss."

1106. Velikonja, Joseph.
"Contributo italiano al carattere geografico di Tontitown, Arkansas, e Rosati, Missouri." *Gli Italiani negli Stati Uniti.* L'emigrazione e l'opera degli Italiani negli Stati Uniti d'America. Atti del III Symposium di Studi Americani, Firenze, 27-29 Maggio 1969. Firenze: Università di Firenze, Istituto di Studi Americani, 1972. Pp. 423-452. Reprinted, New York: Arno Press, 1975.

A contribution to a conference on the emigration and work of Italians in the United States held in Florence in 1969. It describes the history, development and melting away of two villages founded by Fr. Bandini and Italian immigrants.

1107. Venegas, Manuel.
Juan Maria de Salvatierra of the Company of Jesus, Missionary in the Province of New Spain, Apostolic Conqueror of the Californias. Translated by Marguerite Eyer Wilber. Cleveland: A.H. Clark, 1929. Pp. 350.

Salvatierra was Kino's closest co-worker in the Pimería and the Californias and a very successful missionary for several years.

1108. *Venticinque anni di Missione fra gl'Immigrati Italiani di Boston, Mass., 1888-1913.* Milano: Tipografia Santa Lega Eucaristica, 1913. Pp. 395.

This volume was published on the occasion of the 25th anniversary of the founding of Sacred Heart Church, located in Boston's North End. It includes brief biographical sketches of the parish's pastors from 1888 to 1913 as well as accounts of the various activities sponsored by the parish during this period.

1109. Veronesi, Gene P.
Italian Americans and Their Communities of Cleveland. Cleveland: Cleveland Ethnic Heritage Studies, Cleveland State University, 1977. Pp. 358.

The author reviews the role of Italian parishes in Cleveland, Ohio, and views them as "the center of the community's life" (pp. 202-214).

1110. Vicentini, Domenico.
L'Apostolo degli Italiani emigrati nelle Americhe ossia Mons. Scalabrini e l'Istituto dei suoi Missionari. Piacenza: Tipografia Editrice A. Del Maino, 1909. Pp. 80.

A biography of Scalabrini by his first successor in the administration of the Congregation he founded for the care of Italian migrants.

1111. Villa, O.
"L'Alasca e le Missioni dei Gesuiti Italiani." *Civiltà Cattolica* (1926), 444-453.

Italian Jesuit missions in Alaska.

1112. Villari, Luigi.
Gli Stati Uniti d'America e l'Emigrazione Italiana. Milano: Fratelli Treves, Editori, 1912. Pp. 314. Reprinted, New York: Arno Press, 1975.

This is a general study of the Italians in the United States. Pages 207-210 and 286-288 contain some comments on the role of the Church in the life of Italian immigrants.

1113. Villeneuve, Alphonse.
"Les Etats-Unis d'Amerique et l'emigration." Extrait du *XXme Siecle*, VI (Juillet-Aout 1891), 53.

Villeneuve insists on the right of the many ethnic groups in America to preserve their identity, praises Scalabrini and his work, refers to Italian emigration to the United States and to the religious "soul" of the Italian immigrants, and defines Scalabrini's work as a work of faith and patriotism.

1114. Vollmar, Edward R.
"Donato Gasparri, New Mexico — Colorado Mission Founder." *Mid-America*, N.S., IX (April, 1938), 96-102.

Brief sketch of Fr. Donato Maria Gasparri, founder of the New Mexico-Colorado Mission of the Neapolitan Province of the Society of Jesus. The mission was started in 1867.

1115. Vollmar, Edward R.
"First Jesuit School in New Mexico." *New Mexico Historical Review,* XXVII (October, 1952), 296-299.

Recounts efforts by Jesuits of the Province of Naples to open a school in New Mexico.

1116. Vollmar, Edward R.
"Missionary Life in Colorado, 1874." *Mid-America,* XXXV (July, 1953), 175-180.

Translation of a letter from Fr. Baldassare to his superior, describing winter, language difficulties, etc., at Conejos.

1117. Vollmar, Edward R.
"Religious Processions and Penitente Activities at Conejos, 1874." *Colorado Magazine,* XXXI (July, 1954), 172-179.

Based on one of the *Lettere Edificanti* by Fr. Salvatore Persone.

1118. Volpe Landi, Giovanni Battista.
"Emigrazione, Sue Cause, Suoi Bisogni, Suoi Provvedimenti." *Atti del I Congresso Cattolico Italiano degli Studiosi di Scienze Sociali.* Padova: 1893. I, 236-238.

The Marquis Volpe Landi, a close collaborator of Bishop Scalabrini, presents comments and proposals for meeting the emigration problem. See G.B. Volpe Landi. "Il Problema dell'Emigrazione." *Rivista Internazionale di Scienze Sociali e Discipline Ausilierie,* XIII (1897), 500-520.

1119. Volpe Landi, Giovanni Battista.
"Sulla Associazione Detta di San Raffaele per la Protezione degli Immigrati Italiani negli Stati Uniti." *Bollettino dell'Emigrazione,* 1 (1903), 56-58.

An excellent and detailed statement on the St. Raphael Society for the protection of Italian immigrants in the United States.

1120. Volpe Landi, Giovanni Battista and Pietro Maldotti.
"Società di Patronato per gli Emigranti." *Studi Emigrazione,* V (Febbraio-Giugno, 1968), 395-416.

This is the text of a report submitted by the Marchese Giovanni Battista Volpe Landi and Fr. Pietro Maldotti in November, 1896 to the Italian minister for foreign affairs. The report discusses some of the problems faced by the immigrants and calls for better government regulation to deal with these problems.

1121. "Voyage of Very Rev. Fr. John Anthony Grassi, S.J. from Russia to America. January 1805-October 1810." *Woodstock Letters*, IV (1875), 115-136.

Description of how Fr. Grassi never reached his mission in China and instead ended up at Goergetown College, Washington, D.C.

1122. Walker, James B.
"Father Mazzuchelli, Apostle to the Winnebagos." *Catholics in America, 1776-1976*. Edited by Robert Trisco. Washington, D.C.: National Conference of Catholic Bishops Committee for the Bicentennial, 1976. Pp. 51-53.

Brief account of the work of Fr. Mazzuchelli, a missionary in the American Midwest during the nineteenth century.

1123. Walsh, A.T.
"Trinitarians." *New Catholic Encyclopedia*, XIV (1967), 293-295.

Brief account of the history of the Order of the Most Holy Trinity for the Redemption of Captives, founded by John of Matha during the 12th century. The author notes that the Order's "American beginnings date from the attempt of an Italian Trinitarian to open a parish in 1906. He was not successful, but 5 years later another Italian priest arrived and in 1912 he took charge of a parish in Asbury Park, N.J."

1124. Walsh, James J.
"An Apostle of the Italians." *The Catholic World*, CVII (April, 1918), 64-71. Reprinted, Wayne Moquin, ed. *A Documentary History of the Italian Americans*. New York: Praeger Publishers, 1974.

In this brief article, the author summarizes the work of Mother Frances Xavier Cabrini among the Italian immigrants in the New World.

1125. Walsh, James J.
"The Irish and the Italians." *Il Carroccio*, XXVII (January, 1928), 114-116.

"No wonder the Irish and the Italians are getting to realize in recent years the bonds of sympathy that join them. They represent ever so much more than others the progressive elements in a dozen of centuries of civilization and culture..."

1126. Walsh, James J.
American Jesuits. New York: The Macmillan Company, 1934. Pp. ix-336.

Popularly written account of the establishment and work of the Society of Jesus in the United States. It includes some information on the work of Italian Jesuit missionaries.

1127. Walsh, Richard J.
"Pere Marquette — Padre Kino — Father DeSmet." *Records of the American Catholic Historical Society of Philadelphia*, LVII (September, 1946), 169-178.

This brief study compares and evaluates the activities and influence of three Jesuit missionaries, one French, one Italian, and one Belgian. It gives biographical information on each of these missionaries.

1128. Ware, Caroline F.
Greenwich Village, 1920-1930. New York: Harper & Row, 1965. Pp. xii-496.

This well-known community study contains interesting observations on the religious adaptation of Italians to American society (pp. 292-318) and reflects the experience of other urban centers with Italian immigrant concentrations.

1129. Watts, George B.
The Waldenses in the New World. Durham, North Carolina: Duke University Press, 1941. Pp. xi-309.

This is an account of the coming and development of the Waldenses in both North and South America. The author provides a solid bibliography on pp. 263-273.

1130. Watts, George B.
The Waldenses of Valdese. Valdese, N.C.: 1965. Pp. 174.

A detailed, descriptive chronological narrative of the founding of Valdese by Waldenses from the Italian Cottian Alps in 1893 and of the growth of the town, its struggles and adaptation to the American environment. Attached are lists of original settlers and of the pastors of Valdese. See Watts. *The Waldenses in the New World*. Durham, N.C.: 1941.

1131. Weibel, Geo. F.
Rev. Joseph M. Cataldo, S.J. A Short Sketch of a Wonderful Career. N.p., n.d. Pp. 36.

Pamphlet reprinted from *Gonzaga Quarterly*, March 15, 1928, available at the New York Public Library. Biography of Fr. Cataldo who worked among the Indians in the West in the post-Civil War period and founded Gonzaga University in 1881.

1132. Whittier, Isabel.
The Waldensians. Brunswick, Maine: The Brunswick Publishing Co., 1957. Unpaged.

A brief history of the Waldenses in Italy and the United States.

1133. Williams, G.P.
"Italian Work in Chicago." *The Assembly Herald*, (August, 1901), 303.

Offers a sketch on an Italian parish in Chicago as it is administered by its Italian Presbyterian pastor.

1134. Williams, George H.
"Professor George LaPiana (1878-1971), Catholic Modernist at Harvard (1915-1947)." *Harvard Library Bulletin*, XXI (April, 1973), 117-143.

A review of LaPiana's life and writings. Born in Sicily, La Piana moved to the United States in 1913 after initiating his career as a priest, teacher and writer with strong Modernist views. In Milwaukee, he wrote about the Italians there, and then moved to Harvard University where for many years he taught at the Divinity School and became John Hopkins Morison Professor of Church History. No longer a practicing Catholic, he kept writing and was interested in Italian political developments. He died reconciled to the church.

1135. Williams, Phyllis H.
South Italian Folkways in Europe and America, a Handbook for Social Workers, Visiting Nurses, School Teachers, and Physicians. New Haven: Published for the Institute of Human Relations by Yale University Press, 1938. Reprinted, New York: Russell & Russell, 1969. Pp. xviii-216.

This is a study of South Italian customs and cultural patterns as they relate to a variety of areas, such as the home, work, clothing, religion and education. Pages 135-159 deal with South Italian religious practices.

1136. *With a Spirit of Song! Servites Century of Service to America, 1870-1970. A Year of Joy and Jubilee.* Buena Park, California: Servites of the West, Provincial Center, 5210 Somerset St., 1970. Pp. 16.

Brief centennial survey of the founding and work in the United States of the Order of the Friars Servants of Mary (Servites).

1137. Woods, Henry.
"California Missions of the Soc. of Jesus. Founded by the Province of Turin, Italy." *Woodstock Letters*, XIII (1884), 157-164.

Brief description of the beginning of Jesuit missionary and educational work on the West Coast.

1138. *Woodstock Letters, A Record of Current Events and Historical Notes connected with the Colleges and Missions of the Soc. of Jesus in North and South America.* Woodstock, Md.: Woodstock College, 1872-.

A multi-volume series, "printed for private circulation only," which includes many letters and reports by Italian Jesuit missionaries in America. The letters and reports are listed in alphabetical order in this section of the bibliography. alphabetical order in this section of the bibliography and they describe the work and record the personal experiences and achievements of these missionaries mostly active before the period of mass immigration from Italy.

1139. "Work Among the Italians." *The Baptist Home Mission Monthly,* XXIV (August, 1902), 223-224.

Notes need for Baptist work among Italians and points to the work of the Baptist Home Mission Society. *The Baptist Home Mission Monthly* was published by the American Baptist Home Mission Society, 111 Fifth Avenue, New York City.

1140. Workers of the Federal Writers' Project, Works Progress Administration in the City of New York.
The Italians of New York. New York: Random House, 1938. Reprinted, New York: Arno Press, Inc., 1969. Pp. xx-241.

This is a publication in the American Guide Series, written by members of the Federal Writers' Project of the Works Progress Administration. Based on secondary sources, the volume offers a general history of the Italians in New York City. Pages 75-92 describe the religious life of New York's Italians.

1141. Workers of the Writers' Program, Work Projects Administration in the State of Nebraska.
The Italians of Omaha. Omaha, Nebr.: Independent Printing Company, 1941. Pp. 111. Reprinted, New York: Arno Press, 1975.

Chapter V, pp. 81-85, is titled "Religion."

1142. Wright, Frederick H.
The Italians in America. New York: Missionary Education Movement of the United States and Canada, 1913. Pp. 27. Reprinted, *Italians in the United States. A Repository of Rare Tracts and Miscellanea.* New York: Arno Press, 1975.

Twenty-seven page pamphlet by F.H. Wright, the Superintendent of the Italian Missions of the Methodist Episcopal Church.

1143. Wright, Frederick H.
"How to Reach Italians in America. Shall They Be Segregated, 'Missioned,' Neglected or Welcomed?" *The Missionary Review of the World*, XL (August, 1917), 589-594.

Wright, "Late Superintendent of the Italian Mission of the Methodist Episcopal Church in the United States," discusses the need to evangelize the Italians, points out the limited success of evangelical work among Italians, and calls on Protestant missionaries to shed patronizing attitudes.

1144. Wyllys, Rufus K.
"Kino of Pimeria Alta, Apostle of the Southwest." *The Arizona Historical Review*, V (April, July, October, 1932, January, 1933), 5-32, 93-134, 203-225, 308-326.

This study is "an effort to put into convenient form a summary of what is known about Padre Kino, together with some description of his times and the country in which he labored" (p. 6).

1145. Wyllys, Rufus King.
Pioneer Padre: The Life and Times of Eusebio Francisco Kino. Dallas, Texas: The Southwest Press, 1935. Pp. xi-230.

This is "an effort to put into convenient and popular form a summary of what is best known about Padre Kino, together with some description of his times and the country in which he labored."

1146. Yans-McLaughlin, Virginia.
Family and Community: Italian Immigrants in Buffalo, 1880-1930. Ithaca, N.Y.: Cornell University Press, 1977. Pp. 286.

In this study, the author argues that the Italian families in Buffalo made a relatively smooth transition from the Old World to the New. Includes many references on the role of religion among the immigrants.

1147. Yergin, Howard V.
"They of Italy Salute You." *The Assembly Herald*, XXIV (March, 1918), 147-149. Reprinted, *Protestant Evangelism Among Italians in America.* New York: Arno Press, 1975.

A report from Southern Italy by a Presbyterian minister commenting on the place and its religion and some Protestant work there.

1148. "A Young Italian's Story." *The Baptist Home Mission Monthly*, XXXI (March, 1909), 123-125.

Account, by an unidentified young Italian Catholic, of his "life of sin and shame" and his conversion to Protestantism.

1149. Yzermans, Vincent A.
The People I Love: A Biography of Luigi G. Ligutti. Collegeville, Minnesota: The Liturgical Press, 1976. Pp. 325.

The life of an active churchman born in Friuli, Italy, who emigrated to Iowa, founded the National Catholic Rural Life Conference, and later became Vatican observer to Food and Agriculture Organization. Contains interesting remarks concerning his education as an immigrant and his participation in national and international efforts for social justice.

1150. Zanconato, Cesare.
"Nel Centenario della 'St. Raphaels-Verein.' " *Studi Emigrazione*, VIII (Ottobre-Dicembre, 1971), 328-338.

Zanconato, basing himself on correspondence available at the Scalabrini General Archives in Rome, relates the Italian and German situations vis-a-vis assistance to the immigrants in the late nineteenth century. It was published on the occasion of the one hundredth anniversay of the founding of the St. Raphaels-Verein,

1151. Zarrilli, John.
A Prayerful Appeal to the American Hierarchy in Behalf of the Italian Catholic Cause in the United States. Two Harbors, Minnesota: 1924. Pp. 26.

This pamphlet, published by Zarrilli, contains three articles dealing with the "Italian problem." 1) John Zarrilli. "A Suggestion for the Solution of the Italian Problem," pp. 2-11, which originally appeared in *The Ecclesiastical Review*, LXX (January, 1924), 70-77; 2) John Zarrilli. "Pastoral Care of Foreign Catholics in America and the Italian Question," pp. 11-19, Zarrilli's reply to the anonymously written article "Pastoral Care of Foreign Catholics in America," *The Ecclesiastical Review*, LXX (February, 1924), 176-181; and 3) Miles Muredach. "An Experiment in City Home Missions," pp. 19-26, which originally appeared in *Extension Magazine*, XVII (April, 1923), 35-36, 62. Muredach's article describes the efforts of Bishop Thomas J. Walsh of Trenton, New Jersey, to solve the Italian problem through the establishment of bilingual parochial schools. These schools were staffed by the Maestre Pie Filippini, an Italian community of teaching sisters.

1152. Zarrilli, John.
"A Suggestion for the Solution of the Italian Problem." *The Ecclesiastical Review*, LXX (January, 1924), 70-77.

The author, a longtime pastor of Italian parishes in Minnesota, calls for the establishment of bilingual parochial schools in every Italian parish in America, for a Center of Italo-American Catholic culture and activity, and for a few bishops of Italian nationality in the American hierarchy. For a reply, see "Pastoral Care of Foreign Catholics in America." *The Ecclesiastical Review*, LXX (February, 1924), 176-181. The Zarrilli article was reprinted in John Zarrilli, *A Prayerful Appeal to the American Hierarchy in Behalf of the Italian Catholic Cause in the United States*. Two Harbors, Minnesota: 1924. Pp. 2-11.

1153. Zarrilli, John.
"Some More Light on the Italian Problem." *The Ecclesiastical Review*, LXXIX (September, 1928), 256-268.

In this article the author recalls his previous article, "A Suggestion for the Solution of the Italian Problem." *The Ecclesiastical Review*, LXX (January, 1924), 70-77. In the 1928 article the author lists ten points which, if implemented, would help resolve the Italian problem.

1154. Zavatti, Silvio.
P. Pasquale Tosi: missionario ed esploratore nell'Alasca. Milano: Pont. Ist. Missioni estere, 1950. Pp. 64.

Short biography of Fr. Tosi, explorer of Alaska.

1155. Zazzara, Jerome N.
"Pastoral Care of Italian Emigrants." *The Ecclesiastical Review*, LXIV (March, 1921), 279-284.

In this article, Zazzara describes the appointment on September 15, 1920 of Monsignor Michael Cerrati as the first Prelate for Italian Immigration. The task of the Prelate was to supervise and centralize the work of the various religious groups doing welfare work among the Italian immigrants.

1156. Zema, Gabriel A.
"The Italian Immigrant Problem." *America*, LV (May 16, 1936), 129-130.

In this article Zema addresses himself to the question of the leakage of Italian immigrants from the Catholic Church. The author argues that the main cause of such defection is "the neglect of the growing boy and the young man" (p. 130).

1157. Zema, Gabriel A.
"Jottings in Italy." *The American Ecclesiastical Review*, CXXIX (August, 1953), 95-99.

In this article Zema offers disconnected comments on religion in Italy as well as the religious behavior of Italian-Americans in the United States.

1158. Zwierlein, Frederick J.
The Life and Letters of Bishop McQuaid, Prefaced with the History of Catholic Rochester Before His Episcopate. 3 vols. Rochester, N.Y.: The Art Print Shop, 1925-1927. Pp. xii-368, xii-487, xii-513.

This biography of Bishop McQuaid includes an account of the debate at the Third Plenary Council of Baltimore on the Italian immigrants. See vol. II, pp. 333-335.

Index

NOTE — The number indicated refers to the numbered entries of the bibliography. The material is indexed by author and subject.